BISON
BOOKS

DATE DUE

The Blennerhasset Plantation

PRESIDENTIAL EDITION

THE WINNING OF THE WEST

BY

THEODORE ROOSEVELT

VOLUME FOUR

LOUISIANA AND THE NORTHWEST

1791–1807

WITH MAP

Introduction to the Bison Book Edition
by James P. Ronda

University of Nebraska Press
Lincoln and London

Introduction to the Bison Book Edition © 1995
by the University of Nebraska Press

First Bison Book printing: 1995
Most recent printing indicated by the last digit below:
10   9   8   7   6   5   4   3   2   1

Library of Congress Cataloging-in-Publication Data
Roosevelt, Theodore, 1858–1919.
The winning of the West / by Theodore Roosevelt—Presidential
ed.
p.   cm.
Includes index.
Originally published: New York: G. P. Putnam's Sons, 1894.
Contents: v. 1. From the Alleghanies to the Mississippi, 1769–
1776—v. 2. From the Alleghanies to the Mississippi, 1777–
1783—v. 3. The founding of the trans-Alleghany common-
wealths, 1784–1790—v. 4. Louisiana and the Northwest, 1791–
1807.
ISBN 0-8032-8958-8 (set)—ISBN 0-8032-8954-5 (v. 1)—
ISBN 0-8032-8955-3 (v. 2)—ISBN 0-8032-8956-1 (v. 3)—
ISBN 0-8032-8957-X (v. 4)
1. United States—Territorial expansion.   2. Northwest, Old—
History.   3. West (U.S.)—History.   I. Title.
E179.5.R66   1995
976—dc20
94-46645   CIP

The four-volume set of *The Winning of the West* was copyrighted
and published between 1889 and 1896 by G. P. Putnam's Sons,
New York. This Bison Book is a reprint of volume 4, © 1896. The
title-page designation of Presidential Edition and the fron-
tispiece were added later, but in all other respects this is the
original edition.

THIS BOOK IS DEDICATED, WITH HIS PERMISSION

TO

FRANCIS PARKMAN

TO WHOM AMERICANS WHO FEEL A PRIDE IN THE PIONEER HISTORY OF
THEIR COUNTRY ARE SO GREATLY INDEBTED

INTRODUCTION

James P. Ronda

When Theodore Roosevelt wrote the final volume of *The Winning of the West* in the mid-1890s, the discipline of American history was just emerging as a pursuit separate from literature. The study of the American West was still the province of dime novel writers and Wild West show entrepreneurs. Roosevelt came to this uncertain world of the American past armed with three confident certainties. Those certainties—his often unexamined assumptions—were part of Roosevelt's own energetic temperament and nationalist ideology. His certainties, not his doubts and questions, determined not only what he wrote about but how he judged each actor and every action in the historical drama.

As much as Roosevelt welcomed the growing professionalism of American historians and prized his term (1912) as president of the American Historical Association, he never wholly abandoned his conviction that history was really part of literature. Roosevelt found the power of the narrative with all its action and color far more appealing than the quiet "pause and reflect" virtues of scholarly analysis. Even the most casual reader of Roosevelt's works knows instantly that he is in the presence of a writer fully in the grip of grand passion and even grander ideas. Like Francis Parkman and William H. Prescott, Roosevelt wrote history as part of national literature, a literature aimed at a broad middle-class audience. This was a literature intended to educate and inspire.

Having embraced the tradition of literary history, Roosevelt built the final volume of *The Winning of the West* around the sweeping themes of conflict and conquest. Here he followed Parkman, the historian he most admired and sought to emulate. In Roosevelt's historical imagination the conflict pitted the young American nation (and by that he meant white Americans) against a host of enemies. The stakes in the conflict were political and cultural dominion in North America. Roosevelt's plot, his narrative line, was a series of violent encounters leading to eventual American triumph.

If Roosevelt's love for history in the grand manner moved him to accept the stereotypes of savage enemies and civilized Americans, that same certainty assured him that the outcome was inevitable. Roosevelt took pains to let his readers know that the English-speaking, white Protestant Americans were going to win the West, no matter what the cost. The West was the birthright of the American republic, promised by God and bought with the blood of righteous pioneers. Roosevelt's notions about inevitability and conflict are sure to trouble modern readers. He was certain that conflict was inevitable. With his own personal commitment to an expanding American nation, Roosevelt could not allow for compromise. His version of the western past demanded conflict as a means for conquest. There could be no half-way measures. Roosevelt not only celebrated conflict but also praised those he knew as the winners. Roosevelt did not ignore English, Spanish, or Native American participants in the war for America. On his stage they were allowed to fight but not to win. Inevitable conflict and predetermined decision—these were essential parts of Roosevelt's historical faith.

Those certainties made Roosevelt's portrayal of the West a popular one. His readers could see the West as just the first in a glorious series of territorial gains made to secure an American empire. Roosevelt's certainties often carried the hard edge of racist arrogance. Modern readers might feel that *The Winning of the West* is more imperialist apology than history. Roosevelt surely wrote history in the service of American identity. But for all his brash confidence and complacent arrogance, one of Roosevelt's certainties remains as a vital and engaging idea. Always thinking in sweeping terms, Roosevelt appreciated continuity in the American past. He did not consider it a contradiction to assert that conflict preserved and extended the continuity of the American nation. Later writers saw the Mississippi River as a fundamental dividing line in the American experience. The temptation was to separate the history of the East from the West. Roosevelt insisted that the river was neither a historical boundary nor a cultural barrier. Readers quickly discover that most of the West in volume four of *The Winning of the West* lies geographically east of the Mississippi River. Roosevelt, deeply influenced by Parkman, grasped the fundamental continuities in the war for America. The battles waged in Ohio and Tennessee were fought again and again beyond the wide Missouri.

Violence, racial conflict, imperial destiny, and a broad sense of American history all informed Roosevelt's conception of western history. His prejudices were those of his age. His history swaggers just as he did. To his certainties and confident assumptions we should add one more. Roosevelt had a Jeffersonian faith in the power of the West and the frontier experience to keep the republic forever young and virtuous. Like his contemporary Frederick Jackson Turner, Roosevelt thought about the West in terms of cultural renewal. Turner feared that the end of the frontier might spell American decline. Roosevelt seemed to think that the violence and the physical challenges of more distant imperial frontiers would keep the nation ever vigorous. Roosevelt came dangerously close to believing that violence itself was essential for cultural vitality.

The final volume of *The Winning of the West* covers the years between 1791 and 1807. The modest extent of this chronology might lull an unsuspecting reader into thinking that these were uneventful years. But Roosevelt was right in centering his attention on that tumultuous era. These were the years of the Ohio Indian wars, the white settlement of Kentucky and Tennessee, the Louisiana Purchase, and the great exploring journeys of Meriwether Lewis, William Clark, and Zebulon Montgomery Pike. The creation of a western American empire began in those years. Territorial expansion, exploration, the extension of democratic political institutions, and military action against Indians were hallmarks of that era. And those hallmarks stamped the future as well.

While this final volume of *The Winning of the West* touches on many important events and compelling personalities, modern readers will be drawn to three episodes of enduring significance. Film and fiction have given the Indian wars of the Far West near-legendary status. Names like Crazy Horse, Sitting Bull, Geronimo, and Custer loom large on the American historical landscape. But Roosevelt understood that the campaigns waged by the United States against the native peoples of the Ohio country had vast meaning for the future of North America. These wars of conquest set the pattern for generations of conflict. Roosevelt recognized the importance of the Ohio country struggle but he could not escape his own cultural prejudices when writing about it. Roosevelt's Ohio Indians were nameless, faceless "plumed woodland warriors" who stood defiantly in the way of American progress. Their defeat at the Battle of Fallen Timbers (20 August 1794) and the land cessions made at the Treaty of Greeneville (1795) guaranteed native dispossession and American expansion. Roosevelt praised the victory, identified with the victors, and thought the result wholly inevitable.

No single event so dominates the historical landscape that Roosevelt sought to survey as the Louisiana Purchase. Roosevelt's contemporary Henry Adams, a scholar often highly critical of Thomas Jefferson, viewed the purchase as "the single greatest diplomatic success recorded in American history." Roosevelt acknowledged the great importance of the purchase but could not bring himself to praise Jefferson and the American negotiators. He argued that the "true history" of the acquisition of Louisiana could be found in the "western growth of the people of the United

States." Roosevelt ridiculed what he called "the feeble diplomacy of Jefferson's administration." That evaluation
has not stood the test of time and new evidence. Historians
now recognize that Jefferson was guided by a comprehensive and powerful imperial vision. The territorial expansion of the American republic was of the highest priority
for Jefferson. And if he did not bluster and threaten in
quite the way Roosevelt hoped, it was the historian—not
the president—who lacked a keen understanding of international diplomacy.

Roosevelt devoted the final chapter in this volume to exploration in the western countries beyond the Mississippi.
Western expansion was a great adventure and Roosevelt
saw exploration as the greatest adventure of all. By the
time Roosevelt wrote about Lewis, Clark, and Pike, the
reputations of those captains in Jefferson's Corps of Discov-
ery had suffered a long decline. These early explorers had
been replaced in the public imagination by the likes of
John Charles Frémont, Buffalo Bill, and Billy the Kid.
With the publication (1893) of a new edition of the
Nicholas Biddle *History of the Lewis and Clark Expedition,*
edited and annotated by Elliot Coues, Lewis and Clark began to regain prominence in both the popular and the
scholarly mind. An experienced naturalist, Coues emphasized the scientific aspects of the expedition. While Roosevelt appreciated Nature and natural history, he did so as a
hunter, not as a scientist. What fascinated Roosevelt was
strenuous adventure and high drama. Exploration represented both. For Roosevelt, Lewis and Clark were the vanguard of an American empire, one he was sure would have
a global reach.

Theodore Roosevelt dedicated *The Winning of the West* to
Francis Parkman. That dedication put Roosevelt squarely
where he wanted to be as an historian. He belonged in the
camp of the great literary historians. Roosevelt wanted to
do for his western country what Parkman had done for the
woodlands frontier. Both writers fashioned narrative land-
scapes filled with explosive action and colorful characters.

Roosevelt was never Parkman's equal as a literary stylist but he did tell stories with dash and energy. Later generations of historians would tell those stories from different points of view, but Roosevelt was one of the first to struggle with the complexities of a West becoming part of an American empire.

SUGGESTIONS FOR FURTHER READING

Over the years since Theodore Roosevelt wrote the final volume of *The Winning of the West,* historians have learned much about the terrain surveyed in that book. Several books now provide a reliable introduction to the complex events of the period. Malcolm J. Rohrbough, *The Trans-Appalachian Frontier: People, Societies, and Institutions 1775–1850* (New York: Oxford University Press, 1978) and Reginald Horsman, *The Frontier in the Formative Years 1783–1815* (New York: Holt, Rinehart and Winston, 1970) are both well-researched and engagingly written. Also of real value is Elliott West, "American Frontier," in Clyde A. Milner II, Carol A. O'Connor, and Martha A. Sandweiss, eds., *The Oxford History of the American West* (New York: Oxford University Press, 1994). Federal Indian policy for the period is thoroughly discussed in Reginald Horsman, *Expansion and American Indian Policy, 1783–1812* (East Lansing: Michigan State University Press, 1967) and Francis Paul Prucha, *American Indian Policy in the Formative Years: The Indian Trade and Intercourse Acts, 1790–1834* (Cambridge: Harvard University Press, 1962). The Ohio Indian wars are given sound and comprehensive treatment in Wiley Sword, *President Washington's Indian War: The Struggle for the Old Northwest, 1790–1795* (Norman: University of Oklahoma Press, 1985). The Louisiana Purchase has generated a large body of scholarly literature. Perhaps the best book on the origins of the purchase is Alexander DeConde, *This Affair of Louisiana* (New York: Scribner, 1976). No single book does a better job presenting the exploration of the American West for this period than Donald Jackson, *Thomas Jefferson and the Stony Mountains: Exploring the West from Monticello* (Urbana: University of Illinois Press, 1981). Biography remains an engaging way to enter the world Roosevelt struggled to understand. There is no better biography for a figure in this period than John Mack Faragher, *Daniel Boone: The Life and Legend of an American Pioneer* (New York: Holt, Henry, and Company, 1992).

PREFACE TO FOURTH VOLUME.

THIS volume covers the period which opened with the checkered but finally successful war waged by the United States Government against the Northwestern Indians, and closed with the acquisition and exploration of the vast region that lay beyond the Mississippi. It was during this period that the West rose to real power in the Union. The boundaries of the old West were at last made certain, and the new West, the Far West, the country between the Mississippi and the Pacific, was added to the national domain. The steady stream of incoming settlers broadened and deepened year by year; Kentucky, Tennessee, and Ohio became states, Louisiana, Indiana, and Mississippi territories. The population in the newly settled regions increased with a rapidity hitherto unexampled; and this rapidity, alike in growth of population and in territorial expansion, gave the West full weight in the national councils.

The victorious campaigns of Wayne in the north, and the innumerable obscure forays and reprisals of the Tennesseeans and Georgians in the south, so cowed the Indians, that they all, north and south alike, made peace; the first peace the border had known for fifty years. At the same time the treaties of Jay and Pinckney gave us in fact the boundaries which the peace of 1783 had only given us in name. The execution of these treaties put an end in the north to the intrigues of the British, who had stirred the Indians to hostility against the Americans; and in the south to the far more treacherous intrigues of the Spaniards, who showed astounding duplicity, and whose intrigues extended not only to the Indians but also to the baser separatist leaders among the Westerners themselves.

The cession of Louisiana followed. Its true history is to be found, not in the doings of the diplomats who determined merely the terms upon which it was made, but in the western growth of the people of the United States from 1769 to 1803, which made it inevitable. The men who settled and peopled the western wilderness were the men who won Louisiana; for it was surrendered by France merely because it was impossible to hold it against the American advance. Jefferson, through his agents at Paris, asked only for New Orleans; but Napoleon thrust upon him the great West, because Napoleon saw, what the American statesmen and diplomats did not see, but what the Westerners felt; for he saw that no European power could hold the country beyond the Mississippi when the Americans had made good their foothold upon the hither bank.

It remained to explore the unknown land; and this task fell, not to mere wild hunters, such as those who had first penetrated the wooded wilderness beyond the Alleghanies, but to officers of the regular army, who obeyed the orders of the National Government. Lewis, Clark, and Pike were the pioneers in the exploration of the vast territory the United States had just gained.

The names of the Indian fighters, the treaty-makers, the wilderness wanderers, who took the lead in winning and exploring the West, are memorable. More memorable still are the lives and deeds of the settler folk for whom they fought and toiled; for the feats of the leaders were rendered possible only by the lusty and vigorous growth of the young commonwealths built up by the throng of westward-pushing pioneers. The raw, strenuous, eager social life of these early dwellers on the western waters must be studied before it is possible to understand the conditions that determined the continual west-ward extension of the frontier. Tennessee, during the years immediately preceding her admission to statehood, is especially well worth study, both as a typical frontier community, and because of the opportunity afforded to examine in detail the causes and course of the Indian wars.

In this volume I have made use of the material to which reference was made in the first; beside the American State Papers, I have drawn on the Canadian Archives, the Draper Collection, including especially the papers from the Spanish archives, the Robertson MSS., and the Clay MSS. for hitherto unused matter. I have derived much assistance from the various studies and monographs on special phases of Western history; I refer to each in its proper place.   I regret that Mr. Stephen B. Weeks' valuable study of the Martin family did not appear in time for me to use it while writing about the little state of Franklin, in my third volume.

THEODORE ROOSEVELT.

SAGAMORE HILL, LONG ISLAND,
    May, 1896.

CONTENTS.

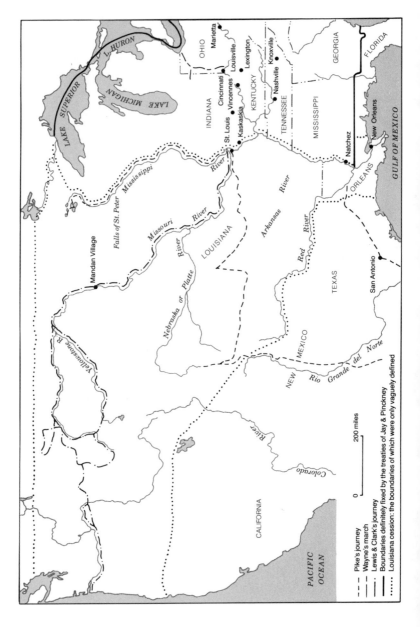

Map Showing the First Explorations of the Great West. Based on a map by G. P. Putnam's Sons, New York and London.

THE WINNING OF THE WEST.

CHAPTER I.

ST. CLAIR'S DEFEAT, 1791.

THE backwoods folk, the stark hunters and tree-fellers, and the war-worn regulars who fought beside them in the forest, pushed ever westward *The West-* the frontier of the Republic. Year after *ward March* year each group of rough settlers and *of the Back-* rough soldiers wrought its part in the great *woodsman.* epic of wilderness conquest.

The people that for one or more generations finds its allotted task in the conquest of a continent, has before it the possibility of splendid victory, and the certainty of incredible toil, suffering, and hardship. The opportunity is great indeed; but the chance of disaster is even greater. Success is for a mighty race, in its vigorous and masterful prime. It is an opportunity such as is offered to an army by a struggle against a powerful foe; only by great effort can defeat be avoided, but triumph means lasting honor and renown.

As it is in the battle, so it is in the infinitely greater contests where the fields of fight are continents, and the ages form the measure of time. In actual life the victors win in spite of brutal blunders and repeated checks. Watched nearby, while the fight stamps to and fro, the doers and the deeds stand out naked and ugly. We see all too clearly the blood and sweat, the craft and cunning and blind luck, the raw cruelty and stupidity, the shortcomings of heart and hand, the mad abuse of victory. Strands of meanness and cowardice are everywhere shot through the warp of lofty and generous daring. There are failures bitter and shameful side by side with feats of triumphant prowess. Of those who venture in the contest some achieve success; others strive feebly and fail ignobly.

The Grimness and Harshness of Frontier Life.

If a race is weak, if it is lacking in the physical and moral traits which go to the makeup of a conquering people, it cannot succeed. For three hundred years the Portuguese possessed footholds in South Africa; but they left to the English and Dutch the task of building free communities able to hold in fact as well as in name the country south of the Zambesi. Temperate South America is as fertile and healthy for the white man as temperate North America, and is so much less in extent as to offer a far simpler problem of conquest and settlement; yet the Spaniard, who came to the Plata two centuries before the American backwoodsman reached the Mississippi, scarcely made as much progress in a decade as his northern rival did in a year.

Only a Mighty Race Fit for the Trial.

The task must be given the race just at the time when it is ready for the undertaking. The whole future of the world would have been changed had the period of trans-oceanic expansion among the nations of Europe begun at a time when the Scandinavians or Germans were foremost in sea-trade and sea-war; if it had begun when the fleets of the Norsemen threatened all coasts, or when the Hanseatic league was in its prime. But in the

No Race can Succeed Save at the Right Moment.

actual event the days of Scandinavian supremacy at sea resulted in no spread of the Scandinavian tongue or culture; and the temporary maritime prosperity of the North German cities bore no permanent fruit of conquest for the German people. The only nations that profited by the expansion beyond the seas, and that built up in alien continents vast commonwealths with the law, the language, the creed, and the culture, no less than the blood, of the parent stocks, were those that during the centuries of expansion, possessed power on the ocean,—Spain, Portugal, France, Holland, and, above all, England.

Even a strong race, in its prime, and given the task at the right moment, usually fails to perform it; for at the moment the immense importance of the opportunity is hardly ever understood, while the selfish interests of the individual and the generation are opposed to the interest of the race as a whole.

Interest of the Race and the Individual Opposed.

Only the most far-seeing and high-minded statesmen can grasp the real weight, from the race-standpoint, of the possibilities which to the men of their day seem so trivial. The conquest and settlement rarely take place save under seldom-occurring conditions

which happen to bring about identity of interest
between the individual and the race. Dutch sea-
men knew the coasts of Australia and New Zealand
generations before they were settled by the English,
and had the people of Holland willed to take possession of them, the Dutch would now be one of the
leading races of mankind; but they preferred the
immediate gains to be derived from the ownership
of the trade with the Spice Islands; and so for the
unimportant over-lordship of a few patches of tropi-
cal soil, they bartered the chance of building a giant
Dutch Republic in the South Seas. Had the
Swedish successors of Gustavus Adolphus devoted
their energies to colonization in America, instead of
squabbling with Slavs and Germans for one or two
wretched Baltic provinces, they could undoubtedly
have built up in the new world a Sweden tenfold
greater than that in the old. If France had sent to
her possessions in America as many colonists as she
sent soldiers to war for petty townships in Germany
and Italy, the French would now be masters of half
the territory north of the Rio Grande. England
alone, because of a combination of causes, was able
to use aright the chances given her for the conquest
and settlement of the world's waste spaces; and in
consequence the English-speaking peoples now have
before them a future more important than that of all
the continental European peoples combined.

It is natural that most nations should be thus
blind to the possibilities of the future. Few indeed
are the men who can look a score of years into the
future, and fewer still those who will make great

sacrifices for the real, not the fancied, good of their children's children; but in questions of race supremacy the look-ahead should be for centuries rather than decades, and the self-sacrifice of the individual must be for the good not of the next generation but perchance of the fourth or fifth in line of descent. The Frenchman and the Hollander of the seventeenth century could not even dimly see the possibilities that loomed vast and vague in the colonization of America and Australia; they did not have, and it was hardly possible that they should have, the remotest idea that it would be well for them to surrender, one the glory gained by his German conquests, the other the riches reaped from his East Indian trade, in order that three hundred years later huge unknown continents should be filled with French and Dutch commonwealths. No nation, taken as a whole, can ever see so far into the future; no nation, even if it could see such a future, would ever sacrifice so much to win it. Hitherto each race in turn has expanded only because the interests of a certain number of individuals of many succeeding generations have made them active and vigorous agents in the work of expansion.

Each Race Indifferent to its Own Future.

This indifference on the part of individuals to the growth of the race is often nearly as marked in new as in old communities, although the very existence of these new communities depends upon that growth. It is strange to see how the new settlers in the new land tend to turn their faces, not towards the

This Indifference as Marked in New as in Old Communities.

world before them, but towards the world they have left behind. Many of them, perhaps most, wish rather to take parts in the struggles of the old civilized powers, than to do their share in laying the obscure but gigantic foundations of the empires of the future. The New Englander who was not personally interested in the lands beyond the Alleghanies often felt indifferent or hostile to the growth of the trans-montane America; and in their turn these over-mountain men, these Kentuckians and Tennesseans, were concerned to obtain a port at the mouth of the Mississippi rather than the right to move westward to the Pacific. There were more men in the new communities than in the old who saw, however imperfectly, the grandeur of the opportunity and of the race-destiny; but there were always very many who did their share in working out their destiny grudgingly and under protest. The race as a whole, in its old homes and its new, learns the lesson with such difficulty that it can scarcely be said to be learnt at all until success or failure has done away with the need of learning it. But in the case of our own people, it has fortunately happened that the concurrence of the interests of the individual and of the whole organism has been normal throughout most of its history.

The Race Grows because its Interests Happen to be Identical with those of the Individual.

The attitude of the United States and Great Britain, as they faced one another in the western wilderness at the beginning of the year 1791, is but another illustration of the truth of this fact. The British held the lake posts, and more or less actively supported the Indians in their efforts to bar the Americans from the Northwest. Nominally, they held the posts because the Americans had themselves left unfulfilled some of the conditions of the treaty of peace; but this was felt not to be the real reason, and the Americans loudly protested that their conduct was due to sheer hatred of the young Republic. The explanation was simpler. The British had no far-reaching design to prevent the spread and growth of the English-speaking people on the American continent. They cared nothing, one way or the other, for that spread and growth, and it is unlikely that they wasted a moment's thought on the ultimate future of the race. All that they desired was to preserve the very valuable fur-trade of the region round the Great Lakes for their own benefit. They were acting from the motives of self-interest that usually control nations; and it never entered their heads to balance against these immediate interests the future of a nation many of whose members were to them mere foreigners.

The majority of the Americans, on their side, were exceedingly loth to enter into aggressive war with the Indians; but were reluctantly forced into the contest by the necessity of supporting the backwoodsmen. The frontier was pushed westward, not because the leading statesmen of America, or the bulk of the American people, foresaw the continental greatness of this country or strove for such greatness; but because the bordermen of the West,

The United States and Great Britain in 1791.

Reluctance of the Americans to Enter into War with the Indians.

and the adventurous land-speculators of the East, were personally interested in acquiring new territory, and because, against their will, the governmental representatives of the nation were finally forced to make the interests of the Westerners their own. The people of the seaboard, the leaders of opinion in the coast towns and old-settled districts, were inclined to look eastward, rather than westward. They were interested in the quarrels of the old-world nations; they were immediatly concerned in the rights of the fisheries they jealously shared with England, or the trade they sought to secure with Spain. They did not covet the Indian lands. They had never heard of the Rocky Mountains—nobody had as yet,—they cared as little for the Missouri as for the Congo, and they thought of the Pacific Slope as a savage country, only to be reached by an ocean voyage longer than the voyage to India. They believed that they were entitled, under the treaty, to the country between the Alleghanies and the Great Lakes; but they were quite content to see the Indians remain in actual occupancy, and they had no desire to spend men and money in driving them out. Nevertheless, they were even less disposed to proceed to extremities against their own people, who in very fact were driving out the Indians; and this was the only alternative, for in the end they had to side with one or the other set of combatants.

The governmental authorities of the newly created Republic shared these feelings. They felt no hunger for the Indian lands; they felt no desire to stretch their boundaries and thereby add to their already heavy burdens and responsibilities. They wished to do strict justice to the Indians; the treaties they held with them were carried on with scrupu- lous fairness and were honorably lived up to by the United States officials. They strove to keep peace, and made many efforts to persuade the frontiersmen to observe the Indian boundary lines, and not to intrude on the territory in dispute; and they were quite unable to foresee the rapidity of the nation's westward growth. Like the people of the eastern seaboard, the men high in governmental authority were apt to look upon the frontiersmen with feelings dangerously akin to dislike and suspicion. Nor were these feel- ings wholly unjustifiable. The men who settle in a new country, and begin subduing the wilderness, plunge back into the very conditions from which the race has raised itself by the slow toil of ages. The conditions cannot but tell upon them. Inevitably, and for more than one lifetime—perhaps for several generations—they tend to retrograde, instead of ad- vancing. They drop away from the standard which highly civilized nations have reached. As with harsh and dangerous labor they bring the new land up towards the level of the old, they themselves partly revert to their ancestral conditions; they sink back towards the state of their ages-dead barbarian forefathers. Few observers can see beyond this temporary retrogression into the future for which it is a preparation. There is small cause for wonder in the fact that so many of the leaders of Eastern

The Gov- ernment Especially Averse to War.

Inevitable Shortcom- ings of the Frontiers- men.

thought looked with coldness upon the effort of the
Westerners to push north of the Ohio.

Yet it was these Western frontiersmen who were
the real and vital factors in the solution of the problems which so annoyed the British Mon-
The West-
erners   archy and the American Republic. They
Solved the   eagerly craved the Indian lands; they
Problem.   would not be denied entrance to the thinly-
peopled territory wherein they intended to make
homes for themselves and their children. Rough,
masterful, lawless, they were neither daunted by the
prowess of the red warriors whose wrath they
braved, nor awed by the displeasure of the Government whose solemn engagements they violated.
The enormous extent of the frontier dividing the
white settler from the savage, and the tangled inac-
cessibility of the country in which it everywhere
lay, rendered it as difficult for the national authorities to control the frontiersmen as it was to chastise
the Indians.

If the separation of interests between the thickly
settled East and the sparsely settled West had been
complete it may be that the East would
Why the
East   have refused outright to support the West,
backed the   in which case the advance would have
West.   been very slow and halting. But the
separation was not complete. The frontiersmen
were numerically important in some of the States, as
in Virginia, Georgia, and even Pennsylvania and
New York; and under a democratic system of government this meant that these States were more or
less responsive to their demands. It was greatly to

the interest of the frontiersmen that their demands should be gratified, while other citizens had no very concrete concern in the matter one way or the other. In addition to this, and even more important, was the fact that there were large classes of the population everywhere who felt much sense of identity with the frontiersmen, and sympathized with them. The fathers or grandfathers of these peoples had themselves been frontiersmen, and they were still under the influences of the traditions which told of a constant march westward through the vast forests, and a no less constant warfare with a hostile savagery. Moreover, in many of the communities there were people whose kinsmen or friends had gone to the border; and the welfare of these adventurers was a matter of more or less interest to those who had stayed behind. Finally, and most important of all, though the nation might be lukewarm originally, and might wish to prevent the settlers from trespassing on the Indian lands or entering into an Indian war, yet when the war had become of real moment and when victory was doubtful, the national power was sure to be used in favor of the hard-pressed pioneers. At first the authorities at the national capital would blame the whites, and try to temporize and make new treaties, or even threaten to drive back the settlers with a strong hand; but when the ravages of the Indians had become serious, when the bloody details were sent to homes in every part of the Union by letter after letter from the border, when the little newspapers began to publish

The Government Ultimately supports the Frontiersmen.

accounts of the worst atrocities, when the county lieutenants of the frontier counties were clamoring for help, when the Congressmen from the frontier districts were appealing to Congress, and the governors of the States whose frontiers were molested were appealing to the President—then the feeling of race and national kinship rose, and the Government no longer hesitated to support in every way the hard-pressed wilderness vanguard of the American people.

The situation had reached this point by the year 1791. For seven years the Federal authorities had been vainly endeavoring to make some final settlement of the question by entering into treaties with the Northwestern and Southwestern tribes. In the earlier treaties the delegates from the Continental Congress asserted that the United States were invested with the fee of all the land claimed by the Indians. In the later treaties the Indian proprietorship of the lands was conceded.[1] This concession at the time seemed important to the whites; but the Indians probably never understood that there had been any change of attitude; nor did it make any practical difference, for, whatever the theory might be, the lands had eventually to be won, partly by whipping the savages in fight, partly by making it better worth their while to remain at peace than to go to war.

The Federal officials under whose authority these treaties were made had no idea of the complexity of

---

[1] American State Papers, Vol. IV., Indian Affairs, I., p. 13. Letter of H. Knox, June 15, 1789. This is the lettering on the back of the volume, and for convenience it will be used in referring to it.

the problem. In 1789 the Secretary of War, the New Englander Knox, solemnly reported to the President that, if the treaties were only observed and the Indians conciliated, they would become attached to the United States, and the expense of managing them, for the next half-century, would be only some fifteen thousand dollars a year.[1] He probably represented, not unfairly, the ordinary Eastern view of the matter. He had not the slightest idea of the rate at which the settlements were increasing, though he expected that tracts of Indian territory would from time to time be acquired. He made no allowance for a growth so rapid that within the half-century six or eight populous States were to stand within the Indian-owned wilderness of his day. He utterly failed to grasp the central features of the situation, which were that the settlers needed the land, and were bound to have it, within a few years; and that the Indians would not give it up, under no matter what treaty, without an appeal to arms.

Knox and the Treaties.

In the South the United States Commissioners, in endeavoring to conclude treaties with the Creeks and Cherokees, had been continually hampered by the attitude of Georgia and the Franklin frontiersmen. The Franklin men made war and peace with the Cherokees just as they chose, and utterly refused to be bound by the treaties concluded on behalf of the United States. Georgia played the same part with regard to the Creeks. The Georgian authorities paid no

Treaties with the Southern Indians.

[1] American State Papers, Vol. IV., Indian Affairs, I., p. 13.

heed whatever to the desires of Congress, and negotiated on their own account a series of treaties with
the Creeks at Augusta, Galphinton, and Shoulder-
bone, in 1783, 1785, and 1786. But these treaties
amounted to nothing, for nobody could tell exactly
which towns or tribes owned a given tract of land,
or what individuals were competent to speak for
the Indians as a whole; the Creeks and Cherokees
went through the form of surrendering the same
territory on the Oconee.[1] The Georgians knew that
the Indians with whom they treated had no power
to surrender the lands; but all they wished was
some shadowy color of title, that might serve as
an excuse for their seizing the coveted territory.
On the other hand the Creeks, loudly though they
declaimed against the methods of the Georgian
treaty-makers, themselves shamelessly disregarded
the solemn engagements which their authorized representatives made with the United States. Moreover their murderous forays on the Georgian settlers
were often as unprovoked as were the aggressions of
the brutal Georgia borderers.

The Creeks were prompt to seize every advantage
given by the impossibility of defining the rights of
the various component parts of their loosely
knit confederacy. They claimed or disclaimed responsibility as best suited their
plans for the moment. When at Galphinton two of the Creek towns signed away a
large tract of territory, McGillivray, the famous half-
breed, and the other chiefs, loudly protested that
the land belonged to the whole confederacy, and

Mutual Wrongs of the Creeks and the Borderers.

[1] American State Papers, IV., 15. Letter of Knox, July 6, 1789.

that the separate towns could do nothing save by
consent of all.   But in May, 1787, a party of Creeks
from the upper towns made an unprovoked foray
into Georgia, killed two settlers, and carried off a
negro and fourteen horses; the militia who followed them attacked the first Indians they fell in
with, who happened to be from the lower towns,
and killed twelve; whereupon the same chiefs disavowed all responsibility for the deeds of the Upper
Town warriors, and demanded the immediate surrender of the militia who had killed the Lower
Town people—to the huge indignation of the
Governor of Georgia.[1]

The United States Commissioners were angered
by the lawless greed with which the Georgians
grasped at the Indian lands; and they
soon found that though the Georgians   **Difficulties
of the**
were always ready to clamor for help from   **Federal
Treaty-
Makers.**
the United States against the Indians, in
the event of hostilities, they were equally
prompt to defy the United States authorities if the
latter strove to obtain justice for the Indians, or if
the treaties concluded by the Federal and the State
authorities seemed likely to conflict.[2]   The Commissioners were at first much impressed by the letters
sent them by McGillivray, and the "talks" they
received through the Scotch, French, and English
half-breed interpreters[3] from the outlandishly-named
Muscogee chiefs—the Hallowing King of the War

[1] American State Papers, Vol. IV., 31, 32, 33.   Letter of Governor
Matthews, August 4, 1787, etc.

[2] *Do.*, p. 49.   Letter of Benjamin Hawkins and Andrew Pickens, December 30, 1785.

[3] *Do.*, *e. g.*, the letter of Galphin and Douzeazeaux, June 14, 1787.

Towns, the Fat King of the White or Peace Towns, the White Bird King, the Mad Dog King, and many more. But they soon found that the Creeks were quite as much to blame as the Georgians, and were playing fast and loose with the United States, promising to enter into treaties, and then refusing to attend; their flagrant and unprovoked breaches of faith causing intense anger and mortification to the Commissioners, whose patient efforts to serve them were so ill rewarded.[1] Moreover, to offset the Indian complaints of lands taken from them under fraudulent treaties, the Georgians submitted lists[2] of hundreds of whites and blacks killed, wounded, or captured, and of thousands of horses, horned cattle, and hogs butchered or driven off by Indian war parties. The puzzled Commissioners having at first been inclined to place the blame of the failure of peace negotiations on the Georgians, next shifted the responsibility to McGillivray, reporting that the Creeks were strongly in favor of peace. The event proved that they were in error; for after McGillivray and his fellow chiefs had come to New York, in the summer of 1790, and concluded a solemn treaty of peace, the Indians whom they nominally represented refused to be bound by it in any way, and continued without a change their war of rapine and murder.

In truth the red men were as little disposed as the white to accept a peace on any terms that were possible. The Secretary of War, who knew nothing of Indians by actual contact, wrote that it

---

[1] American State Papers, Vol. IV., p. 74, September 26, 1789.

[2] *Do.*, p. 77, October 5, 1789.

would be indeed pleasing "to a philosophic mind
to reflect that, instead of exterminating a part of the
human race by our modes of population
. . . we had imparted our knowledge of
cultivation and the arts to the aboriginals
of the country," thus preserving and civ-
ilizing them [1]; and the public men who
represented districts remote from the frontier shared
these views of large, though vague, beneficence. But
neither the white frontiersmen nor their red antagonists possessed "philosophic minds." They represented two stages of progress, ages apart; and it
would have needed many centuries to bring the
lower to the level of the higher. Both sides recognized the fact that their interests were incompatible;
and that the question of their clashing rights had to
be settled by the strong hand.

The
Indians as
Much to
Blame as
the Whites.

In the Northwest matters culminated sooner than
in the Southwest. The Georgians, and the settlers
along the Tennessee and Cumberland, were
harassed rather than seriously menaced by
the Creek war parties; but in the north
the more dangerous Indians of the Miami,
the Wabash, and the Lakes gathered in bodies so
large as fairly to deserve the name of armies. Moreover, the pressure of the white advance was far
heavier in the north. The pioneers who settled in
the Ohio basin were many times as numerous as those
who settled on the lands west of the Oconee and
north of the Cumberland, and were fed from States
much more populous. The advance was stronger,

The Trouble
Most Seri-
ous in the
North.

[1] American State Papers, Vol. IV., pp. 53, 57, 60, 77, 79, 81, etc.

the resistance more desperate; naturally the open break occurred where the strain was most intense.

There was fierce border warfare in the south. In the north there were regular campaigns carried on, and pitched battles fought, between Federal armies as large as those commanded by Washington at Trenton or Greene at Eutaw Springs, and bodies of Indian warriors more numerous than had ever yet appeared on any single field.

The newly created Government of the United States was very reluctant to make formal war on **The United** the northwestern Indians. Not only were **States Gov-** President Washington and the National **ernment** **Driven** Congress honorably desirous of peace, but **to War.** they were hampered for funds, and dreaded any extra expense. Nevertheless they were forced into war. Throughout the years 1789 and 1790 an increasing volume of appeals for help came from the frontier countries. The governor of the Northwestern Territory, the brigadier-general of the troops on the Ohio, the members of the Kentucky Convention, and all the county lieutenants of Kentucky, the lieutenants of the frontier counties of Virginia proper, the representatives from the counties, the field officers of the different districts, the General Assembly of Virginia, all sent bitter complaints and long catalogues of injuries to the President, the Secretary of War, and the two Houses of Congress; complaints which were redoubled after Harmar's failure. With heavy hearts the national authorities prepared for war.[1]

[1] American State Papers, IV., pp. 83, 94, 109, and 111.

Their decision was justified by the redoubled fury of the Indian raids during the early part of 1791. Among others the settlements near Mari- Raid on the etta were attacked, a day or two after the Marietta Settle- new year began, in bitter winter weather. ments. A dozen persons, including a woman and two children, were killed, and five men were taken prisoners. The New England settlers, though brave and hardy, were unused to Indian warfare. They were taken completely by surprise, and made no effective resistance; the only Indian hurt was wounded with a hatchet by the wife of a frontier hunter in the employ of the company.[1] There were some twenty-five Indians in the attacking party; they were Wyandots and Delawares, who had been mixing on friendly terms with the settlers throughout the preceding summer, and so knew how best to deliver the assault. The settlers had not only treated these Indians with much kindness, but had never wronged any of the red race; and had been lulled into a foolish feeling of security by the apparent good-will of the treacherous foes. The assault was made in the twilight, on the 2nd of January, the Indians crossing the frozen Muskingum and stealthily approaching a block-house and two or three cabins. The inmates were frying meat for supper, and did not suspect harm, offering food to the Indians; but the latter, once they were within doors, dropped the garb of friendliness, and shot or tomahawked all save a couple of men who escaped and the five who were made prisoners. The captives were all taken

[1] " The American Pioneer," II., 110. American State Papers, IV., 122.

to the Miami, or Detroit, and as usual were treated
with much kindness and humanity by the British
officers and traders with whom they came in contact.
McKee, the British Indian agent, who was always
ready to incite the savages to war against the Americans as a nation, but who was quite as ready to
treat them kindly as individuals, ransomed one
prisoner; the latter went to his Massachusetts home
to raise the amount of his ransom, and returned to
Detroit to refund it to his generous rescuer. Another prisoner was ransomed by a Detroit trader,
and worked out his ransom in Detroit itself. Yet
another was redeemed from captivity by the famous
Iroquois chief Brant, who was ever a terrible and
implacable foe, but a great-hearted and kindly
victor. The fourth prisoner died; while the Indians took so great a liking to the fifth that they
would not let him go, but adopted him into the
tribe, made him dress as they did, and, in a spirit of
pure friendliness, pierced his ears and nose. After
Wayne's treaty he was released, and returned to
Marietta to work at his trade as a stone mason, his
bored nose and slit ears serving as mementos of his
captivity.

The squalid little town of Cincinnati also suffered
from the Indian war parties in the spring of this
Cincinnati year,[1] several of the townsmen being killed
Also by the savages, who grew so bold that they
Suffers. lurked through the streets at nights, and lay
in ambush in the gardens where the garrison of Fort
Washington raised their vegetables. One of the

[1] " American Pioneer," II., 149.

Indian attacks, made upon a little palisaded "station" which had been founded by a man named Dunlop, some seventeen miles from Cincinnati, was noteworthy because of an act of not uncommon cruelty by the Indians. In the station there were some regulars. Aided by the settlers they beat back their foes; whereupon the enraged savages brought one of their prisoners within ear-shot of the walls and tortured him to death. The torture began at midnight, and the screams of the wretched victim were heard until daylight.[1]

Until this year the war was not general. One of the most bewildering problems to be solved by the Federal officers on the Ohio was to find out which tribes were friendly and which hostile. Many of the inveterate enemies of the Americans were as forward in professions of friendship as the peaceful Indians, and were just as apt to be found at the treaties, or lounging about the settlements; and this widespread treachery and deceit made the task of the army officers puzzling to a degree. As for the frontiersmen, who had no means whatever of telling a hostile from a friendly tribe, they followed their usual custom and lumped all the Indians, good and bad, together; for which they could hardly be blamed. Even St. Clair, who had small sympathy with the backwoodsmen, acknowledged[2] that they could not and ought not to submit patiently to the cruelties and depredations of the savages; "they are in the habit of retaliation, perhaps without attend-

Difficulties in Discriminating between Hostile and Friendly Indians.

[1] McBride, I., 88.   [2] American State Papers, IV., 58.

ing precisely to the nations from which the injuries are received," said he. A long course of such aggressions and retaliations resulted, by the year 1791, in all the Northwestern Indians going on the war-path. The hostile tribes had murdered and plundered the frontiersmen; the vengeance of the latter, as often as not, had fallen on friendly tribes; and these justly angered friendly tribes usually signalized their taking the red hatchet by some act of treacherous hostility directed against the settlers who had not molested them.

In the late winter of 1791 the hitherto friendly Delawares who hunted or traded along the western frontiers of Pennsylvania and Virginia proper took this manner of showing that they had joined the open foes of the Americans. A big band of warriors spread up and down the Alleghany for about forty miles, and on the 9th of February attacked all the outlying settlements. The Indians who delivered this attack had long been on intimate terms with the Alleghany settlers, who were accustomed to see them in and about their houses; and as the savages acted with seeming friendship to the last moment, they were able to take the settlers completely unawares, so that no effective resistance was made.[1] Some settlers were killed and some captured. Among the captives was a lad named John Brickell, who, though at first maltreated, and forced to run the gauntlet, was afterwards adopted into the tribe, and was not released until after Wayne's victory. After his

Treachery of the Friendly Delawares.

---

[1] "American Pioneer," I., 44; Narrative of John Brickell.

adoption, he was treated with the utmost kindness, and conceived a great liking for his captors, admiring their many good qualities, especially their courage and their kindness to their children. Long afterwards he wrote down his experiences, which possess a certain value as giving, from the Indian standpoint, an account of some of the incidents of the forest warfare of the day.

The warriors who had engaged in this raid on their former friends, the settlers along the Alleghany, retreated two or three days' journey into the wilderness to an appointed place, where they found their families. One of the Girtys was with the Indians. No sooner had the last of the warriors come in, **Utter Untrustworthiness of the Indians.** with their scalps and prisoners, including the boy Brickell, than ten of their number deliberately started back to Pittsburgh, to pass themselves as friendly Indians, and trade. In a fortnight they returned laden with goods of various kinds, including whiskey. Some of the inhabitants, sore from disaster, suspected that these Indians were only masquerading as friendly, and prepared to attack them; but one of the citizens warned them of their danger and they escaped. Their effrontery was as remarkable as their treachery and duplicity. They had suddenly attacked and massacred settlers by whom they had never been harmed, and with whom they preserved an appearance of entire friendship up to the very moment of the assault. Then, their hands red with the blood of their murdered friends, they came boldly into Pittsburgh, among the near neighbors of these same murdered men, and stayed there several days to trade, pretending to be peaceful allies of the whites. With savages so treacherous and so ferocious it was a mere impossibility for the borderers to distinguish the hostile from the friendly, as they hit out blindly to revenge the blows that fell upon them from unknown hands. Brutal though the frontiersmen often were, they never employed the systematic and deliberate bad faith which was a favorite weapon with even the best of the red tribes.

The people who were out of reach of the Indian tomahawk, and especially the Federal officers, were **The Federal Authorities Misjudge the Settlers.** often unduly severe in judging the borderers for their deeds of retaliation. Brickell's narrative shows that the parties of seemingly friendly Indians who came in to trade were sometimes—and indeed in this year 1791 it was probable they were generally—composed of Indians who were engaged in active hostilities against the settlers, and who were always watching for a chance to murder and plunder. On March 9th, a month after the Delawares had begun their attacks, the grim backwoods captain Brady, with some of his Virginian rangers, fell on a party of them who had come to a block-house to trade, and killed four. The Indians asserted that they were friendly, and both the Federal Secretary of War and the Governor of Pennsylvania denounced the deed, and threatened the offenders; but the frontiersmen stood by them.[1] Soon afterwards a delegation of

[1] State Department MSS., Washington Papers, Ex. C., p. 11, etc. Presly Neville to Richard Butler, March 19, 1791 ; Isaac Craig to Secretary of War, March 16, 1791 ; Secretary of War to President, March 31, 1791.

chiefs from the Seneca tribe of the Iroquois arrived at Fort Pitt, and sent a message to the President, complaining of the murder of these alleged friendly Indians.[1] On the very day these Seneca chiefs started on their journey home another Delaware war party killed nine settlers, men, women, and children, within twenty miles of Fort Pitt; which so enraged the people of the neighborhood that the lives of the Senecas were jeopardized. The United States authories were particularly anxious to keep at peace with the Six Nations, and made repeated efforts to treat with them; but the Six Nations stood sullenly aloof, afraid to enter openly into the struggle, and yet reluctant to make a firm peace or cede any of their lands.[2]

The intimate relations between the Indians and the British at the Lake Posts continued to perplex and anger the Americans. While the Intimate frontiers were being mercilessly ravaged, Relations the same Indians who were committing the British and ravages met in council with the British Indians. agent, Alexander McKee, at the Miami Rapids; the council being held in this neighborhood for the special benefit of the very towns which were most hostile to the Americans, and which had been partially destroyed by Harmar the preceding fall. The Indian war was at its height, and the murderous forays never ceased throughout the spring and sum-

---

[1] American State Papers, IV., 145, Cornplanter and others to the President, March 17, 1791.

[2] State Department MSS., Washington Papers, Knox to the President, April 10, 1791; American State Papers, IV., pp. 139–170, 225–233, 477–482, etc.

mer. McKee came to Miami in April, and was
forced to wait nearly three months, because of the
absence of the Indian war parties, before the principal
chiefs and headmen gathered to meet him. At last,
on July 1st, they were all assembled; not only the
Shawnees, Delawares, Wyandots, Ottawas, Pottawatamies and others who had openly taken the
hatchet against the Americans, but also representatives of the Six Nations, and tribes of savages from
lands so remote that they carried no guns, but
warred with bows, spears, and tomahawks, and were
clad in buffalo-robes instead of blankets. McKee
in his speech to them did not incite them to war.
On the contrary, he advised them, in guarded language, to make peace with the United States; but
only upon terms consistent with their "honor and
interest." He assured them that, whatever they did,
he wished to know what they desired; and that the
sole purpose of the British was to promote the welfare of the confederated Indians. Such very cautious
advice was not of a kind to promote peace; and the
goods furnished the savages at the council included
not only cattle, corn, and tobacco, but also quantities
of powder and balls. [1]

The chief interest of the British was to preserve
the fur trade for their merchants, and it was mainly
The Fur   for this reason that they clung so tenaciously
Trade the   to the Lake Posts. For their purposes it
Prime Ob-
ject of the   was essential that the Indians should re-
British.   main lords of the soil. They preferred to
see the savages at peace with the Americans, pro-

---

[1] Canadian Archives, McKee's speech to the Indians, July 1, 1791; and
Francis Lafontaine's account of sundries to Indians.

vided that in this way they could keep their lands; but, whether through peace or war, they wished the lands to remain Indian, and the Americans to be barred from them. While they did not at the moment advise war, their advice to make peace was so faintly uttered, and so hedged round with conditions as to be of no weight; and they furnished the Indians not only with provisions but with munitions of war. While McKee, and other British officers, were at the Miami Rapids, holding councils with the Indians, and issuing to them goods and weapons, bands of braves were continually returning from forays against the American frontier, bringing in scalps and prisoners; and the wilder subjects of the British King, like the Girtys, and some of the French from Detroit, went off with the war parties on their forays.[1] The authorities at the capital of the new Republic were deceived by the warmth with which the British insisted that they were striving to bring about a peace; but the frontiersmen were not deceived, and they were right in their belief that the British were really the mainstay and support of the Indians in their warfare.

Peace could only be won by the unsheathed sword. Even the National Government was reluctantly driven to this view. As all the Northwestern tribes were banded in open war, it was useless to let the conflict remain a succession of raids and counter-raids. Only a severe stroke, delivered by a formidable army,

The Americans Draw the Sword.

[1] American State Papers, IV., 196. Narrative of Thomas Rhea, July 2, 1791. This narrative was distrusted; but it is fully borne out by McKee's letter, and the narrative of Brickell. He saw Brickell, whom he calls "Brittle," at the Miami.

could cow the tribes. It was hopeless to try to deliver such a crippling blow with militia alone, and it was very difficult for the infant government to find enough money or men to equip an army composed exclusively of regulars. Accordingly preparations were made for a campaign with a mixed force of regulars, special levies, and militia; and St. Clair, already Governor of the Northwestern Territory, was put in command of the army as Major-General.

Before the army was ready the Federal Government was obliged to take other measures for the **Rangers** defence of the border. Small bodies of **and Scouts** rangers were raised from among the frontier **are Raised.** militia, being paid at the usual rate for soldiers in the army, a net sum of about two dollars a month while in service. In addition, on the repeated and urgent request of the frontiersmen, a few of the most active hunters and best woodsmen, men like Brady, were enlisted as scouts, being paid six or eight times the ordinary rate. These men, because of their skill in woodcraft and their thorough knowledge of Indian fighting, were beyond comparison more valuable than ordinary militia or regulars, and were prized very highly by the frontiersmen.[1]

Besides thus organizing the local militia for defense, the President authorized the Kentuckians to **Raid of** undertake two offensive expeditions against **Scott.** the Wabash Indians so as to prevent them from giving aid to the Miami tribes, whom St. Clair was to attack. Both expeditions were carried on by bands of mounted volunteers, such as had

---

[1] American State Papers, IV., 107, Jan. 5, 1791.

followed Clark on his various raids. The first was
commanded by Brigadier-General Charles Scott;
Colonel John Hardin led his advance guard, and
Wilkinson was second in command. Towards the
end of May, Scott crossed the Ohio, at the head of
eight hundred horse-riflemen, and marched rapidly
and secretly towards the Wabash towns. A mounted
Indian discovered the advance of the Americans and
gave the alarm; and so most of the Indians escaped
just as the Kentucky riders fell on the town. But
little resistance was offered by the surprised and
outnumbered savages. Only five Americans were
wounded, while of the Indians thirty-two were slain,
as they fought or fled, and forty-one prisoners, chiefly
women and children, were brought in, either by
Scott himself or by his detachments under Hardin
and Wilkinson. Several towns were destroyed, and
the growing corn cut down. There were not a few
French living in the town, in well-finished log-
houses, which were burned with the wigwams.[1]
The second expedition was under the command of
Wilkinson, and consisted of over five hundred men. He marched in August, and Raid of
Wilkinson.
repeated Scott's feats, again burning down
two or three of the towns, and destroying the goods
and the crops. He lost three or four men killed or
wounded, but killed ten Indians and captured some
thirty.[2] In both expeditions the volunteers behaved
well and committed no barbarous act, except that in
the confusion of the actual onslaught two or three

[1] American State Papers, IV., 131, Scott's Report, June 28, 1791.
[2] *Do.*, Wilkinson's Letter, August 24, 1791.

non-combatants were slain. The Wabash Indians were cowed and disheartened by their punishment, and in consequence gave no aid to the Miami tribes; but beyond this the raids accomplished nothing, and brought no nearer the wished-for time of peace.

Meanwhile St. Clair was striving vainly to hasten the preparations for his own far more formidable task. There was much delay in forwarding him the men and the provisions and munitions. Congress hesitated and debated; the Secretary of War, hampered by a newly created office and insufficient means, did not show to advantage in organizing the campaign, and was slow in carrying out his plans; while there was positive dereliction of duty on the part of the quartermaster, and the contractors proved both corrupt and inefficient. The army was often on short commons, lacking alike food for the men and fodder for the horses; the powder was poor, the axes useless, the tents and clothing nearly worthless; while the delays were so extraordinary that the troops did not make the final move from Fort Washington until mid-September.[1]

St. Clair himself was broken in health; he was a sick, weak, elderly man, high minded, and zealous to do his duty, but totally unfit for the terrible responsibilities of such an expedition against such foes. The troops were of wretched stuff. There were two small regiments of regular infantry, the rest of the army

St. Clair's Difficulty in Organizing his Campaign.

Wretched Condition of St. Clair's Army.

---

[1] St. Clair Papers, II., 286, Report of Special Committee of Congress, March 27, 1792.

being composed of six months' levies and of militia
ordered out for this particular campaign. The pay
was contemptible. Each private was given three
dollars a month, from which ninety cents was
deducted, leaving a net payment of two dollars and
ten cents a month.[1] Sergeants netted three dollars
and sixty cents; while the lieutenants received
twenty-two, the captains thirty, and the colonels
sixty dollars. The mean parsimony of the nation in
paying such low wages to men about to be sent on
duties at once very arduous and very dangerous met
its fit and natural reward. Men of good bodily
powers, and in the prime of life, and especially men
able to do the rough work of frontier farmers, could
not be hired to fight Indians in unknown forests for
two dollars a month. Most of the recruits were
from the streets and prisons of the seaboard cities.
They were hurried into a campaign against peculiarly
formidable foes before they had acquired the rudiments of a soldier's training, and, of course, they
never even understood what woodcraft meant.[2] The
officers were men of courage, as in the end most of
them showed by dying bravely on the field of battle;
but they were utterly untrained themselves, and had
no time in which to train their men. Under such
conditions it did not need keen vision to foretell disaster. Harmar had learned a bitter lesson the preceding year; he knew well what Indians could do,
and what raw troops could not; and he insisted with

[1] American State Papers, IV., 118, Report of Secy. of War, January 22,
1791.
[2] Denny's Journal, 374.

emphasis that the only possible outcome to St. Clair's expedition was defeat.

As the raw troops straggled to Pittsburgh they were shipped down the Ohio to Fort Washington; and St. Clair made the headquarters of his army at a new fort some twenty-five miles northward, which he christened Fort Hamilton. During September the army slowly assembled; two small regiments of regulars, two of six months' levies, a number of Kentucky militia, a few cavalry, and a couple of small batteries of light guns. After wearisome delays, due mainly to the utter inefficiency of the quartermaster and contractor, the start for the Indian towns was made on October the 4th.

The Troops Gather at Fort Washington.

The army trudged slowly through the deep woods and across the wet prairies, cutting out its own road, and making but five or six miles a day. It was in a wilderness which abounded with game; both deer and bear frequently ran into the very camps; and venison was a common food.[1] On October 13th a halt was made to build another little fort, christened in honor of Jefferson. There were further delays, caused by the wretched management of the commissariat department, and the march was not resumed until the 24th, the numerous sick being left in Fort Jefferson. Then the army once more stumbled northward through the wilderness. The regulars,

The Army Begins its March.

---

[1] Bradley MSS. The journal and letters of Captain Daniel Bradley; shown me by the courtesy of his descendants, Mr. Daniel B. Bradley of Southport, Conn., and Mr. Arthur W. Bradley of Cincinnati, Ohio.

though mostly raw recruits, had been reduced to
some kind of discipline; but the six months' levies
were almost worse than the militia.[1] Owing to the
long delays, and to the fact that they had been
enlisted at various times, their terms of service were
expiring day by day; and they wished to go home,
and tried to, while the militia deserted in squads and
bands. Those that remained were very disorderly.
Two who attempted to desert were hung; and another, who shot a comrade, was hung also; but even
this severity in punishment failed to stop the demoralization.

With such soldiers there would have been grave
risk of disaster under any commander; but St. Clair's
leadership made the risk a certainty. There   St. Clair
was Indian sign, old and new, all through   a Broken-
the woods; and the scouts and stragglers   down Man.
occasionally interchanged shots with small parties of
braves, and now and then lost a man, killed or captured. It was, therefore, certain that the savages
knew every movement of the army, which, as it
slowly neared the Miami towns, was putting itself
within easy striking range of the most formidable
Indian confederacy in the Northwest. The density
of the forest was such that only the utmost watchfulness could prevent the foe from approaching
within arm's length unperceived. It behooved St.
Clair to be on his guard, and he had been warned by
Washington, who had never forgotten the scenes of
Braddock's defeat, of the danger of a surprise. But
St. Clair was broken down by the worry and by con-

[1] Denny, October 29, 1791, etc.

tinued sickness; time and again it was doubtful whether he could so much as stay with the army. The **His Subordinates.** second in command, Major-General Richard Butler, was also sick most of the time; and, like St. Clair, he possessed none of the qualities of leadership save courage. The whole burden fell on the Adjutant-General, Colonel Winthrop Sargent, an old Revolutionary officer; without him the expedition would probably have failed in ignominy even before the Indians were reached, and he showed not only cool courage but ability of a good order; yet in the actual arrangements for battle he was, of course, unable to remedy the blunders of his superiors.

St. Clair should have covered his front and flanks for miles around with scouting parties; but he rarely **His Shortcomings.** sent any out, and, thanks to letting the management of those that did go devolve on his subordinates, and to not having their reports made to him in person, he derived no benefit from what they saw. He had twenty Chickasaws with him; but he sent these off on an extended trip, lost touch of them entirely, and never saw them again until after the battle. He did not seem to realize that he was himself in danger of attack. When some fifty miles or so from the Miami towns, on the last day of October, sixty of the militia deserted; and he actually sent back after them one of his two regular regiments, thus weakening by one half the only trustworthy portion of his force.[1]

[1] Bradley MSS. In his journal Captain Bradley expresses his astonishment at seeing the regiment and his inability to understand the object in sending it back. Captain Bradley was not over-pleased with his life at the fort; as one of the minor ills he mentions in one of his letters to Ebenezer

On November 3d the doomed army, now reduced to a total of about fourteen hundred men, camped on the eastern fork of the Wabash, high up, where it was but twenty yards wide. **The Last Camp.** There was snow on the ground and the little pools were skimmed with ice. The camp was on a narrow rise of ground, where the troops were cramped together, the artillery and most of the horse in the middle. On both flanks, and along most of the rear, the ground was low and wet. All around, the wintry woods lay in frozen silence. In front the militia were thrown across the creek, and nearly a quarter of a mile beyond the rest of the troops.[1] Parties of Indians were seen during the afternoon, and they skulked around the lines at night, so that the sentinels frequently fired at them; yet neither St. Clair nor Butler took any adequate measures to ward off the impending blow. It is improbable that, as things actually were at this time, they could have won a victory over their terrible foes; but they might have avoided overwhelming disaster.

On November 4th the men were under arms, as usual, by dawn, St. Clair intending to throw up entrenchments and then make a forced march in light order against the Indian **The Indians** towns. But he was forestalled. Soon **Surprise** after sunrise, just as the men were dis- **the Camp** missed from parade, a sudden assault was **at Dawn.** made upon the militia, who lay unprotected beyond the creek. The unexpectedness and fury of the

Banks: "Please deliver the enclosed letter to my wife. Not a drop of cider have I drinked this twelve month."

[1] St. Clair's Letter to the Secretary of War, Nov. 9, 1791.

onset, the heavy firing, and the appalling whoops and yells of the throngs of painted savages threw the militia into disorder. After a few moments' resistance they broke and fled in wild panic to the camp of the regulars, among whom they drove in a frightened herd, spreading dismay and confusion.

The drums beat, and the troops sprang to arms, as soon as they heard the heavy firing at the front; and their volleys for a moment checked the onrush of the plumed woodland warriors. But the check availed nothing. The braves filed off to one side and the other, completely surrounded the camp, killed or drove in the guards and pickets, and then advanced close to the main lines.[1]

A furious battle followed. After the first onset the Indians fought in silence, no sound coming from **Desperate** them save the incessant rattle of their fire, **Fighting** as they crept from log to log, from tree to **Follows.** tree, ever closer and closer. The soldiers stood in close order, in the open; their musketry and artillery fire made a tremendous noise, but did little damage to a foe they could hardly see. Now and then, through the hanging smoke, terrible figures flitted, painted black and red, the feathers of the hawk and eagle braided in their long scalp-locks; but save for these glimpses, the soldiers knew the presence of their sombre enemy only from the fearful rapidity with which their comrades fell dead and wounded in the ranks. They never even knew the numbers or leaders of the Indians. At the time it

[1] Denny, November 4th; also p. 221.

was supposed that they outnumbered the whites;
but it is probable that the reverse was the case, and
it may even be that they were not more than half as
numerous. It is said that the chief who led them,
both in council and battle, was Little Turtle, the
Miami. At any rate, there were present all the
chiefs and picked warriors of the Delawares, Shawnees, Wyandots, and Miamis, and all the most reckless and adventurous young braves from among the
Iroquois and the Indians of the Upper Lakes, as
well as many of the ferocious whites and half-breeds
who dwelt in the Indian villages.

The Indians fought with the utmost boldness and
ferocity, and with the utmost skill and caution.
Under cover of the smoke of the heavy but
harmless fire from the army they came up
so close that they shot the troops down as
hunters slaughter a herd of standing buffalo. Watching their chance, they charged again and again with
the tomahawk, gliding into close quarters while their
bewildered foes were still blindly firing into the
smoke-shrouded woods. The men saw no enemy as
they stood in the ranks to load and shoot; in a
moment, without warning, dark faces frowned
through the haze, the war-axes gleamed, and on the
frozen ground the weapons clattered as the soldiers
fell. As the comrades of the fallen sprang forward
to avenge them, the lithe warriors vanished as
rapidly as they had appeared; and once more the
soldiers saw before them only the dim forest and the
shifting smoke wreaths, with vague half glimpses of
the hidden foe, while the steady singing of the

Indian bullets never ceased, and on every hand the bravest and steadiest fell one by one.

At first the army as a whole fought firmly; indeed there was no choice, for it was ringed by a wall of

The Troops at First Fight Resolutely.

flame. The officers behaved very well, cheering and encouraging their men; but they were the special targets of the Indians, and fell rapidly. St. Clair and Butler by their cool fearlessness in the hour of extreme peril made some amends for their shortcomings as commanders. They walked up and down the lines from flank to flank, passing and repassing one another; for the two lines of battle were facing outward, and each general was busy trying to keep his wing from falling back. St. Clair's clothes were pierced by eight bullets, but he was himself untouched. He wore a blanket coat with a hood; he had a long queue, and his thick gray hair flowed from under his three-cornered hat; a lock of his hair was carried off by a bullet.[1] Several times he headed the charges, sword in hand. General Butler had his arm broken

Bravery of the Officers in Command.

early in the fight, but he continued to walk to and fro along the line, his coat off and the wounded arm in a sling. Another bullet struck him in the side, inflicting a mortal wound; and he was carried to the middle of the camp, where he sat propped up by knapsacks. Men and horses were falling around him at every moment. St. Clair sent an aide, Lieutenant Ebenezer Denny,

---

[1] McBride's "Pioneer Biography," I., 165. Narrative of Thomas Irwin, a packer, who was in the fight. There are of course discrepancies between the various accounts; in the confusion of such a battle even the most honest eye-witnesses could not see all things alike.

to ask how he was; he displayed no anxiety, and answered that he felt well. While speaking, a young cadet, who stood nearby, was hit on the knee-cap by a spent ball, and at the shock cried aloud; whereat the General laughed so that his wounded side shook. The aide left him; and there is no further certain record of his fate except that he was slain; but it is said that in one of the Indian rushes a warrior bounded towards him and sunk the toma-hawk in his brain before any one could interfere.

Instead of being awed by the bellowing artillery, the Indians made the gunners a special object of attack. Man after man was picked off, until every officer was killed but one, who was wounded; and most of the privates also were slain or disabled. The artillery was thus almost silenced, and the Indians, embold-ened by success, swarmed forward and seized the guns, while at the same time a part of the left wing of the army began to shrink back. But the Indians were now on comparatively open ground, where the regulars could see them and get at them; and under St. Clair's own leadership the troops rushed fiercely at the savages, with fixed bayonets, and drove them back to cover. By this time the confusion and dis-order were great; while from every hollow and grass patch, from behind every stump and tree and fallen log, the Indians continued their fire. Again and again the officers led forward the troops in bayonet charges; and at first the men followed them with a will. Each charge seemed for a moment to be suc-cessful, the Indians rising in swarms and running in

The In-dians Cap-ture the Artillery.

headlong flight from the bayonets. In one of the
earliest, in which Colonel Darke led his battalion,
the Indians were driven several hundred
yards, across the branch of the Wabash;
but when the Colonel halted and rallied his
men, he found that the savages had closed in
behind him, and he had to fight his way back, while
the foe he had been driving at once turned and harassed his rear. He was himself wounded, and lost
most of his command. On re-entering camp he found
the Indians again in possession of the artillery and
baggage, from which they were again driven; they
had already scalped the slain who lay about the
guns. Major Thomas Butler had his thigh broken
by a bullet; but he continued on horseback, in command of his battalion, until the end of the fight, and
led his men in one of the momentarily successful
bayonet charges. The only regular regiment present
lost every officer, killed or wounded. The commander of the Kentucky militia, Colonel Oldham,
was killed early in the action, while trying to rally
his men and damning them for cowards.

The charging troops could accomplish nothing permanent. The men were too clumsy and ill-trained
in forest warfare to overtake their fleet,
half-naked antagonists. The latter never
received the shock; but though they fled
they were nothing daunted, for they turned
the instant the battalion did, and followed firing.
They skipped out of reach of the bayonets, and came
back as they pleased; and they were only visible
when raised by a charge.

*Charges
and
Counter-
Charges.*

*Inferiority
of the
Troops to
the Indians.*

Among the packhorsemen were some who were accustomed to the use of the rifle and to life in the woods; and these fought well. One, named Benjamin Van Cleve, kept a journal, in which he described what he saw of the fight.[1] He had no gun, but five minutes after the firing began he saw a soldier near him with his arm swinging useless; and he borrowed the wounded man's musket and cartridges. The smoke had settled to within three feet of the ground, so he knelt, covering himself behind a tree, and only fired when he saw an Indian's head, or noticed one running from cover to cover. He fired away all his ammunition, and the bands of his musket flew off; he picked up another just as two levy officers ordered a charge, and followed the charging party at a run. By this time the battalions were broken, and only some thirty men followed the officers. The Indians fled before the bayonets until they reached a ravine filled with down timber; whereupon they halted behind the impenetrable tangle of fallen logs. The soldiers also halted, and were speedily swept away by the fire of the Indians, whom they could not reach; but Van Cleve, showing his skill as a woodsman, covered himself behind a small tree, and gave back shot for shot until all his ammunition was gone. Before this happened his less skilful companions had been slain or driven off, and he ran at full speed back to camp. Here he found that the artillery had been taken and re-taken again and again. Stricken men lay in heaps everywhere, and the charging

Feats of Some of the Pack-horsemen.

[1] " American Pioneer," II., 150 ; Van Cleve's memoranda.

troops were once more driving the Indians across the creek in front of the camp. Van Cleve noticed that the dead officers and soldiers who were lying about the guns had all been scalped and that "the Indians had not been in a hurry, for their hair was all skinned off." Another of the packers who took part in the fight, one Thomas Irwin, was struck with the spectacle offered by the slaughtered artillerymen, and with grewsome homeliness compared the reeking heads to pumpkins in a December cornfield.

As the officers fell the soldiers, who at first stood up bravely enough, gradually grew disheartened. No **The Sol-** words can paint the hopelessness and horror **diers Lose** of such a struggle as that in which they **Heart.** were engaged. They were hemmed in by foes who showed no mercy and whose blows they could in no way return. If they charged they could not overtake the Indians; and the instant the charge stopped the Indians came back. If they stood they were shot down by an unseen enemy; and there was no stronghold, no refuge to which to flee. The Indian attack was relentless, and could neither be avoided, parried, nor met by counter assault. For two hours or so the troops kept up a slowly lessening resistance; but by degrees their hearts failed. The wounded had been brought towards the middle of the lines, where the baggage and tents were, and an **Panic** ever growing proportion of unwounded **Seizes the** men joined them. In vain the officers tried, **Army.** by encouragement, by jeers, by blows, to drive them back to the fight. They were unnerved. As in all cases where large bodies of men are put

in imminent peril of death, whether by shipwreck,
plague, fire, or violence, numbers were swayed by a
mad panic of utterly selfish fear, and others became
numbed and callous, or snatched at any animal gratification during their last moments. Many soldiers
crowded round the fires and stood stunned and confounded by the awful calamity; many broke into
the officers' marquees and sought for drink, or devoured the food which the rightful owners had left
when the drums beat to arms.

There was but one thing to do. If possible the
remnant of the army must be saved, and it could
only be saved by instant flight, even at the St. Clair
cost of abandoning the wounded. The Resolves
broad road by which the army had ad- on Retreat.
vanced was the only line of retreat. The artillery
had already been spiked and abandoned. Most of
the horses had been killed, but a few were still left,
and on one of these St. Clair mounted. He gathered
together those fragments of the different battalions
which contained the few men who still kept heart and
head, and ordered them to charge and regain the road
from which the savages had cut them off. Repeated
orders were necessary before some of the men could
be roused from their stupor sufficiently to follow the
charging party; and they were only induced to move
when told that it was to retreat.

Colonel Darke and a few officers placed themselves at the head of the column, the coolest and
boldest men drew up behind them, and they fell
on the Indians with such fury as to force them
back well beyond the road. This made an opening

through which, said Van Cleve the packer, the rest
of the troops "pressed like a drove of bullocks."
The The Indians were surprised by the vigor
Troops of the charge, and puzzled as to its object.
Break
through They opened out on both sides and half
the Indian the men had gone through before they
Ring. fired more than a chance shot or two.
They then fell on the rear, and began a hot pursuit.
St. Clair sent his aide, Denny, to the front to try to
keep order, but neither he nor anyone else could
check the flight. Major Clark tried to rally his battalion to cover the retreat, but he was killed and the
effort abandoned.

There never was a wilder rout. As soon as the
men began to run, and realized that in flight there
Wild Rout lay some hope of safety, they broke into a
of the stampede which soon became uncontrol-
Army. lable. Horses, soldiers, and the few camp
followers and women who had accompanied the army
were all mixed together. Neither command nor
example had the slightest weight; the men were
abandoned to the terrible selfishness of utter fear.
They threw away their weapons as they ran. They
thought of nothing but escape, and fled in a huddle,
the stronger and the few who had horses trampling
their way to the front through the old, the weak, and
the wounded; while behind them raged the Indian
tomahawk. Fortunately the attraction of plundering the camp was so overpowering that the savages
only followed the army about four miles; otherwise
hardly a man would have escaped.

St. Clair was himself in much danger, for he tried

to stay behind and stem the torrent of fugitives; but
he failed, being swept forward by the crowd, and
when he attempted to ride to the front to   Story of
rally them, he failed again, for his horse   Van Cleve
could not be pricked out of a walk.   The   the Packer.
packer, Van Cleve, in his journal, gives a picture of
the flight. He was himself one of the few who
lost neither courage nor generosity in the rout.

Among his fellow packers were his uncle and a
young man named Bonham, who was his close and
dear friend. The uncle was shot in the wrist, the
ball lodging near his shoulder; but he escaped.
Bonham, just before the retreat began, was shot
through both hips, so that he could not walk.
Young Van Cleve got him a horse, on which he
was with difficulty mounted; then, as the flight
began, Bonham bade Van Cleve look to his safety,
as he was on foot, and the two separated. Bonham
rode until the pursuit had almost ceased; then, weak
and crippled, he was thrown off his horse and slain.
Meanwhile Van Cleve ran steadily on foot. By the
time he had gone two miles most of the mounted
men had passed him. A boy, on the point of falling
from exhaustion, now begged his help; and the kind-
hearted backwoodsman seized the lad and pulled
him along nearly two miles farther, when he himself
became so worn-out that he nearly fell. There were
still two horses in the rear, one carrying three men,
and one two; and behind the latter Van Cleve, summoning his strength, threw the boy, who escaped.
Nor did Van Cleve's pity for his fellows cease with
this; for he stopped to tie his handkerchief around

the knee of a wounded man. His violent exertions gave him a cramp in both thighs, so that he could barely walk; and in consequence the strong and active passed him until he was within a hundred yards of the rear, where the Indians were tomahawking the old and wounded men. So close were they that for a moment his heart sunk in despair; but he threw off his shoes, the touch of the cold ground seemed to revive him, and he again began to trot forward. He got around a bend in the road, passing half a dozen other fugitives; and long afterwards he told how well he remembered thinking that it would be some time before they would all be massacred and his own turn came. However, at this point the pursuit ceased, and a few miles farther on he had gained the middle of the flying troops, and like them came to a walk. He fell in with a queer group, consisting of the sole remaining officer of the artillery, an infantry corporal, and a woman called Red-headed Nance. Both of the latter were crying, the corporal for the loss of his wife, the woman for the loss of her child. The worn-out officer hung on the corporal's arm, while Van Cleve " carried his fusee and accoutrements and led Nance; and in this sociable way arrived at Fort Jefferson a little after sunset."

Before reaching Fort Jefferson the wretched army encountered the regular regiment which had been so unfortunately detached a couple of days before the battle. The most severely wounded were left in the fort;[1] and then the flight was renewed, until the

---

[1] Bradley MSS. The addition of two hundred sick and wounded brought the garrison to such short commons that they had to slaughter the pack-horses for food.

disorganized and half-armed rabble reached Fort Washington, and the mean log huts of Cincinnati. Six hundred and thirty men had been killed and over two hundred and eighty wounded; less than five hundred, only about a third of the whole number engaged in the battle, remained unhurt. But one or two were taken prisoners, for the Indians butchered everybody, wounded or unwounded, who fell into their hands. There is no record of the torture of any of the captives, but there was one singular instance of cannibalism. The savage Chippewas from the far-off north devoured one of the slain soldiers, probably in a spirit of ferocious bravado; the other tribes expressed horror at the deed.[1] The Indians were rich with the spoil. They got horses, tents, guns, axes, powder, clothing, and blankets—in short everything their hearts prized. Their loss was comparatively slight; it may not have been one twentieth that of the whites. They did not at the moment follow up their victory, each band going off with its own share of the booty. But the triumph was so overwhelming, and the reward so great, that the war spirit received a great impetus in all the tribes. The bands of warriors that marched against the frontier were more numerous, more formidable, and bolder than ever.

The Remnant of the Army Reaches Cincinnati.

Exultation of the Victors.

In the following January Wilkinson with a hundred and fifty mounted volunteers marched to the battle-field to bury the slain. The weather was bit-

[1] Brickell's Narrative.

terly cold, snow lay deep on the ground, and some of the volunteers were frost bitten.[1] Four miles

from the scene of the battle, where the pursuit had ended, they began to find the bodies on the the road, and close alongside, in the woods, whither some of the hunted creatures had turned at the last, to snatch one more moment of life. Many had been dragged from under the snow and devoured by wolves. The others lay where they had fallen, showing as mounds through the smooth white mantle that covered them. On the battle-field itself the slain lay thick, scalped, and stripped of all their clothing which the conquerors deemed worth taking. The bodies, blackened by frost and exposure, could not be identified; and they were buried in a shallow trench in the frozen ground. The volunteers then marched home.

When the remnant of the defeated army reached the banks of the Ohio, St. Clair sent his aide, Denny,

to carry the news to Philadelphia, at that time the national capital. The river was swollen, there were incessant snowstorms, and ice formed heavily, so that it took twenty days of toil and cold before Denny reached Wheeling and got horses. For ten days more he rode over the bad winter roads, reaching Philadelphia with the evil tidings on the evening of December 19th. It was thus six weeks after the defeat of

[1] McBride's " Pioneer Biography," John Reily's narrative. This expedition, in which not a single hostile Indian was encountered, has been transmuted by Withers and one or two other border historians into a purely fictitious expedition of revenge in which hundreds of Indians were slain on the field of St. Clair's disaster.

the army before the news was brought to the anxious Federal authorities.

The young officer called first on the Secretary of War; but as soon as the Secretary realized the importance of the information he had it conveyed to the President. Washington was at dinner, with some guests, and was called from the table to listen to the tidings of ill fortune. He returned with unmoved face, and at the dinner, and at the reception which followed, he behaved with his usual stately courtesy to those whom he was entertaining, not so much as hinting at what he had heard. But when the last guest had gone, his pent-up wrath **Washington's Wrath.** broke forth in one of those fits of volcanic fury which sometimes shattered his iron outward calm. Walking up and down the room he burst out in wild regret for the rout and disaster, and bitter invective against St. Clair, reciting how, in that very room, he had wished the unfortunate commander success and honor and had bidden him above all things beware of a surprise.[1] " He went off with that last solemn warning thrown into his ears,"

[1] Tobias Lear, Washington's Private Secretary as quoted by both Custis and Rush. The report of an eyewitness. See also Lodge's " Washington," p. 94. Denny, in his journal, merely mentions that he went at once to the Secretary of War's office on the evening of the 19th, and does not speak of seeing Washington until the following morning. On the strength of this omission one or two of St. Clair's apologists have striven to represent the whole account of Washington's wrath as apocryphal ; but the attempt is puerile ; the relation comes from an eyewitness who had no possible motive to distort the facts. The Secretary of War, Knox, was certain to inform Washington of the disaster the very evening he heard of it ; and whether he sent Denny, or another messenger, or went himself is unimportant. Lear might very well have been mistaken as to the messenger who brought the news ; but he could not have been mistaken about Washington's speech.

spoke Washington, as he strode to and fro, " and yet to suffer that army to be cut to pieces, hacked, butchered, tomahawked, by a surprise, the very thing I guarded him against! O God, O God, he 's worse than a murderer! How can he answer it to his country!" Then, calming himself by a mighty effort: " General St. Clair shall have justice. . . . he shall have full justice." And St. Clair did receive full justice, and mercy too, from both Washington and Congress. For the sake of his courage and honorable character they held him guiltless of the disaster for which his lack of capacity as a general was so largely accountable.

Washington and his administration were not free from blame. It was foolish to attempt the campaign The Blame against the Northwestern Indians with for the men who had only been trained for six Disaster. months, and who were enlisted at the absurd price of two dollars a month. Moreover, there were needless delays in forwarding the troops to Fort Washington; and the commissary department was badly managed. Washington was not directly responsible for any of these shortcomings; he very wisely left to the Secretary of War, Knox, the immediate control of the whole matter, seeking to avoid all interference with him, so that there might be no clashing or conflict of authority[1]; but he was of course ultimately responsible for the little evil, no less than for the great good, done by his administration.

[1] State Dep. MSS., Washington Papers. War Dept. Ex. C., Washington to Knox, April 1, 1791.

The chief blunder was the selection of St. Clair. As a commander he erred in many ways. He did not, or could not, train his troops; and he had no business to challenge a death fight with raw levies. It was unpardonable of him to send back one of his two regular regiments, the only trustworthy portion of his force, on the eve of the battle. He should never have posted the militia, his poorest troops, in the most exposed situation. Above all he should have seen that the patrols and pickets were so numerous, and performed their duty so faithfully, as to preclude the possibility of surprise. With the kind of army furnished him he could hardly have won a victory under any circumstances; but the overwhelming nature of the defeat was mainly due to his incompetence.

Incompetence of St. Clair.

CHAPTER II.

MAD ANTHONY WAYNE; AND THE FIGHT OF THE FALLEN TIMBERS, 1792–1795.

THE United States Government was almost as much demoralized by St. Clair's defeat as was St. Clair's own army. The loosely-knit nation was very poor, and very loath to undertake any work which involved sustained effort and pecuniary sacrifice; while each section was jealous of every other and was unwilling to embark in any enterprise unlikely to inure to its own immediate benefit. There was little national glory or reputation to be won by even a successful Indian war; while another defeat might prove a serious disaster to a government which was as yet far from firm in its seat. The Eastern people were lukewarm about a war in which they had no direct interest; and the foolish frontiersmen, instead of backing up the administration, railed at it and persistently supported the party which desired so to limit the powers and energies of the National Government as to produce mere paralysis. Under such conditions the national administration, instead of at once redoubling its efforts to ensure success by shock of arms, was driven to the ignoble necessity of yet again striving for a hopeless peace.

Demoralization Caused by St. Clair's Defeat.

It would be impossible to paint in too vivid colors the extreme reluctance of the Government to enter into, or to carry on, war with the Indians. It was only after every other shift had been vainly tried that resort was had to the edge of the sword. The United States would gladly have made a stable peace on honorable terms, and strove with weary patience to bring about a friendly understanding. But all such efforts were rendered abortive partly by the treachery and truculence of the savages, who could only be cowed by a thorough beating, and partly by the desire of the settlers for lands which the red men claimed as their hunting grounds.

In pursuance of their timidly futile policy of friendliness, the representatives of the National Government, in the spring of 1792, sent peace envoys, with a flag of truce, to the hostile tribes. The unfortunate ambassadors thus chosen for sacrifice were Colonel John Hardin, the gallant but ill-starred leader of Kentucky horse, who had so often and with such various success encountered the Indians on the field of battle; and a Federal officer, Major Alexander Trueman. In June they started towards the hostile towns, with one or two companions, and soon fell in with some Indians, who on being shown the white flag, and informed of the object of their visit, received them with every appearance of good will. But this was merely a mask. A few hours later the treacherous savages suddenly fell upon and slew the messengers of

peace.[1] It was never learned whether the deed was
the mere wanton outrage of some blood-thirsty young
braves, or the result of orders given by one of the
Indian councils. At any rate, the Indians never
punished the treachery; and when the chiefs wrote
to Washington they mentioned with cool indifference that "you sent us at different times different
speeches, the bearers whereof our foolish young men
killed on their way"[2]; not even expressing regret
for the occurrence.

The truculent violence and bad faith of the savages merited severe chastisement; but the United
States Government was long-suffering and
Treachery forbearing to a degree. There was no at-
of the tempt to avenge the murder of the flag-of-
Savages. truce men. On the contrary, renewed efforts were
made to secure a peace by treaty. In the fall of 1792
Rufus Putnam, on behalf of the United States, succeeded in concluding a treaty with the Wabash and
Illinois tribes,[3] which at least served to keep many
of their young braves out of actual hostilities. In the
following spring three commissioners — Benjamin
Lincoln, Beverly Randolph, and Timothy Pickering,
all men of note,—were sent to persuade the Miami
tribes and their allies to agree to a peace. In his
letter of instructions the Secretary of War impressed
upon them the desire of the people of the United
States for peace in terms that were almost humili-

---

[1] American State Papers, IV., 238, 239, etc. ; also Marshall.

[2] Canadian Archives, Indian affairs, M. 2, p. 224. The Michigan and
Wisconsin historical societies have performed a great service by publishing
so many of these papers.

[3] American State Papers, IV., 338.

ating, and even directed them if necessary to cede some of the lands already granted by the Indians at previous treaties.

In May, 1793, the Commissioners went to Niagara, where they held meetings with various Iroquois chiefs and exchanged friendly letters with the British officers of the posts, who assured them that they would help in the effort to conclude a peace. Captain Brant, the Iro- quois chief, acted as spokesman for a deputation of the hostile Indians from the Miami, where a great council was being held, at which not only the Northwestern tribes, but the Five Nations, were in attendance. The commissioners then sailed to the Detroit River, having first sent home a strong remon- strance against the activity displayed by the new commander on the Ohio, Wayne, whose vigorous measures, they said, had angered the Indians and were considered by the British "unfair and unwarrantable." This was a preposterous complaint; throughout our history, whether in dealing with Indians or with other foes, our Peace Commissioners have invariably shown to disadvantage when compared with the military commandants, for whom they always betray such jealously. Wayne's conduct was eminently proper; and it is difficult to understand the mental attitude of the commissioners who criticised it be- cause the British considered it "unwarrantable." However, a few weeks later they learned to take a more just view of Wayne, and to thank him for the care with which he had kept the peace while they were vainly trying to treat; for at the Detroit

Peace Com- missioners Go to Niagara.

they found they could do nothing. Brant and the
Iroquois urged the Northwestern tribes not to yield
Failure of any point, and promised them help, telling
the Nego- the British agent, McKee, evidently to his
tiations.   satisfaction, "we came here not only to
assist with our advice, but other ways, ... we
came here with arms in our hands"; and they
insisted that the country belonged to the confederated tribes in common, and so could not be surrendered save by all.[1]   Brant was the inveterate foe of
the Americans, and the pensioner of the British;
and his advice to the tribes was sound, and was
adopted by them—though he misled them by his
never-fulfilled promise of support. They refused to
consider any proposition which did not acknowledge
the Ohio as the boundary between them and the
United States; and so, towards the end of August,
the commissioners returned to report their failure.[2]
The final solution of the problem was thus left to
the sword of Wayne.

The attitude of the British gradually changed
from passive to active hostility. In 1792 and 1793
Attitude of they still wished the Indians to make
the British peace with the Americans, provided always
Becomes   there were no such concessions made to the
Progres-
sively More latter as would endanger the British con-
Hostile.   trol of the fur trade. But by the beginning of 1794 the relations between Great Britain
and the United States had become so strained that
open war was threatened; for the advisers of the

[1] Draper MSS., Brant to McKee, Aug. 4, 1793.
[2] American State Papers, IV., 340–360.

King, relying on the weakness of the young Federal
Republic, had begun to adopt that tone of brutal insolence, which reflected well the general attitude of
the British people towards the Americans, and
which finally brought on the second war between
the two nations.

The British officials in Canada were quick to
reflect the tone of the home government, and, as
always in such cases, the more zealous and Lord Dor-
belligerent went a little farther than they chester's
were authorized. On February 10th Lord Speech.
Dorchestor, Governor of Canada, in an address of
welcome to some of the chiefs from the tribes of
the north and west said, speaking of the boundary :
" Children, since my return I find no appearance of a
line remains ; and from the manner in which the
people of the United States push on and act and
talk . . . I shall not be surprised if we are at
war with them in the course of the present year ; and
if so a line must then be drawn by the warriors . . .
we have acted in the most peaceable manner and
borne the language and conduct of the people of the
United States with patience ; but I believe our
patience is almost exhausted." [1] Of course such a
speech, delivered to such an audience, was more than
a mere incitement to war ; it was a direct appeal to
arms. Nor did the encouragement given the Indians
end with words ; for in April, Simcoe, the Lieuten-

[1] Rives' " Life and Times of James Madison," III., 418. A verified copy
of the speech from the archives of the London foreign office.   The authenticity of the speech was admitted at the time by the British Minister ; yet,
extraordinary to say, not only British, but American historians, have spoken
of it as spurious.

ant Governor, himself built a fort at the Miami
Rapids, in the very heart of the hostile tribes, and
garrisoned it with British regulars, infantry and
artillery ; which, wrote one of the British officials
to another, had " put all the Indians here in great
spirits "[1] to resist the Americans.

The same official further reported that the Spaniards also were exciting the Indians to war, and were
in communication with Simcoe, their messengers coming to him at his post on the Miami.
At this time the Spanish Governor, Carondelet, was alarmed over Clark's threatened
invasion of Louisiana on behalf of the
French Republic. He wrote to Simcoe asking for
English help in the event of such invasion. Simcoe,
in return, wrote expressing his good will, and enclosing a copy of Dorchester's speech to the Northern
Indians ; which, Carondelet reported to the Court
of Spain, showed that the English were following
the same system adopted by the Spaniards in reference to the Indians, whom they were employing with
great success against the Americans.[2] Moreover, the
Spaniards, besides communicating with the British,
sent messages to the Indians at the Miami, urging
them to attack the Americans, and promising help ;[3]
a promise which they never fulfilled, save that in a
covert way they furnished the savages with arms
and munitions of war.

The Canadians themselves were excited and

The British and Spaniards Join in Intriguing with the Indians.

---

[1] Canadian Archives, Thomas Duggan to Joseph Chew, Detroit, April 16, 1794.

[2] Draper MSS., Spanish Documents, letter of Carondelet, July 9, 1794.

[3] Canadian Archives, letter of McKee, May 7, 1794.

alarmed by Dorchester's speech,[1] copies of which were distributed broadcast; for the general feeling was that it meant that war was about to be declared between Great Britain and the United States. The Indians took the same view, as to what the speech meant; but to

Effect of Dorches-ter's Speech.

them it gave unmixed pleasure and encouragement. The British officials circulated it everywhere among the tribes, reading it aloud to the gathered chiefs and fighting men. "His Excellency Governor Simcoe has just now left my house on his way to Detroit with Lord Dorchester's speech to the Seven Nations," wrote Brant the Iroquois chief to the Secretary of Indian Affairs for Canada, "and I have every reason to believe when it is delivered that matters will take an immediate change to the Westward, as it will undoubtedly give those Nations high spirits and enable them by a perfect union to check General Wayne."[2]   In April, Lieutenant Colonel John Butler, of the British army, addressed a great council of chiefs near Buffalo, beginning, "I have now a speech to deliver to you from your father Lord Dorchester, which is of the utmost consequence, therefore desire you will pay strict attention to it."[3]   He then delivered the speech, to the delight of the Indians, and continued: "You have heard the great talk of our going to war with the United States, and by the speech of your Father just now delivered to you, you cannot help seeing there is a great prospect of it, I

[1] Canadian Archives, Joseph Chew to Thomas Aston Coffin, Montreal, February 27, 1794.

[2] Canadian Archives, Brant to Chew, April 21, 1794.

[3] Canadian Archives, Butler to Chew, April 27, 1794.

have therefore to recommend you to be all unanimous as one man, and to call in all your people that
may be scattered about the Territories of the United
States."   McKee, the British Indian agent

The Indi-
ans Greatly among the Northwestern tribes who were
Encour- at war with the Americans, reported with
aged. joy the rapid growth of warlike spirit
among the savages in consequence of Dorchester's
speech, and of the building of the British fort on the
Miami.   He wrote, "The face of the Indian affairs in
this country, I have the greatest satisfaction in informing you, seems considerably altered for the better.
His Excellency Lord Dorchester's speech and the
arrival here of speeches from the Spaniards induce
me to believe that a very extensive union of the
Indian Nations will be the immediate consequence.
The Lieutenant Governor has ordered a strong detachment of the 24th Regt. to take post a mile & a half
below this place, this step has given great spirits to
the Indians and impressed them with a hope of our
ultimately acting with them and affording a security
for their families, should the enemy penetrate to their
villages." [1]

Nor did the British confine their encouragement
to words.   The Canadian authorities forwarded to

The British the Miami tribes, through the agent McKee,
Furnish
Them with quantities of guns, rifles, and gunlocks, be-
Arms and sides vermillion paint and tobacco. [2]   McKee
Munitions. was careful to get from the home authori-
ties the best firearms he could, explaining that his
red protégés preferred the long to the short rifles,

[1] Canadian Archives, McKee to Chew, May 8, 1794.
[2] Canadian Archives, Chew to Coffin, June 23, 1794.

and considered the common trade guns makeshifts, to be used only until they could get better ones.

The Indians made good use of the weapons thus furnished them by the "neutral" British. A party of Delawares and Shawnees, after a success-ful skirmish with the Americans, brought to McKee six of the scalps they had taken; and part of the speech of presentation at the solemn council where they were received **British Agents Greet the Scalping Parties.** by McKee, ran : "We had two actions with [some of Wayne's troops who were guarding convoys] in which a great many of our enemies were killed. Part of their flesh we have brought here with us to convince our friend of the truth of their being now in great force on their march against us; therefore, Father, [addressing McKee] we desire you to be strong and bid your children make haste to our assistance as was promised by them." The speaker, a Dela-ware chief, afterwards handed the six scalps to a Huron chief, that he might distribute them among the tribes. McKee sent to the home authorities a full account of this council, where he had assisted at the reception and distribution of the scalps the savages had taken from the soldiers of a nation with which the British still pretended to be at peace ; and a few days later he reported that the Lake Indians were at last gathering, and that when the fighting men of the various tribes joined forces, as he had reason to believe they shortly would, the British posts would be tolerably secure from any attacks by Wayne.[1]

[1] Canadian Archives, McKee's letters May 25 and May 30, 1794.

The Indians served the British, not only as a barrier, against the Americans, but as a police for their own soldiers, to prevent their deserting. An Englishman who visited the Lake Posts at this time recorded with a good deal of horror the fate that befell one of a party of deserters from the British garrison at Detroit. The commander, on discovering that they had gone, ordered the Indians to bring them back dead or alive. When overtaken one resisted, and was killed and scalped. The Indians brought in his scalp and hung it outside the fort, where it was suffered to remain, that the ominous sight might strike terror to other discontented soldiers.[1]

Indians Serve the British as Police.

The publication of Lord Dorchester's speech caused angry excitement in the United States. Many thought it spurious; but Washington, then President, with his usual clear-sightedness, at once recognized that it was genuine, and accepted it as proof of Great Britain's hostile feeling towards his country. Through the Secretary of State he wrote to the British Minister, calling him to sharp account, not only for Dorchester's speech but for the act of building a fort on the Miami, and for the double-dealing of his government, which protested friendship, with smooth duplicity, while their agents urged the savages to war. "At the very moment when the British Ministry were forwarding assurances of good will, does Lord Dorchester foster and encourage in the Indians

Anger of the Americans over Dorchester's Speech.

[1] Draper MSS. From Parliament Library in Canada, MS. "Canadian Letters," descriptive of a tour in Canada in 1792–93.

hostile dispositions towards the United States," ran the letter, " but this speech only forebodes hostility; the intelligence which has been received this morning is, if true, hostility itself . . . governor Simcoe has gone to the foot of the Rapids of the Miami, followed by three companies of a British regiment, in order to build a fort there." The British Minister, Hammond, in his answer said he was " willing to admit the authenticity of the speech," and even the building of the fort; but sought to excuse both by recrimination, asserting that the Americans had themselves in various ways shown hostility to Great Britain.[1] In spite of this explicit admission, however, the British statesmen generally, both in the House of Lords and the House of Commons, disavowed the speech, though in guarded terms;[2] and many Americans were actually convinced by their denials.

Throughout this period, whatever the negotiators might say or do, the ravages of the Indian war parties never ceased. In the spring following St. Clair's defeat the frontiers of Pennsylvania suffered as severely as those of Virginia, from bands of savages who were seeking for scalps, prisoners, and horses. Boats were way-laid and attacked as they descended the Ohio; and the remote settlements were mercilessly scourged. The spies or scouts, the trained Indian fighters, were out all the while, watching for the war bands; and

Severity of the Indian Ravages.

---

[1] Wait's State Papers and Publick Documents, I., 449, 451. Letters of Randolph, May 20, 1794, and Hammond, May 22, 1794.

[2] Am. State Papers, Foreign Relations, I., Randolph to Jay, Aug. 18, 1794.

when they discovered one, a strong party of rangers
or militia was immediately gathered to assail it, if it
could be overtaken. Every variety of good and
bad fortune attended these expeditions. Thus, in

Raids and August, 1792, the spies discovered an In-
Counter- dian party in the lower settlements of
raids. Kentucky. Thirty militia gathered, followed the trail, and overtook the marauders at Roll-
ing Fork, killing four, while the others scattered;
of the whites one was killed and two wounded.
About the same time Kenton found a strong Indian
camp which he attacked at dawn, killing three warriors; but when they turned out in force, and one
of his own scouts was killed, he promptly drew back
out of danger. Neither the Indians nor the wild
white Indian fighters made any point of honor about
retreating. They wished to do as much damage as
possible to their foes, and if the fight seemed doubtful they at once withdrew to await a more favorable
opportunity. As for the individual adventures,
their name was legion. All the old annalists, all the
old frontiersmen who in after life recorded their
memories of the Indian wars, tell with interminable
repetition stories, grewsome in their blood-thirstiness,
and as monotonous in theme as they are varied in
detail:—how such and such a settler was captured
by two Indians, and, watching his chance, fell on his
captors when they sat down to dinner and slew
them " with a squaw-axe"; how another man was
treacherously attacked by two Indians who had
pretended to be peaceful traders, and how, though
wounded, he killed them both; how two or three

cabins were surprised by the savages and all the inhabitants slain; or how a flotilla of flatboats was
taken and destroyed while moored to the bank of
the Ohio; and so on without end.[1]

The United States authorities vainly sought peace;
while the British instigated the tribes to war, and
the savages themselves never thought of   The Fron-
ceasing their hostilities.   The frontiersmen   tiersmen
also wished war, and regarded the British   Wish War.
and Indians with an equal hatred.   They knew that
the presence of the British in the Lake Posts meant
Indian war; they knew that the Indians would war
on them, whether they behaved well or ill, until the
tribes suffered some signal overthrow; and they
coveted the Indian lands with a desire as simple as
it was brutal.   Nor were land hunger and revenge
the only motives that stirred them to aggression;
meaner feelings were mixed with the greed for un-
tilled prairie and unfelled forest, and the fierce longing for blood.   Throughout our history as a nation,
as long as we had a frontier, there was always a
class of frontiersmen for whom an Indian war meant
the chance to acquire wealth at the expense of the
Government: and on the Ohio in 1792 and '93 there
were plenty of men who, in the event of a campaign,
hoped to make profit out of the goods, horses, and
cattle they supplied the soldiers.   One of Madison's
Kentucky friends wrote him with rather startling
frankness that the welfare of the new State hinged

[1] Draper MSS., Major McCully to Captain Biddle, Pittsburgh, May 5,
1792; B. Netherland to Evan Shelby, July 5, 1793, etc., etc.   Also Kentucky *Gazette*, Sept. 1, 1792; Charleston *Gazette*, July 22, 1791, etc.

on the advent of an army to assail the Indians, first, because of the defence it would give the settlers, and, secondly, because it would be the chief means for introducing into the country a sufficient quantity of money for circulation.[1] Madison himself evidently saw nothing out of the way in this twofold motive of the frontiersmen for wishing the presence of an army. In all the border communities there was a lack of circulating medium, and an earnest desire to obtain more by any expedient.

Like many other frontiersmen, Madison's correspondent indulged almost equally in complaints of the Indian ravages, and in denunciations of the regular army which alone could put an end to them and of the national party which sustained the army.[2]

Major General Anthony Wayne, a Pennsylvanian, had been chosen to succeed St. Clair in the command **Wayne Appointed to Command Western Army.** of the army; and on him devolved the task of wresting victory from the formidable forest tribes, fighting as the latter were in the almost impenetrable wilderness of their own country. The tribes were aided by the support covertly, and often openly, yielded them by the British. They had even more effective allies in the suspicion with which the backswoodsmen regarded the regular army, and the supine indifference of the people at large, which forced the administration to try every means to obtain peace before adopting the only manly and honorable course, a vigorous war.

[1] State Dep. MSS., Madison Papers, Hubbard Taylor to Madison, Jan. 3, 1792.

[2] *Do.*, Taylor to Madison, April 16, 1792; May 8 and 17, 1792; May 23, 1793, etc.

Of all men, Wayne was the best fitted for the work. In the Revolutionary War no other general, American, British, or French, won such a reputation for hard fighting, and for daring energy and dogged courage. He felt very keenly that delight in the actual shock of battle which the most famous fighting generals have possessed. He gloried in the excitement and danger, and shone at his best when the stress was sorest; and because of his magnificent courage his soldiers had affectionately christened him "Mad Anthony." But his head was as cool as his heart was stout. He was taught in a rough school; for the early campaigns in which he took part were waged against the gallant generals and splendid soldiery of the British King. By experience he had grown to add caution to his dauntless energy. Once, after the battle of Brandywine, when he had pushed close to the enemy, with his usual fearless self-confidence, he was surprised in a night attack by the equally daring British general Grey, and his brigade was severely punished with the bayonet. It was a lesson he never forgot; it did not in any way abate his self-reliance or his fiery ardor, but it taught him the necessity of forethought, of thorough preparation, and of ceaseless watchfulness. A few days later he led the assault at Germantown, driving the Hessians before him with the bayonet. This was always his favorite weapon; he had the utmost faith in coming to close quarters, and he trained his soldiers to trust the steel. At Monmouth he turned the fortunes of the day by his stubborn and successful resistance to

the repeated bayonet charges of the Guards and
Grenadiers. His greatest stroke was the storming
of Stony Point, where in person he led the midnight
rush of his troops over the walls of the British fort.
He fought with his usual hardihood against Corn-
wallis; and at the close of the Revolutionary War
he made a successful campaign against the Creeks
in Georgia. During this campaign the Creeks one
night tried to surprise his camp, and attacked with
resolute ferocity, putting to flight some of the troops;
but Wayne rallied them and sword in hand he led
them against the savages, who were overthrown and
driven from the field. In one of the charges he cut
down an Indian chief; and the dying man, as he
fell, killed Wayne's horse with a pistol shot.

As soon as Wayne reached the Ohio, in June,
1792, he set about reorganizing the army. He had
Wayne   as a nucleus the remnant of St. Clair's
Reorganizes beaten forces; and to this were speedily
the Army.   added hundreds of recruits enlisted under
new legislation by Congress, and shipped to him as
fast as the recruiting officers could send them. The
men were of precisely the same general character as
those who had failed so dismally under St. Clair,
and it was even more difficult to turn them into
good soldiers, for the repeated disasters, crowned by
the final crushing horror, had unnerved them and
made them feel that their task was hopeless, and
that they were foredoomed to defeat.[1] The mortality
among the officers had been great, and the new offi-

[1] Bradley MSS. Letters and Journal of Captain Daniel Bradley; see
entry of May 7, 1793, etc.

cers, though full of zeal, needed careful training. Among the men desertions were very common; and on the occasion of a sudden alarm Wayne found that many of his sentries left their posts and fled.[1] Only rigorous and long continued discipline and exercise under a commander both stern and capable, could turn such men into soldiers fit for the work Wayne had before him. He saw this at once, and realized that a premature movement meant nothing but another defeat; and he began by careful and patient labor to turn his horde of raw recruits into a compact and efficient army, which he might use with his customary energy and decision. When he took command of the army—or "Legion," as he preferred to call it—the one stipulation he made was that the campaign should not begin until his ranks were full and his men thoroughly disciplined.

Towards the end of the summer of '92 he established his camp on the Ohio about twenty-seven miles below Pittsburgh. He drilled both officers and men with unwearied patience, and gradually the officers became able to do the drilling themselves, while the men acquired the soldierly self-confidence of veterans. As the new recruits came in they found themselves with an army which was rapidly learning how to manœuvre with precision, to obey orders unhesitatingly, and to look forward eagerly to a battle with the foe. Throughout the winter Wayne kept at work, and by the spring he had under him twenty-five hundred regular soldiers who were already

He Makes a Winter Camp on the Ohio.

[1] " Major General Anthony Wayne," by Charles J. Stillé, p. 323.

worthy to be trusted in a campaign. He never re-
laxed his efforts to improve them; though a man of
weaker stuff might well have been discouraged by
the timid and hesitating policy of the National Government. The Secretary of War, in writing to him,
laid stress chiefly on the fact that the American
people desired at every hazard to avert an Indian
war, and that on no account should offensive operations be undertaken against the tribes. Such orders
tied Wayne's hands, for offensive operations offered
the only means of ending the war; but he patiently
bided his time, and made ready his army against the
day when his superiors should allow him to use the
weapon he had tempered.

In May, '93, he brought his army down the Ohio
to Fort Washington, and near it established a camp
which he christened Hobson's Choice.
**In Spring
He Shifts** Here he was forced to wait the results of
His Camp the fruitless negotiations carried on by the
**to Near
Cincinnati.** United States Peace Commissioners, and
it was not until about the 1st of October
that he was given permission to begin the campaign.
Even when he was allowed to move his army forward he was fettered by injunctions not to run any
risks—and of course a really good fighting general
ought to be prepared to run risks. The Secretary
of War wrote him that above all things he was to remember to hazard nothing, for a defeat would be
fraught with ruinous consequences to the country.
Wayne knew very well that if such was the temper
of the country and the Government, it behooved him
to be cautious, and he answered that, though he

would at once advance towards the Indian towns, to threaten the tribes, he would not run the least unnecessary risk. Accordingly he shifted his army to a place some eighty miles north of Cin- His Second cinnati, where he encamped for the winter,   Winter building a place of strength which he   Camp at named Greeneville in honor of his old com- Greeneville. rade in arms, General Greene. He sent forward a strong detachment of his troops to the site of St. Clair's defeat, where they built a post which was named Fort Recovery. The discipline of the army steadily improved, though now and then a soldier deserted, usually fleeing to Kentucky, but in one or two cases striking through the woods to Detroit. The bands of auxiliary militia that served now and then for short periods with the regulars, were of course much less well trained and less dependable.

The Indians were always lurking about the forts, and threatening the convoys of provisions and muni- tions as they marched slowly from one to the other. Any party that left a fort was Indians At- in imminent danger. On one occasion the   tack the commander of Fort Jefferson and his or- Convoys. derly were killed and scalped but three hundred yards from the fort. A previous commander of this fort while hunting in this neighborhood had been attacked in similar fashion, and though he escaped, his son and a soldier were slain. On another occasion a dozen men, near the same fort, were surprised while haying; four were killed and the other eight cap- tured, four of whom were burned at the stake.[1]

[1] Bradley MSS., Journal, entries of Feb. 11, Feb. 24, June 24, July 12, 1792.

Before Wayne moved down the Ohio a band of
Kentucky mounted riflemen, under major John
Adair, were attacked under the walls of one of the
log forts—Fort St. Clair—as they were convoying a
large number of packhorses. The riflemen were in
camp at the time, the Indians making the assault at
dawn. Most of the horses were driven off or killed,
and the men fled to the fort, which, Adair dryly
remarked, proved "a place of safety for the bash-
ful"; but he rallied fifty, who drove off the Indians,
killing two and wounding others. Of his own men
six were killed and five wounded.[1]

Wayne's own detachments occasionally fared as
badly. In the fall of 1793, just after he had ad-
Defeat of a vanced to Greeneville, a party of ninety
Detach- regulars, who were escorting twenty heavily
ment. laden wagons, were surprised and scattered,
a few miles from the scene of Adair's misadventure.[2]
The lieutenant and ensign who were in command
and five or six of their men were slain, fighting
bravely; half a dozen were captured; the rest were
panic struck and fled without resistance. The Indians took off about seventy horses, leaving the
wagons standing in the middle of the road, with
their contents uninjured; and a rescue party brought
them safely to Wayne. The victors were a party
of Wyandots and Ottawas under the chief Little
Otter. On October 24th the British agent at the
Miami towns met in solemn council with these Indians and with another successful war party. The

---

[1] Am. State Papers, IV., 335.   Adair to Wilkinson, Nov. 6, 1792.
[2] Bradley MSS., Journal, entry of October 17, 1793.

Indians had with them ten scalps and two prisoners.
Seven of the scalps they sent off, by an Indian runner,
a special ally friend of the British agent, to be distributed among the different Lake Indians, to rouse
them to war.   One of their prisoners, an Irishman,
they refused to surrender ; but the other they gave
to the agent.   He proved to be a German, a mer-
cenary who had originally been in Burgoyne's army.[1]
Later one of the remaining captives made his escape,
killing his two Indian owners, a man and a woman,
both of whom had been leaders of war parties.

In the spring of 1794, as soon as the ground was
dry, Wayne prepared to advance towards the hostile
towns and force a decisive battle.   He was delayed
for a long time by lack of provisions, the soldiers
being on such short rations that they could not move.
The mounted riflemen of Kentucky, who had been
sent home at the beginning of winter, again joined
him.   Among the regulars, in the rifle company, was
a young Kentuckian, Captain William Clark, brother
of George Rogers Clark, and afterwards
one of the two famous explorers who first
crossed the continent to the Pacific.   In
his letters home Clark dwelt much on the
laborious nature of his duties, and mentioned that he was "like to have starved," and had
to depend on his rifle for subsistence.[2]   In May he
was sent from Fort Washington with twenty dra-

*Another
Detach-
ment De-
feats a
Body of
Indians.*

[1] Canadian Archives, Duggan to Chew, February 3, 1794, inclosing his
journal for the fall of 1793.   American State Papers, IV., 361, Wayne to
Knox, October 23, 1793.   The Americans lost 13 men ; the Indian reports
of course exaggerated this.

[2] Draper MSS., William Clark to Jonathan Clark, May 25, 1794

goons and sixty infantry to escort 700 packhorses to
Greeneville.   When eighteen miles from Fort Washington Indians attacked his van, driving off a few
packhorses; but Clark brought up his men from the
rear and after a smart skirmish put the savages to
flight.   They left behind one of their number dead,
two wounded, and seven rifles ; Clark lost two men
killed and two wounded.[1]

On the last day of June a determined assault was
made by the Indians on Fort Recovery, which was
garrisoned by about two hundred men.
Thanks to the efforts of the British agents,
and of the runners from the allied tribes
of the Lower Lakes, the Chippewas and
all the tribes of the Upper Lakes had
taken the tomahawk, and in June they gathered at
the Miami.   Over two thousand warriors, all told,[2]
assembled ; a larger body than had ever before
marched against the Americans.[3]   They were eager
for war, and wished to make a stroke of note against
their foes ; and they resolved to try to carry Fort
Recovery, built on the scene of their victory over
St. Clair.   They streamed down through the woods

A Large
War Party
Attacks
Fort
Recovery.

[1] *Do.*   Also Canadian Archives, Duggan to Chew, May 30, 1794.   As
an instance of the utter untrustworthiness of these Indian or British accounts
of the American losses, it may be mentioned that Duggan says the Indians
brought off forty scalps, and killed an unknown number of Americans in
addition ; whereas in reality only two were slain.   Even Duggan admits
that the Indians were beaten off.

[2] Canadian Archives, McKee to Chew, July 7, 1794.

[3] Am. State Papers, IV., 488, Wayne to the Secretary of War, 1794.

He says they probably numbered from 1500 to 2000 men, which was apparently about the truth.   Throughout this campaign the estimate of the
Americans as to the Indian forces and losses were usually close to the facts,
and were often under rather than over statements.

in long columns, and silently neared the fort. With them went a number of English and French rangers, most of whom were painted and dressed like the Indians.

When they reached the fort they found camped close to the walls a party of fifty dragoons and ninety riflemen. These dragoons and riflemen had escorted a brigade of packhorses from Greeneville the day before, and having left the supplies in the fort were about to return with the unladen packhorses. But soon after daybreak the Indians rushed their camp. Against such overwhelming numbers no effective resistance could be made. After a few moments' fight the men broke and ran to the fort. The officers, as usual, showed no fear, and were the last to retreat, half of them being killed or wounded,—one of the honorably noteworthy features of all these Indian fights was the large relative loss among the officers. Most of the dragoons and riflemen reached the fort, including nineteen who were wounded; nineteen officers and privates were killed, and two of the packhorsemen were killed and three captured. Two hundred packhorses were captured. The Indians, flushed with success and rendered over-confident by their immense superiority in numbers, made a rush at the fort, hoping to carry it by storm. They were beaten back at once with severe loss; Repulse for in such work they were no match for of the their foes. They then surrounded the Savages. fort, kept up a harmless fire all day, and renewed it the following morning. In the night they bore off their dead, finding them with the help of torches;

eight or ten of those nearest the fort they could not get. They then drew off and marched back to the Miami towns. At least twenty-five [1] of them had been killed, and a great number wounded ; whereas they had only succeeded in killing one and wounding eleven of the garrison. They were much disheartened at the check, and the Upper Lake Indians began to go home. The savages were as fickle as they were ferocious ; and though terrible antagonists when fighting on their own ground and in their own manner, they lacked the stability necessary for undertaking a formidable offensive movement in mass. This army of two thousand warriors, the largest they had ever assembled, was repulsed with loss in an attack on a wooden fort with a garrison not one sixth their strength, and then dissolved without accomplishing anything at all.

Three weeks after the successful defence of Fort Recovery, Wayne was joined by a large force of **Wayne** mounted volunteers from Kentucky, un- **Starts on** der General Scott ; and on July 27th he **his March.** set out towards the Miami towns. The Indians who watched his march brought word to the British that his army went twice as far in a day

[1] Canadian Archives, G. La Mothe to Joseph Chew, Michilimackinac, July 19, 1794. McKee says, " 17 men killed " ; evidently he either wilfully understated the truth, or else referred only to the particular tribes with which he was associated. La Mothe says, " they have lost twenty-five people amongst different nations," but as he was only speaking of the Upper Lake Indians, it may be that the total Indian loss was 25 plus 17, or 42. McKee always understates the British force and loss, and greatly overstates the loss and force of the Americans. In this letter he says that the Americans had 50 men killed, instead of 22 ; and that 60 " drivers " (pack-horsemen) were taken and killed; whereas in reality 3 were taken and 2 killed.

as St. Clair's, that he kept his scouts well out and his troops always in open order and ready for battle; that he exercised the greatest precaution to avoid an ambush or surprise, and that every night the camps of the different regiments were surrounded by breastworks of fallen trees so as to render a sudden assault hopeless. Wayne was determined to avoid the fates of Braddock and St. Clair. His " legion " of regular troops, was over two thousand strong. His discipline was very severe, yet he kept the loyal affection of his men. He had made the officers devote much of their time to training the infantry in marksmanship and the use of the bayonet and the cavalry in the use of the sabre. He impressed upon the cavalry and infantry alike that their safety lay in charging home with the utmost resolution. By steady drill he had turned his force, which was originally not of a promising character, into as fine an army, for its size, as a general could wish to command.

Severity of Wayne's Discipline.

The perfection of fighting capacity to which he had brought his forces caused much talk among the frontiersmen themselves. One of the contingent of Tennessee militia wrote home in the highest praise of the horsemanship and swordsmanship of the cavalry, who galloped their horses at speed over any ground, and leaped them over formidable obstacles, and of the bayonet practice, and especially of the marksmanship, of the infantry. He remarked that hunters were apt to undervalue the soldiers as marksmen, but that Wayne's riflemen were as good shots as any hunters

Excellence of his Troops.

he had ever seen at any of the many matches he had attended in the backwoods.[1]

Wayne showed his capacity as a commander by the use he made of his spies or scouts. A few of **Wayne's** these were Chickasaw or Choctaw Indians; **Scouts.** the rest, twenty or thirty in number, were drawn from the ranks of the wild white Indian-fighters, the men who plied their trade of warfare and the chase right on the hunting grounds of the hostile tribes. They were far more dangerous to the Indians, and far more useful to the army, than the like number of regular soldiers or ordinary rangers.

It was on these fierce backwoods riflemen that Wayne chiefly relied for news of the Indians, and **Efficiency** they served him well. In small parties, or **of the** singly, they threaded the forest scores of **Scouts.** miles in advance or to one side of the marching army, and kept close watch on the Indians' movements. As skilful and hardy as the red warriors, much better marksmen, and even more daring, they took many scalps, harrying the hunting parties, and hanging on the outskirts of the big wigwam villages. They captured and brought in Indian after Indian; from whom Wayne got valuable information. The use of scouts, and the consequent knowledge gained by the examination of Indian prisoners, emphasized the difference between St. Clair and Wayne. Wayne's reports are accompanied by many examinations of Indian captives.[2]

[1] *Knoxville Gazette*, August 27, 1793.

[2] American State Papers, IV., 489, 94. Examination of two Pottawatamies captured on the 5th of June; of two Shawnees captured on the 22d of June; of a Shawnee captured on Aug. 11th, etc., etc.

Among these wilderness warriors who served under Wayne were some who became known far and wide along the border for their feats of reckless personal prowess and their strange adventures. They were of course all men of remarkable bodily strength and agility, with almost unlimited power of endurance, and the keenest eyesight; and they were masters in the use of their weapons. Several had been captured by the Indians when children, and had lived for years with them before rejoining the whites; so that they knew well the speech and customs of the different tribes.

One of these men was the captain of the spies, William Wells. When a boy of twelve he had been captured by the Miamis, and had grown Feats of to manhood among them, living like any the Scouts. other young warrior; his Indian name was Black Snake, and he married a sister of the great war-chief, Little Turtle. He fought with the rest of the Miamis, and by the side of Little Turtle, in the victories the Northwestern Indians gained over Harmar and St. Clair, and during the last battle he killed several soldiers with his own hand. Afterwards, by some wayward freak of mind, he became harassed by the thought that perhaps he had slain some of his own kinsmen; dim memories of his childhood came back to him; and he resolved to leave his Indian wife and half-breed children and rejoin the people of his own color. Tradition relates that on the eve of his departure he made his purpose known to Little Turtle, and added, "We have long been friends; we are friends yet, until the sun stands so high [indicating the place] in the heavens; from that time we are enemies and may kill one another." Be this as it may, he came to Wayne, was taken into high favor, and made chief of scouts, and served loyally and with signal success until the end of the campaign. After the campaign he was joined by his Indian wife and his children; the latter grew up and married well in the community, so that their blood now flows in the veins of many of the descendants of the old pioneers. Wells himself was slain by the Indians long afterwards, in 1812, at the Chicago massacre.

One of Wells' fellow spies was William Miller. Miller, like Wells, had been captured by the Indians Surprise of when a boy, together with his brother an Indian Christopher. When he grew to manhood Party. he longed to rejoin his own people, and finally did so, but he could not persuade his brother to come with him, for Christopher had become an Indian at heart. In June, 1794, Wells, Miller, and a third spy, Robert McClellan, were sent out by Wayne with special instructions to bring in a live Indian. McClellan, who a number of years afterwards became a famous plainsman and Rocky Mountain man, was remarkably swift of foot. Near the Glaize River they found three Indians roasting venison by a fire, on a high open piece of ground, clear of brushwood. By taking advantage of the cover yielded by a fallen treetop the three scouts crawled within seventy yards of the camp fire; and Wells and Miller agreed to fire at the two outermost Indians, while McClellan, as soon as they had fired, was to dash in and run down the third. As the rifles cracked the two doomed warriors fell dead in their tracks; while McClellan bounded forward at full speed, tomahawk in hand. The Indian had no time to pick up his gun; fleeing for his life he reached the bank of the river, where the bluffs were twenty feet high, and sprang over into the stream-bed. He struck a miry place, and while he was floundering McClellan came to the top of the bluff and instantly sprang down full on him, and overpowered him. The others came up and secured the prisoner, whom they found to be a white man; and to Miller's astonishment it proved to be his brother Christopher. The scouts brought their prisoner, and the scalps of the two slain warriors, back to Wayne. At first Christopher was sulky and refused to join the whites; so at Greeneville he was put in the guard house. After a few days he grew more cheerful, and said he had changed his mind. Wayne set him at liberty, and he not only served valiantly as a scout through the campaign, but acted as Wayne's interpreter. Early in July he showed his good faith by assisting McClellan in the capture of a Pottawatamie chief.

On one of Wells' scouts he and his companions came across a family of Indians in a canoe by the river bank. The white wood rangers were as ruthless as their red foes, sparing neither sex nor age; and the scouts were cocking their rifles when Wells recognized the Indians as being the family into which he had been adopted, and by which he had been treated as a son and brother. Springing forward he swore immediate

An Unexpected Act of Mercy.

death to the first man who fired; and then told his
companions who the Indians were. The scouts at
once dropped their weapons, shook hands with the
Miamis, and sent them off unharmed.

Wells' last scouting trip was made just before the
final battle of the campaign. As it was the eve of
the decisive struggle, Wayne was anxious
**Last
Scouting
Trip be-
fore the
Battle.** to get a prisoner. Wells went off with
three companions—McClellan, a man named
Mahaffy, and a man named May. May, like
Wells and Miller, had lived long with the
Indians, first as a prisoner, and afterwards as an
adopted member of their tribe, but had finally made
his escape. The four scouts succeeded in capturing
an Indian man and woman, whom they bound
securely. Instead of returning at once with their
captives, the champions, in sheer dare-devil, ferocious
love of adventure, determined, as it was already
nightfall, to leave the two bound Indians where
they could find them again, and go into one of the
Indian camps to do some killing. The camp they
selected was but a couple of miles from the British
fort. They were dressed and painted like Indians,
and spoke the Indian tongues; so, riding boldly forward, they came right among the warriors who stood
grouped around the camp fires. They were at arm's-
length before their disguise was discovered. Immediately each of them, choosing his man, fired into an
Indian, and then they fled, pursued by a hail of
bullets. May's horse slipped and fell in the bed of
a stream, and he was captured. The other three,
spurring hard and leaning forward in their saddles

to avoid the bullets, escaped, though both Wells and McClellan were wounded; and they brought their Indian prisoners into Wayne's camp that night. May was recognized by the Indians as their former pris-oner; and next day they tied him up, made a mark on his breast for a target, and shot him to death.[1]

With his advance effectually covered by his scouts, and his army guarded by his own ceaseless vigilance, Wayne marched without opposition to the confluence of the Glaize and the Maumee, where the hostile Indian villages began, and whence they stretched to below the British fort. The savages were taken by surprise and fled without offering opposition; while Wayne halted, on August 8th, and spent a week in building a strong log stockade, with four good block-houses as bastions; he christened the work Fort Defiance.[2] The Indians had cleared and tilled im-mense fields, and the troops revelled in the fresh vegetables and ears of roasted corn, and enjoyed the

Wayne Reaches the Mau-mee and Builds Fort Defiance.

---

[1] McBride collects or reprints a number of narratives dealing with these border heroes; some of them are by contemporaries who took part in their deeds. Brickell's narrative corroborates these stories; the differences are such as would naturally be explained by the fact that different observers were writing of the same facts from memory after a lapse of several years. In their essentials the narratives are undoubtedly trustworthy. In the Draper collection there are scores of MS. narratives of similar kind, written down from what the pioneers said in their old age; unfortunately it is difficult to sift out the true from the false, unless the stories are corroborated from out-side sources; and most of the tales in the Draper MSS. are evidently hope-lessly distorted. Wells' daring attack on the Indian camp is alluded to in the Bradley MSS.; the journal, under date of August 12th, recites how four white spies went down almost to Lake Erie, captured two Indians, and then attacked the Indians in their tents, three of the spies being wounded.

[2] American State Papers, IV., 490, Wayne to Secretary of War, Aug. 14, 1794.

rest; [1] for during the march the labor of cutting a road through the thick forest had been very severe, while the water was bad and the mosquitoes were exceedingly troublesome. At one place a tree fell on Wayne and nearly killed him; but though somewhat crippled he continued as active and vigilant as ever.[2]

From Fort Defiance Wayne sent a final offer of peace to the Indians, summoning them at once to send deputies to meet him. The letter was carried by Christopher Miller, and a Shawnee prisoner; and in it Wayne explained that Miller was a Shawnee by adoption, whom his soldiers had captured "six month since," while the Shawnee warrior had been taken but a couple of days before; and he warned the Indians that he had seven Indian prisoners, who had been well treated, but who would be put to death if Miller were harmed. The Indians did not molest Miller, but sought to obtain delay, and would give no definite answer; whereupon Wayne advanced against them, having laid waste and destroyed all their villages and fields.

The Indians Decline to Make Peace.

His army marched on the 15th, and on the 18th reached Roche du Bout, by the Maumee Rapids, only a few miles from the British fort. Next day was spent in building rough breast-work to protect the stores and baggage, and in reconnoitring the Indian position.[3]

Wayne Marches Forward.

[1] Bradley MSS. Letter of Captain Daniel Bradley to Ebenezer Banks, Grand Glaize, August 28, 1794.

[2] American Pioneer, I., 317, Daily Journal of Wayne's Campaign. By Lieutenant Boyer. Reprinted separately in Cincinnati in 1866.

[3] American State Papers, 491, Wayne's Report to Secretary of War, August 28, 1794.

The Indians—Shawnees, Delawares, Wyandots, Ottawas, Miamis, Pottawatamies, Chippewas, and Iroquois—were camped closed to the British. There were between fifteen hundred and two thousand warriors; and in addition there were seventy rangers from Detroit, French, English, and refugee Americans, under Captain Caldwell, who fought with them in the battle. The British agent McKee was with them; and so was Simon Girty, the "white renegade," and another partisan leader, Elliott. But McKee, Girty, and Elliott did not actually fight in the battle.[1]

On August 20, 1794, Wayne marched to battle against the Indians.[2] They lay about six miles down the river, near the British fort, in a place known as the Fallen Timbers, because there the thick forest had been overturned by a whirlwind, and the dead trees lay piled across one another in rows. All the baggage was left behind in the breastwork, with a sufficient guard. The army numbered about three thousand men; two thousand were regulars, and

The Indians' Stand at the Fallen Timbers.

---

[1] Canadian Archives, McKee to Chew, August 27, 1794. McKee says there were 1300 Indians, and omits all allusion to Caldwell's rangers. He always underestimates the Indian numbers and loss. In the battle one of Caldwell's rangers, Antoine Lasselle, was captured. He gave in detail the numbers of the Indians engaged ; they footed up to over 1500. A deserter from the fort, a British drummer of the 24th Regiment, named John Bevin, testified that he had heard both McKee and Elliott report the number of Indians as 2000, in talking to Major Campbell, the commandant of the fort, after the battle. He and Lasselle agree as to Caldwell's rangers. See their depositions, American State Papers, IV., 494.

[2] Draper MSS., William Clark to Jonathan Clark, August 28, 1794. McBride, II., 129 ; "Life of Paxton." Many of the regulars and volunteers were left in Fort Defiance and the breastworks on the Maumee as garrisons.

there were a thousand mounted volunteers from Kentucky under General Scott.

The army marched down the left or north branch of the Maumee. A small force of mounted volun-**March of** teers—Kentucky militia—were in front. **the Army.** On the right flank the squadron of dragoons, the regular cavalry, marched next to the river. The infantry, armed with musket and bayonet, were formed in two long lines, the second some little distance behind the first; the left of the first line being continued by the companies of regular riflemen and light troops. Scott, with the body of the mounted volunteers, was thrown out on the left with instructions to turn the flank of the Indians, thus effectually preventing them from performing a similar feat at the expense of the Americans. There could be no greater contrast than that between Wayne's carefully trained troops, marching in open order to the attack, and St. Clair's huddled mass of raw soldiers receiving an assault they were powerless to repel.

The Indians stretched in a line nearly two miles long at right angles to the river, and began the battle **Heavy** confidently enough. They attacked and **Skirmish-** drove in the volunteers who were in advance **ing,** and the firing then began along the entire front. But their success was momentary. Wayne ordered the first line of the infantry to advance with trailed arms, so as to rouse the savages from their cover, then to fire into their backs at close range, and to follow them hard with the bayonet, so as to give them no time to load. The regular cavalry were directed to charge the left flank of the enemy; for

Wayne had determined "to put the horse hoof on the moccasin." Both orders were executed with spirit and vigor.

It would have been difficult to find more unfavorable ground for cavalry; nevertheless the dragoons rode against their foes at a gallop, with broad-swords swinging, the horses dodging in and out among the trees and jumping the fallen logs. They received a fire at close quarters which emptied a dozen saddles, both captains being shot down. One, the commander of the squadron, Captain Mis Campbell,[1] was killed; the other, Captain Van Rensselaer, a representative of one of the old Knickerbocker families of New York, who had joined the army from pure love of adventure, was wounded. The command devolved on Lieutenant Covington, who led forward the troopers, with Lieutenant Webb alongside him; and the dragoons burst among the savages at full speed, and routed them in a moment. Covington cut down two of the Indians with his own hand, and Webb one.

At the same time the first line of the infantry charged with equal impetuosity and success. The Indians delivered one volley and were then roused from their hiding places with the bayonet; as they fled they were shot down, and if they attempted to halt they were at once assailed and again driven with the bayonet. They could make no stand at all, and the battle was won with ease. So complete was the success that only the first line of regulars was able to take part in the

---

[1] A curious name, but so given in all the reports.

fighting; the second line, and Scott's horse-riflemen, on the left, in spite of their exertions were unable to reach the battle-field until the Indians were driven from it; "there not being a sufficiency of the enemy for the Legion to play on," wrote Clark. The entire action lasted under forty minutes.[1] Less than a thousand of the Americans were actually engaged. They pursued the beaten and fleeing Indians for two miles, the cavalry halting only when under the walls of the British fort.

Thirty-three of the Americans were killed and one hundred wounded.[2] It was an easy victory. The A Complete Indians suffered much more heavily than and Easy the Americans; in killed they probably Victory. lost two or three times as many. Among the dead were white men from Caldwell's company; and one white ranger was captured. It was the

---

[1] Bradley MSS., entry in the journal for August 20th.

[2] Wayne's report; of the wounded 11 afterwards died. He gives an itemized statement. Clark in his letter makes the dead 34 (including 8 militia instead of 7) and the wounded only 70. Wayne reports the Indian loss as twice as great as that of the whites; and says the woods were strewn with their dead bodies and those of their white auxiliaries. Clark says 100 Indians were killed. The Englishman, Thomas Duggan, writing from Detroit to Joseph Chew, Secretary of the Indian Office, says officially that "great numbers" of the Indians were slain. The journal of Wayne's campaign says 40 dead were left on the field, and that there was considerable additional, but unascertained, loss in the rapid two miles pursuit. The member of Caldwell's company who was captured was a French Canadian; his deposition is given by Wayne. McKee says the Indians lost but 19 men, and that but 400 were engaged, specifying the Wyandots and Ottawas as being those who did the fighting and suffered the loss; and he puts the loss of the Americans, although he admits that they won, at between 300 and 400. He was furious at the defeat, and was endeavoring to minimize it in every way. He does not mention the presence of Caldwell's white company; he makes the mistake of putting the American cavalry on the wrong wing, in trying to show that only the Ottawas and Wyandots were engaged; and if his figures,

most complete and important victory ever gained over the Northwestern Indians, during the forty years' warfare to which it put an end; and it was the only considerable pitched battle in which they lost more than their foes. They suffered heavily among their leaders; no less than eight Wyandot chiefs were slain.

From the fort the British had seen, with shame and anger, the rout of their Indian allies. Their commander wrote to Wayne to demand his intentions; Wayne responded that he thought they were made sufficiently evi- **The British in the Fort.** dent by his successful battle with the savages. The Englishman wrote in resentment of this curt reply, complaining that Wayne's soldiers had approached within pistol shot of the fort, and threatening to fire upon them if the offence was repeated. Wayne responded by summoning him to abandon the fort; a summons which he of course refused to heed. Wayne then gave orders to destroy everything up to the very walls of the fort, and his commands were carried out to the letter; not only were the Indian villages burned and their crops cut down, but all the houses and buildings of the British agents and traders, in-

19 dead, have any value at all, they refer only to those two tribes; above I have repeatedly shown that he invariably underestimated the Indian losses, usually giving the losses suffered by the band he was with as being the entire loss. In this case he speaks of the fighting and loss as being confined to the Ottawas and Wyandots; but Brickell, who was with the Delawares, states that " many of the Delawares were killed and wounded." All the Indians were engaged; and doubtless all the tribes suffered proportionately; and much more than the Americans. Captain Daniel Bradley in his above quoted letter of Aug. 28th to Ebenezer Banks (Bradley MSS.) says that between 50 and 100 Indians were killed.

cluding McKee's, were levelled to the ground. The British commander did not dare to interfere or make good his threats; nor, on the other hand, did Wayne dare to storm the fort, which was well built and heavily armed.

After completing his work of destruction Wayne marched his army back to Fort Defiance. Here he
The Army Marches Back. was obliged to halt for over a fortnight while he sent back to Fort Recovery for provisions. He employed the time in work on the fort, which he strengthened so that it would stand an attack by a regular army. The mounted volunteers were turned to account in a new manner, being employed not only to escort the pack-animals but themselves to transport the flour on their horses. There was much sickness among the soldiers, especially from fever and ague, and but for the corn and vegetables they obtained from the Indian towns which were scattered thickly along the Maumee they would have suffered from hunger. They were especially disturbed because all the whiskey was used up.[1]

On September 14th the legion started westward towards the Miami Towns at the junction of the St. Mary's and St. Joseph's rivers, the scene of Harmar's disaster. In four days the towns were reached, the Indians being too cowed to offer resistance. Here the army spent six weeks, burned the towns and destroyed the fields and stores of the hostile tribes, and built a fort which was christened Fort Wayne. British deserters came in from time to time; some of the Canadian traders made overtures to the army

[1] Daily Journal of Wayne's Campaign, "American Pioneer," I., 351

and agreed to furnish provisions at a moderate price; and of the savages only straggling parties were seen. The mounted volunteers grew mutinous, but were kept in order by their commander Scott, a rough, capable backwoods soldier. Their term of service at length expired and they were sent home; and the regulars of the Legion, leaving a garrison at Fort Wayne, marched back to Greeneville, and reached it on November 2d, just three months and six days after they started from it on their memorable and successful expedition. Wayne had shown himself the best general ever sent to war with the Northwestern Indians; and his victorious campaign was the most noteworthy ever carried on against them, for it brought about the first lasting peace on the border, and put an end to the bloody turmoil of forty years' fighting. It was one of the most striking and weighty feats in the winning of the West.

The army went into winter quarters at Greeneville. There was sickness among the troops, and there were occasional desertions; the discipline was **Winter** severe, and the work so hard and dangerous **Quarters at** that the men generally refused to re-enlist.[1] **Greeneville.** The officers were uneasy lest there should be need of a further campaign. But their fears were groundless. Before winter set in heralds arrived from the hostile tribes to say that they wished peace.

The Indians were utterly downcast over their defeat.[2] The destruction of their crops, homes, and stores of provisions was complete, and they were put

[1] Draper MSS., William Clark to Jonathan Clark, November 23, 1794.

[2] Canadian Archives, William Johnson Chew to Joseph Chew, December 7, 1794.

to sore shifts to live through the winter. Their few cattle, and many even of their dogs, died; they could not get much food from the British; and as winter wore on they sent envoy after envoy to the Americans, exchanged prisoners, and agreed to make a permanent peace in the spring. They were exasperated with the British, who, they said, had not fulfilled a single promise they had made.[1]

The Indians Utterly Downcast.

The anger of the Indians against the British was as just as it was general. They had been lured and goaded into war by direct material aid, and by indirect promises of armed assistance; and they were abandoned as soon as the fortune of war went against them. Brant, the Iroquois chief, was sorely angered by the action of the British in deserting the Indians whom they had encouraged by such delusive hopes; and in his letter to the British officials[2] he reminded them of the fact that but for their interference the Indians would have concluded "an equitable and honorable peace in June 1793"— thus offering conclusive proof that the American commissioners, in their efforts to make peace with the Indians in that year, had been foiled by the secret machinations of the British agents, as Wayne had always thought. Brant blamed the British agent McKee for ever having interfered in the Indian councils, and misled the tribes to their hurt; and in writing to the Secretary of the Indian Office for Canada he reminded him in plain terms of the

Their Anger with the British.

---

[1] Brickell's Narrative.

[2] Canadian Archives, Joseph Brant to Joseph Chew, Oct. 22, 1794; William J. Chew to J. Chew, Oct. 24, 1794.

treachery with which the British had behaved to the Indians at the close of the Revolutionary War, and expressed the hope that it would not be repeated; saying:[1] "If there is a treaty between Great Britain and the Yankees I hope our Father the King will not forget the Indians as he did in the year '83." When his forebodings came true and the British, in assenting to Jay's treaty, abandoned their Indian allies, Brant again wrote to the Secretary of the Indian Office, in repressed but bitter anger at the conduct of the King's agents in preventing the Indians from making peace with the Americans while they could have made it on advantageous terms, and then in deserting them. He wrote: "This is the second time the poor Indians have been left in the lurch & I cannot avoid lamenting that they were prevented at a time when they had it in their power to make an Honorable and Advantageous Peace."[2]

McKee, the British Indian agent, was nearly as frank as Brant in expressing his views of the conduct of the British towards their allies; he doubtless felt peculiar bitterness as he had been made the active instrument in carrying out the policy of his chiefs, and had then seen that policy abandoned and even disavowed.

Wrath of the British Indian Agents.

In fact he suffered the usual fate of those who are chosen to do some piece of work which unscrupulous men in power wish to have done, but wish also to avoid the responsibility of doing. He foretold evil results from the policy adopted, a policy under which, as he put it, "the distressed situation of the

[1] Canadian Archives, Brant to Joseph Chew, Feb. 24, and March 17, 1795.
[2] *Do.*, Brant to Chew, Jan. 19, 1796.

poor Indians who have long fought for us and bled
farely for us [is] no bar to a Peaceable accommoda-
tion with America and . . . they [are] left to
shift for themselves." [1] That a sentence of this kind
could be truthfully written by one British official to
another was a sufficiently biting comment on the
conduct of the British Government.

The battle of the Fallen Timbers opened the eyes
of the Indians to more facts than one. They saw

The
Indians
Resolve to
Treat.
that they could not stand against the
Americans unassisted. Furthermore, they
saw that though the British would urge
them to fight, and would secretly aid them,
yet that in the last resort the King's troops would
not come to their help by proceeding to actual war.
All their leaders recognized that it was time to make
peace. The Americans found an active ally in the
French Canadian, Antoine Lasselle, whom they had
captured in the battle. He worked hard to bring
about a peace, inducing the Canadian traders to
come over to the American side, and making every
effort to get the Indians to agree to terms. Being a
thrifty soul, he drove a good trade with the savages
at the councils, selling them quantities of liquor.

In November the Wyandots from Sandusky sent
ambassadors to Wayne at Greeneville. Wayne spoke

They Send
Ambassa-
dors to
Wayne.
to them with his usual force and frankness.
He told them he pitied them for their folly
in listening to the British, who were very
glad to urge them to fight and to give them
ammunition, but who had neither the power nor
the inclination to help them when the time of trial

[1] Canadian Archives, McKee to Chew, March 27, 1795.

came; that hitherto the Indians had felt only the weight of his little finger, but that he would surely destroy all the tribes in the near future if they did not make peace.[1]

The Hurons went away much surprised, and resolved on peace; and the other tribes followed their example. In January, 1795, the Miamis, Chippewas, Sacs, Delawares, Pottawatomies, and Ottawas sent ambassadors to Greeneville and agreed to treat.[2] The Shawnees were bent on continuing the war; but when their allies deserted them they too sent to Greeneville and asked to be included in the peace.[3] On February 11th the Shawnees, Delawares, and Miamis formally entered into a preliminary treaty.

This was followed in the summer of 1795 by the formal Treaty of Greeneville, at which Wayne, on behalf of the United States, made a defi-   Treaty of nite peace with all the Northwestern tribes. Greeneville. The sachems, war chiefs, and warriors of the different tribes began to gather early in June; and formal proceedings for a treaty were opened on June 17th. But many of the tribes were slow in coming to the treaty ground, others vacillated in their course, and unforeseen delays arose; so that it was not until August 7th that it was possible to come to a unanimous agreement and ratify the treaty. No less than eleven hundred and thirty Indians were present at the treaty grounds, including a full delegation from every hostile tribe. All solemnly covenanted to keep the peace; and they agreed to surrender to

[1] Canadian Archives, Geo. Ironside to McKee, Dec. 13, 1794.

[2] *Do.*, Antoine Lasselle to Jacques Lasselle, Jan. 31, 1795.

[3] *Do.*, Letter of Lt.-Col. England, Jan. 30, 1795 ; also copy of treaty of peace of Feb. 11th.

the whites all of what is now southern Ohio and south eastern Indiana, and various reservations elsewhere, as at Fort Wayne, Fort Defiance, Detroit, and Michilimackinac, the lands around the French towns, and the hundred and fifty thousand acres near the Falls of the Ohio which had been allotted to Clark and his soldiers. The Government, in its turn, acknowledged the Indian title to the remaining territory, and agreed to pay the tribes annuities aggregating nine thousand five hundred dollars. All prisoners on both sides were restored. There were interminable harangues and councils while the treaty was pending, the Indians invariably addressing Wayne as Elder Brother, and Wayne in response styling them Younger Brothers. In one speech a Chippewa chief put into terse form the reasons for making the treaty, and for giving the Americans title to the land, saying, "Elder Brother, you asked who were the true owners of the land now ceded to the United States. In answer I tell you, if any nations should call themselves the owners of it they would be guilty of falsehood; our claim to it is equal; our Elder Brother has conquered it." [1]

Wayne had brought peace by the sword. It was the first time the border had been quiet for over a generation; and for fifteen years the quiet lasted unbroken. The credit belongs to Wayne and his army, and to the Government which stood behind both. Because it thus finally stood behind them we can forgive its manifold shortcomings and vacillations, its futile

Wayne's Great Achievement.

[1] American State Papers, IV., 562–583.

efforts to beg a peace, and its reluctance to go to war. We can forgive all this; but we should not forget it. Americans need to keep in mind the fact that as a nation they have erred far more often in not being willing enough to fight than in being too willing. Once roused, they have always been dangerous and hard-fighting foes; but they have been over-difficult to rouse. Their educated classes, in particular, need to be perpetually reminded that, though it is an evil thing to brave a conflict needlessly, or to bully and bluster, it is an even worse thing to flinch from a fight for which there is legitimate provocation, or to live in supine, slothful, unprepared ease, helpless to avenge an injury.

The conduct of the Americans in the years which closed with Wayne's treaty did not shine very brightly; but the conduct of the British was black, indeed. On the Northwestern frontier they behaved in a way which can scarcely be too harshly stigmatized. This does not apply to the British civil and military officers at the Lake Posts; for they were merely doing their duty as they saw it, and were fronting their foes bravely, while with loyal zeal they strove to carry out what they understood to be the policy of their superiors. The ultimate responsibility rested with these superiors, the Crown's high advisers, and the King and Parliament they represented. Their treatment both of the Indians, whom they professed to protect, and of the Americans, with whom they professed to be friendly, forms one of the darkest pages in the annals of the British in America. Yet they have

been much less severely blamed for their behaviour
in this matter, than for far more excusable offences.
American historians, for example, usually condemn
them without stint because in 1814 the army of Ross
and Cockburn burned and looted the public buildings
of Washington ; but by rights they should keep all
their condemnation for their own country, so far as
the taking of Washington is concerned ; for the sin
of burning a few public buildings is as nothing compared with the cowardly infamy of which the politicians of the stripe of Jefferson and Madison, and
the people whom they represented, were guilty in
not making ready, by sea and land, to protect their
Capital and in not exacting full revenge for its
destruction. These facts may with advantage be
pondered by those men of the present day who are
either so ignorant or of such lukewarm patriotism
that they do not wish to see the United States keep
prepared for war and show herself willing and able
to adopt a vigorous foreign policy whenever there is
need of furthering American interests or upholding
the honor of the American flag. America is bound
scrupulously to respect the rights of the weak ; but
she is no less bound to make stalwart insistance on
her own rights as against the strong.

The count against the British on the Northwestern
frontier is, not that they insisted on their rights, but
that they were guilty of treachery to both friend
and foe. The success of the British was incompatible with the good of mankind in general, and of
the English-speaking races in particular ; for they
strove to prop up savagery, and to bar the westward

march of the settler-folk whose destiny it was to
make ready the continent for civilization.   But the
British cannot be seriously blamed because   Their
they failed to see this.   Their fault lay in   Treachery
their aiding and encouraging savages in a   towards
warfare which was necessarily horrible;   Both the
and still more in their repeated breaches   and the
of faith.   The horror and the treachery   Americans.
were the inevitable outcome of the policy on which
they had embarked; it can never be otherwise when
a civilized government endeavors to use, as allies in
war, savages whose acts it cannot control and for
whose welfare it has no real concern.

Doubtless the statesmen who shaped the policy of
Great Britain never deliberately intended to break
faith, and never fully realized the awful nature of
the Indian warfare for which they were in part
responsible; they thought very little of the matter at
all in the years which saw the beginning of their
stupendous struggle with France.   But the acts of
their obscure agents on the far interior frontier were
rendered necessary and inevitable by their policy.
To encourage the Indians to hold their own against
the Americans, and to keep back the settlers, meant
to encourage a war of savagery against the border
vanguard of white civilization; and such a war was
sure to teem with fearful deeds.   Moreover, where
the interests of the British Crown were so manifold
it was idle to expect that the Crown's advisers
would treat as of much weight the welfare of the
scarcely-known tribes whom their agents had urged
to enter a contest which was hopeless except for

British assistance. The British statesmen were engaged in gigantic schemes of warfare and diplomacy ;
and to them the Indians and the frontiersmen alike
were pawns on a great chessboard, to be sacrificed
whenever necessary. When the British authorities
deemed it likely that there would be war with
America, the tribes were incited to take up the
hatchet ; when there seemed a chance of peace with
America the deeds of the tribes were disowned ;
and peace was finally assured by a cynical abandon-
ment of their red allies. In short, the British, while
professing peace with the Americans, treacherously
incited the Indians to war against them ; and, when
it suited their own interests, they treacherously
abandoned their Indian allies to the impending ruin.[1]

---

[1] The ordinary American histories, often so absurdly unjust to England,
are right in their treatment of the British actions on the frontier in 1793–94.
The ordinary British historians simply ignore the whole affair. As a type of
their class, Mr. Percy Gregg may be instanced. His "History of the
United States" is a silly book ; he is often intentionally untruthful, but his
chief fault is his complete ignorance of the facts about which he is writing.
It is, of course, needless to criticise such writers as Mr. Gregg and his fellows. But it is worth while calling attention to Mr. Goldwin Smith's " The
United States," for Mr. Goldwin Smith is a student, and must be taken
seriously. He says : " That the British government or anybody by its
authority was intriguing with the Indians against the Americans is an assertion of which there seems to be no proof." If he will examine the Canadian
Archives, from which I have quoted, and the authorities which I cite, he
will find the proof ready to hand. Prof. A. C. McLaughlin has made a
capital study of this question in his pamphlet on " The Western Posts and
the British Debts." What he says cannot well be controverted.

CHAPTER III.

TENNESSEE BECOMES A STATE, 1791–1796.

" The Territory of the United States of America
South of the River Ohio " was the official title of
the tract of land which had been ceded by The South-
North Carolina to the United States, and   western
which a few years later became the State   Territory.
of Tennessee.   William Blount, the newly appointed
Governor, took charge late in 1790.   He made a tour
of the various counties, as laid out under authority
of the State of North Carolina, rechristening them
as counties of the Territory, and summoning before
him the persons in each county holding commissions
from North Carolina, at the respective court-houses,
where he formally notified them of the change.   He
read to them the act of Congress accepting the cessions of the claims of North Carolina; then he read
his own commission from President Washington;
and informed them of the provision by North Carolina that Congress should assume and execute the
government of the new Territory "in a manner
similar to that which they support northwest of
the River Ohio."   Following this he formally read
the ordinance for the government of the Northwestern Territory.   He commented upon and explained this proclamation, stating that under it the

President had appointed the Governor, the Judges, and the Secretary of the new Territory, and that he himself, as Governor, would now appoint the necessary county officers.

The remarkable feature of this address was that he read to the assembled officers in each county, as part of the law apparently binding upon them, Article 6 of the Ordinance of 1787, which provided that there should be neither slavery nor involuntary servitude in the Northwestern Territory.[1] It had been expressly stipulated that this particular provision as regards slavery should not apply to the Southwestern Territory, and of course Blount's omission to mention this fact did not in any way alter the case; but it is a singular thing that he should without comment have read, and his listeners without comment have heard, a recital that slavery was abolished in their territory. It emphasizes the fact that at this time there was throughout the West no very strong feeling on the subject of slavery, and what feeling there was, was if anything hostile. The adventurous backwoods farmers who composed the great mass of the population in Tennessee, as elsewhere among and west of the Alleghanies, were not a slave-owning people, in the sense that the planters of the seaboard were. They were preeminently folk who did their work with their own hands. Master and man chopped and ploughed and reaped and builded side by side, and even the leaders

Blount Inaugurated as Governor.

Slavery in the New Territory.

[1] Blount MSS., Journal of Proceedings of William Blount, Esq., Governor in and over the Territory of the United States of America South of the River Ohio, in his executive department, October 23, 1790.

of the community, the militia generals, the legislators, and the judges, often did their share of farm
work, and prided themselves upon their capacity to
do it well. They had none of that feeling which
makes slave-owners look upon manual labor as a
badge of servitude. They were often lazy and shiftless, but they never deified laziness and shiftlessness
or made them into a cult. The one thing they prized
beyond all others was their personal freedom, the
right of the individual to do whatsoever he saw fit.
Indeed they often carried this feeling so far as to
make them condone gross excesses, rather than insist
upon the exercise of even needful authority. They
were by no means entirely logical, but they did see
and feel that slavery was abhorrent, and that it was
utterly inconsistent with the theories of their own
social and governmental life. As yet there was no
thought of treating slavery as a sacred institution,
the righteousness of which must not be questioned.
At the Fourth of July celebrations toasts such as
" The total abolition of slavery " were not uncommon.[1] It was this feeling which prevented any manifestation of surprise at Blount's apparent acquiescence
in a section of the ordinance for the government of
the Territory which prohibited slavery.

Nevertheless, though slaves were not numerous,
they were far from uncommon, and the moral conscience of the community was not really **Dulness of**
roused upon the subject. It was hardly **the Public**
possible that it should be roused, for no **Conscience about**
civilized people who owned African slaves **Slavery.**

---

[1] *Knoxville Gazette*, July 17, 1795, etc. See also issue Jan. 28, 1792.

had as yet abolished slavery, and it was too much to hope that the path toward abolition would be pointed out by poor frontiersmen engaged in a life and death struggle with hostile savages. The slave-holders were not interfered with until they gradually grew numerous enough and powerful enough to set the tone of thought, and make it impossible to root out slavery save by outside action.

Blount recommended the appointment of Sevier and Robertson as brigadier-generals of militia of the **Blount's** Eastern and Western districts of the Ter-**First Ap-** ritory, and issued a large number of com-**pointments.** missions to the justices of the peace, militia officers, sheriffs, and clerks of the county courts in the different counties.[1] In his appointments he shrewdly and properly identified himself with the natural leaders of the frontiersmen. He made Sevier and Robertson his right-hand men, and strove always to act in harmony with them, while for the minor military and civil officers he chose the persons whom the frontiersmen themselves desired. In consequence he speedily became a man of great influence for good. The Secretary of the Territory reported to the Federal Government that the effect of Blount's character on the frontiersmen was far greater than was the case with any other man, and that he was able to get them to adhere to the principles of order and to support the laws by his influence in a way which it was hopeless to expect from their own respect for governmental authority. Blount was felt by the frontiersmen to be thoroughly in sym-

[1] Blount MSS., Journal of the Proceedings, etc.

pathy with them, to understand and appreciate them, and to be heartily anxious for their welfare; and yet at the same time his influence could be counted upon on the side of order, while the majority of the frontier officials in any time of commotion were apt to remain silent and inactive, or even to express their sympathy with the disorderly element.[1]

No one but a man of great tact and firmness could have preserved as much order among the frontiersmen as Blount preserved. He **Blount's** was always under fire from both sides. **Tact in** The settlers were continually complaining **with Dif-** that they were deserted by the Federal **ficulties.** authorities, who favored the Indians, and that Blount himself did not take sufficiently active steps to subdue the savages; while on the other hand the National Administration was continually upbraiding him for being too active against the Indians, and for not keeping the frontiersmen sufficiently peaceable. Under much temptations, and in a situation that would have bewildered any one, Blount steadfastly followed his course of, on the one hand, striving his best to protect the people over whom he was placed as governor, and to repel the savages, while, on the other hand, he suppressed so far as lay in his power, any outbreak against the authorities, and tried to inculcate a feeling of loyalty and respect for the National Government.[2]   He did much in cre-

---

[1] American State Papers, iv. ; Daniel Smith to the Secretary of War, Knoxville, July 19, 1793.

[2] Robertson MSS., Blount to Robertson, Feb. 13, 1793.

ating a strong feeling of attachment to the Union among the rough backwoodsmen with whom he had thrown in his lot.

Early in 1791 Blount entered into negotiations with the Cherokees, and when the weather grew warm he summoned them to a treaty. They met on the Holston, all of the noted Cherokee chiefs and hundreds of their warriors being present, and concluded the treaty of Holston, by which, in consideration of numerous gifts and of an annuity of a thousand (afterwards increased to fifteen hundred) dollars, the Cherokees at last definitely abandoned their disputed claims to the various tracts of land which the whites claimed under various former treaties. By this treaty with the Cherokees, and by the treaty with the Creeks entered into at New York the previous summer, the Indian title to most of the present State of Tennessee, was fairly and legally extinguished. However the westernmost part, was still held by the Chickasaws, and certain tracts in the southeast, by the Cherokees; while the Indian hunting grounds in the middle of the territory were thrust in between the groups of settlements on the Cumberland and the Holston.

On the ground where the treaty was held Blount proceeded to build a little town, which he made the capital of the Territory, and christened Knoxville, in honor of Washington's Secretary of War. At this town there was started, in 1791, under his own supervision, the first newspaper of Tennessee, known as the *Knoxville Gazette*. It

was four or five years younger than the only other
newspaper of the then far West, the *Kentucky
Gazette*. The paper gives an interesting glimpse of
many of the social and political conditions of the
day. In political tone it showed Blount's influence
very strongly, and was markedly in advance of most
of the similar papers of the time, including the *Kentucky Gazette ;* for it took a firm stand in favor of
the National Government, and against every form
of disorder, of separatism, or of mob law. As with
all of the American papers of the day, even in the
backwoods, there was much interest taken in European news, and a prominent position was given to
long letters, or extracts from seaboard papers, containing accounts of the operations of the English
fleets and the French armies, or of the attitude of the
European governments. Like most Americans, the
editorial writers of the paper originally   The
sympathized strongly with the French "Knoxville
Revolution ; but the news of the behead-   Gazette."
ing of Marie Antoinette, and the recital of the
atrocities committed in Paris, worked a reaction
among those who loved order, and the *Knoxville
Gazette* ranged itself with them, taking for the
time being strong grounds against the French, and
even incidentally alluding to the Indians as being
more blood-thirsty than any man "not a Jacobin."[1]
The people largely shared these sentiments. In
1793 at the Fourth of July celebration at Jones-
borough there was a public dinner and ball, as there
was also at Knoxville ; Federal troops were paraded

[1] *Knoxville Gazette*, March 27, 1794.

and toasts were drunk to the President, to the
Judges of the Supreme Court, to Blount, to General
Wayne, to the friendly Chickasaw Indians, to Sevier,
to the ladies of the Southwestern Territory, to the
American arms, and, finally, "to the true liberties of
France and a speedy and just punishment of the
murderers of Louis XVI." The word "Jacobin"
was used as a term of reproach for some time.

The paper was at first decidedly Federalist in sentiment. No sympathy was expressed with Genet or
with the efforts undertaken by the West-
The "Gazette" ern allies of the French Minister to organ-
Sound in ize a force for the conquest of Louisiana; and
its Politics. the Tennessee settlers generally took the
side of law and order in the earlier disturbances in
which the Federal Government was concerned. At
the Fourth of July celebration in Knoxville, in
1795, one of the toasts was "The four western counties of Pennsylvania; may they repent their folly
and sin no more"; the Tennesseeans sympathizing
as little with the Pennsylvania whiskey revolution-
ists as four years later they sympathized with the
Kentuckians and Virginians in their nullification agi-
Its Gradual tation against the alien and sedition laws.
Change Gradually, however, the tone of the paper
of Tone. changed, as did the tone of the community,
at least to the extent of becoming Democratic and
anti-Federal; for the people felt that the Easterners
did not sympathize with them either in their contests with the Indians or in their desire to control
the Mississippi and the farther West. They grew
to regard with particular vindictiveness the Feder-

alists,—the aristocrats, as they styled them,—of the Southern seaboard States, notably of Virginia and South Carolina.

One pathetic feature of the paper was the recurrence of advertisements by persons whose friends and kinsfolk had been carried off by the Indians, and who anxiously sought any trace of them.

But the *Gazette* was used for the expression of opinions not only by the whites, but occasionally even by an Indian. One of the Cherokee chiefs, the Red Bird, put into the *Gazette*, for two buckskins, a talk to the Cherokee chief of the Upper Towns, in which he especially warned him to leave alone one William Cocke, "the white man who lived among the mulberry trees," for, said Red Bird, "the mulberry man talks very strong and runs very fast"; this same Cocke being afterwards one of the first two senators from Tennessee. The Red Bird ended his letter by the expression of the rather quaint wish, "that all the bad people on both sides were laid in the ground, for then there would not be so many mush men trying to make people to believe they were warriors."[1]

Queer Use of the "Gazette."

Blount brought his family to Tennessee at once, and took the lead in trying to build up institutions for higher education. After a good deal of difficulty an academy was organized under the title of Blount College, and was opened as soon as a sufficient number of pupils could be gotten together; there were already two other colleges in the Territory, Greeneville and

Efforts to Promote Higher Education.

[1] *Knoxville Gazette*, November 3, 1792.

Washington, the latter being the academy founded by Doak. Like almost all other institutions of learning of the day these three were under clerical control; but Blount College was chartered as a non-denomination institution, the first of its kind in the United States.[1] The clergyman and the lawyer, with the school-master, were still the typical men of letters in all the frontier communities. The doctor was not yet a prominent feature of life in the backwoods, though there is in the *Gazette* an advertisement of one who announces that he intends to come to practise "with a large stock of genuine medicines."[2]

The ordinary books were still school books, books of law, and sermons or theological writings. The first

Books of the Backwoods. books, or pamphlets, published in Eastern Tennessee were brought out about this time at the *Gazette* office, and bore such titles as "A Sermon on Psalmody, by Rev. Hezekiah Balch"; "A Discourse by the Rev. Samuel Carrick"; and a legal essay called "Western Justice."[3] There was also a slight effort now and then at literature of a lighter kind. The little Western papers, like those in the East, had their poets' corners, often with the heading of "Sacred to the Muses," the poems ranging from "Lines to Myra" and "An Epitaph on John Topham" to "The Pernicious Consequences of Smoking Cigars." In one of the issues of the *Knoxville Gazette* there is adver-

[1] See Edward T. Sanford's "Blount College and the University of Tennessee," p. 13.

[2] *Knoxville Gazette*, June 19, 1794.

[3] *Knoxville Gazette*, Jan. 30 and May 8, 1794.

tised for sale a new song by "a gentleman of Col. McPherson's Blues, on a late Expedition against the Pennsylvania Insurgents"; and also, in rather incongruous juxtaposition, "Toplady's Translation of Zanchi on Predestination."

Settlers were thronging into East Tennessee, and many penetrated even to the Indian-harassed western district. In travelling to the western parts the immigrants generally banded together in large parties, led by some man of note. Among those who arrived in 1792 was the old North Carolina Indian fighter, General Griffith Rutherford. He wished to settle on the Cumberland, and to take thither all his company, with a large number of wagons, and he sent to Blount begging that a road might be cut through the wilderness for the wagons; or, if this could not be done, that some man would blaze the route, "in which case," said he "there would be hands of our own that could cut as fast as wagons could march."[1]

Settlers Throng into Tennessee.

In 1794, there being five thousand free male inhabitants, as provided by law, Tennessee became entitled to a Territorial legislature, and the Governor summoned the Assembly to meet at Knoxville on August 17th. So great was the danger from the Indians that a military company had to accompany the Cumberland legislators to and from the seat of government. For the same reason the judges on their circuits had to go accompanied by a military guard.

Meeting of the Territorial Legislature.

Among the first acts of this Territorial Legisla-

---

[1] Blount MSS., Rutherford to Blount, May 25, 1792.

ture was that to establish higher institutions of learning; John Sevier was made a trustee in both Blount and Greeneville Colleges. A lottery was established for the purpose of building the Cumberland road to Nashville, and another one to build a jail and stocks in Nashville. A pension act was passed for disabled soldiers and for widows and orphans, who were to be given an adequate allowance at the discretion of the county court. A poll tax of twenty-five cents on all taxable white polls was laid, and on every taxable negro poll fifty cents. Land was taxed at the rate of twenty-five cents a hundred acres, town lots one dollar; while a stud horse was taxed four dollars. Thus, taxes were laid exclusively upon free males, upon slaves, lands, town lots, and stud horses, a rather queer combination.[1]

Various industries were started, as the people began to demand not only the necessaries of life but

Many Industries Established. the comforts, and even occasionally the luxuries. There were plenty of blacksmith shops; and a goldsmith and jeweller set up his establishment. In his advertisement he shows that he was prepared to do some work which would be alien to his modern representative, for he notifies the citizens that he makes "rifle guns in the neatest and most approved fashion."[2]

Ferries were established at the important crossings, and taverns in the county-seats and small towns. One of the Knoxville taverns advertises its rates,

---

[1] Laws of Tennessee, Knoxville, 1803.   First Session of Territorial Legislature, 1794.

[2] *Knoxville Gazette*, Oct. 20, 1792.

which were one shilling for breakfast, one shilling
for supper, and one and sixpence for dinner; board
and lodging for a week costing two dol-   **Ferries**
lars, and board only for the same space   **and**
of time nine shillings. Ferriage was three   **Taverns.**
pence for a man and horse and two shillings for a
wagon and team.

Various stores were established in the towns, the
merchants obtaining most of their goods in the great
trade centres of Philadelphia and Balti-
more, and thence hauling them by wagon   **Trade.**
to the frontier. Most of the trade was carried on
by barter. There was very little coin in the country
and but few bank-notes. Often the advertisement
specified the kind of goods that would be taken
and the different values at which they would be
received. Thus, the salt works at Washington,
Virginia, in advertising their salt, stated that they
would sell it per bushel for seven shillings and
sixpence if paid in cash or prime furs; at ten shillings if paid in bear or deer skins, beeswax, hemp,
bacon, butter, or beef cattle ; and at twelve shillings
if in other trade and country produce, as was usual.[1]
The prime furs were mink, coon, muskrat, wildcat,
and beaver. Besides this the stores advertised that
they would take for their articles cash, beeswax, and country produce or tallow, hogs'   **Currency.**
lard in white walnut kegs, butter, pork, new feathers,
good horses, and also corn, rye, oats, flax, and "old
Congress money," the old Congress money being
that issued by the Continental Congress, which had

[1] *Knoxville Gazette*, June 1, 1793.

depreciated wonderfully in value. They also took certificates of indebtedness either from the State or the nation because of services performed against the Indians, and certificates of land claimed under various rights. The value of some of these commodities was evidently mainly speculative. The storekeepers often felt that where they had to accept such dubious substitutes for cash they desired to give no credit, and some of the advertisements run : " Cheap, ready money store, where no credit whatever will be given," and then proceed to describe what ready money was,—cash, furs, bacon, etc. The stores sold salt, iron-mongery, pewterware, corduroys, rum, brandy, whiskey, wine, ribbons, linen, calamancos, and in fact generally what would be found at that day in any store in the smaller towns of the older States. The best eight by ten crown-glass "was regularly imported," and also "beautiful assortments of fashionable coat and vest buttons," as well as "brown and loaf sugar, coffee, chocolate, tea, and spices." In the towns the families had ceased to kill their own meat, and beef markets were established where fresh meat could be had twice a week.

Houses and lots were advertised for sale, and one result of the method of allowing the branded stock **Stock on** to range at large in the woods was that **the Range.** there were numerous advertisements for strayed horses, and even cattle, with descriptions of the brands and ear marks. The people were already beginning to pay attention to the breeding of their horses, and fine stallions with pedigrees were advertised, though some of the advertisements show a certain indifference to purity of strain; one stallion being quoted as of "mixed fox-hunting and dray" breed. Rather curiously the Chickasaw horses were continually mentioned as of special merit, together with those of imported stock. Attention was paid both to pacers and trotters.

The lottery was still a recognized method of raising money for every purpose, including the advancement of education and religion. One of the advertisements gives as one of the prizes a negro, valued at one hundred and thirty pounds, a horse at ten pounds, and five hundred acres of fine land without improvements at twelve hundred pounds.

Journeying to the long-settled districts of the East, persons went as they wished, in their own wagons or on their own horses; but to go **Government** from East Tennessee either to Kentucky, **Escort for** or to the Cumberland district, or to New **Immigrants.** Orleans, was a serious matter because of the Indians. The Territorial authorities provided annually an escort for immigrants from the Holston country to the Cumberland, a distance of one hundred and ten miles through the wilderness, and the departure of this annual escort was advertised for weeks in advance.

Sometimes the escort was thus provided by the authorities. More often adventurers simply banded together; or else some enterprising man advertised that on a given date he should start and would provide protection for those who chose to accompany him. Thus, in the *Knoxville Gazette* for February 6, 1795, a boat captain gives public notice to all persons who wish to sail from the Holston country to New Orleans, that on March 1st, if the waters answer, his two boats will start, the *Mary* of twenty-five tons, and the *Little Polly* of fifteen tons. Those who had contracted for freight and passage are desired to attend previous to that period.

There was of course a good deal of lawlessness and a strong tendency to settle assault and battery **Lawless-** cases in particular out of court. The offi-**ness.** cers of justice at times had to subdue criminals by open force. Andrew Jackson, who was District Attorney for the Western District, early acquired fame by the energy and success with which he put down any criminal who resisted the law. The worst offenders fled to the Mississippi Territory, there to live among Spaniards, Creoles, Indians, and lawless Americans. Lawyers drove a thriving business; but they had their own difficulties, to judge by one advertisement, which appears in the issue of the *Gazette* for March 23, 1793, where six of them give notice that thereafter they will give no legal advice unless it is legally paid for.

All the settlers, or at least all the settlers who had any ambition to rise in the world, were absorbed in **Endless** land speculations; Blount, Robertson, and **Land** the other leaders as much so as anybody. **Specula-** They were continually in correspondence **tions.** with one another about the purchase of land warrants, and about laying them out in the best localities. Of course there was much jealousy and rivalry in the effort to get the best sites. Robertson, being farthest on the frontier, where there was most wild land, had peculiar advantages. Very soon after he settled in the Cumberland district at the close of the Revoluntionary War, Blount had entered into an agreement with him for a joint land speculation. Blount was to purchase land claims from both officers and soldiers amounting in all to fifty thousand acres and enter them for the Western Territory, while Robertson was to survey and locate the claims, receiving one fourth of the whole for his reward.[1] Their connection continued during Blount's term as Governor, and Blount's letters to Robertson contain much advice as to how the warrants shall be laid out. Wherever possible they were of course laid outside the Indian boundaries; but, like every one else, Blount and Robertson knew that eventually the Indian lands would come into the possession of the United States, and in view of the utter confusion of the titles, and especially in view of the way the Indians as well as the whites continually broke the treaties and rendered it necessary to make new ones, both Blount and Robertson were willing to place claims on the Indian lands and trust to luck to make the claims good if ever a cession was made. The lands thus located were not lands upon which any Indian village stood. Generally they were tracts of wilderness through which the Indians occasionally hunted, but as to which there was a question whether they had yet been formally ceded to the government.[2]

---

[1] Blount MSS., Agreement between William Blount and James Robertson, Oct. 30, 1783.

[2] Robertson MSS., Blount to Robertson, April 29, 1792.

Blount also corresponded with many other men on the question of these land speculations, and it is

Land Tax and Land Sales.

amusing to read the expressions of horror of his correspondents when they read that Tennessee had imposed a land tax.[1] By his activity he became a very large landed proprietor, and when Tennessee was made a State he was taxed on 73,252 acres in all. The tax was not excessive, being but $179.72.[2] It was of course entirely proper for Blount to get possession of the land in this way. The theory of government on the frontier was that each man should be paid a small salary, and be allowed to exercise his private business just so long as it did not interfere with his public duties. Blount's land speculations were similar to those in which almost every other prominent American, in public or private life, was engaged. Neither Congress nor the States had as yet seen the wisdom of allowing the land to be sold only in small parcels to actual occupants, and the favorite kind of speculation was the organization of land companies. Of course there were other kinds of business in which prominent men took part. Sevier was interested not only in land, but in various mercantile ventures of a more or less speculative kind ; he acted as an intermediary with the big importers, who were willing to furnish some of the stores with six months' credit if they could be guaranteed a settlement at the end of that time.[3]

---

[1] Blount MSS., Thomas Hart to Blount, Lexington, Ky., March 29, 1795.

[2] *Do.*, Return of taxable property of Blount, Nashville, Sept. 9, 1796.

[3] *Do.*, David Allison to Blount, Oct. 16, 1791.

One of the characteristics of all the leading frontiersmen was not only the way in which they combined business enterprises with their work
as Government officials and as Indian
fighters, but the readiness with which
they turned from one business enterprise
to another.   One of Blount's Kentucky correspondents, Thomas Hart, the grandfather of Benton, in
his letter to Blount shows these traits in typical
fashion.   He was engaged in various land speculations with Blount,[1] and was always writing to him
about locating land warrants, advertising the same
as required by law, and the like.   He and Blount
held some tens of thousands of acres of the Henderson claim, and Hart proposed that they should lay
it out in five-hundred-acre tracts, to be rented to
farmers, with the idea that each farmer should
receive ten cows and calves to start with; a proposition which was of course hopeless, as the pioneers
would not lease lands when it was so easy to obtain
freeholds.   In his letters, Hart mentioned cheerfully
that though he was sixty-three years old he was just
as well able to carry on his manufacturing business,
and, on occasion, to leave it, and play pioneer, as he
ever had been, remarking that he "never would be
satisfied in the world while new countries could be
found," and that his intention, now that he had
moved to Kentucky, was to push the mercantile
business as long as the Indian war continued and
money was plenty, and when that failed, to turn his

*Business
Versatility
of the Fron-
tiersman.*

---

[1] Clay MSS., Blount to Hart, Knoxville, February 9, 1794. This was
just as Hart was moving to Kentucky.

attention to farming and to divide up those of his lands he could not till himself, to be rented by others.[1]

This letter to Blount shows, by the way, as was shown by Madison's correspondent from Kentucky, that the Indian war, scourge though it was to the frontiersmen as a whole, brought some attendant benefits in its wake by putting a stimulus on the trade of the merchants and bringing ready money into the country. It must not be forgotten, however, that men like Hart and Blount, though in some ways they were benefited by the war, were in other ways very much injured, and that, moreover, they consistently strove to do justice to the Indians and to put a stop to hostilities.

In his letters Colonel Hart betrays a hearty, healthy love of life, and capacity to enjoy it, and make the best of it, which fortunately exist in many Kentucky and Tennessee families to this day. He wanted money, but the reason he wanted it was to use it in having a good time for himself and his friends, writing: "I feel all the ardor and spirit for business I did forty years ago, and see myself more capable to conduct it. Oh, if my old friend Uncle Jacob was but living and in this country, what pleasure we should have in raking up money and spending it with our friends!" and he closed by earnestly entreating Blount and his family to come to Kentucky, which he assured him was the finest country in the world, with moreover, "a very pleasant society, for," said he, "I can say with truth

[1] Blount MSS., Thomas Hart to Blount, Dec. 23, 1793.

that the society of this place is equal, if not superior, to any that can be found in any inland town in the United States, for there is not a day that passes over our heads but I can have half a dozen strange gentlemen to dine with us, and they are from all parts of the Union." [1]

The one overshadowing fact in the history of Tennessee during Blount's term as governor was the Indian warfare. Hostilities with the Indians were never ceasing, and, so far as Tennessee was concerned, during these six years it was the Indians, and not the whites who were habitually the aggressors and wrongdoers. The Indian warfare in the Territory during these years deserves some study because it was typical of what occurred elsewhere. It illustrates forcibly the fact that under the actual conditions of settlement wars were inevitable; for if it is admitted that the land of the Indians had to be taken and that the continent had to be settled by white men, it must be further admitted that the settlement could not have taken place save after war. The whites might be to blame in some cases, and the Indians in others; but under no combination of circumstances was it possible to obtain possession of the country save as the result of war, or of a peace obtained by the fear of war. Any peace which did not surrender the land was sure in the end to be broken by the whites; and a peace which did surrender the land would be broken by the Indians. The history

The Never Ending Indian Warfare.

Incessant Violation of the Treaties by Both the Red Men and the White.

[1] Blount MSS., Hart to Blount, Lexington, Feb. 15, 1795.

of Tennessee during the dozen years from 1785 to 1796 offers an admirable case in point. In 1785 the United States Commissioners concluded the treaty of Hopewell with the Indians, and solemnly guaranteed them certain lands. The whites contemptuously disregarded this treaty and seized the lands which it guaranteed to the Indians, being themselves the aggressors, and paying no heed to the plighted word of the Government, while the Government itself was too weak to make the frontiersmen keep faith. The treaties of New York and of Holston with the Creeks and Cherokees in 1790 and 1791 were fairly entered into by fully authorized representatives of the tribes. Under them, for a valuable consideration, and of their own motion, the Creeks and Cherokees solemnly surrendered all title to what is now the territory of Tennessee, save to a few tracts mostly in the west and southeast; and much of the land which was thus ceded they had ceded before. Nevertheless, the peace thus solemnly made was immediately violated by the Indians themselves. The whites were not the aggressors in any way, and, on the contrary, thanks to the wish of the United States authorities for peace, and to the care with which Blount strove to carry out the will of the Federal Government, they for a long time refrained even from retaliating when injured; yet the Indians robbed and plundered them even more freely than when the whites themselves had been the aggressors and had broken the treaty.

Before making the treaty of Holston Blount had been in correspondence with Benjamin Hawkins, a

man who had always been greatly interested in
Indian affairs. He was a prominent politician in
North Carolina, and afterwards for many   Confusion
years agent among the Southern Indians.   of the
He had been concerned in several of the   Treaties.
treaties. He warned Blount that since the treaty of
Hopewell the whites, and not the Indians, had been
the aggressors; and also warned him not to try to
get too much land from the Indians, or to take away
too great an extent of their hunting grounds, which
would only help the great land companies, but to be
content with the thirty-fifth parallel for a southern
boundary.[1] Blount paid much heed to this advice,
and by the treaty of Holston he obtained from the
Indians little more than what the tribes had previously granted; except that they confirmed to the
whites the country upon which the pioneers were
already settled. The Cumberland district had
already been granted over and over again by the
Indians in special treaties, to Henderson, to the
North Carolinians and to the United States. The
Creeks in particular never had had any claim to
this Cumberland country, which was a hundred
miles and over from any of their towns. All the
use they had ever made of it was to visit it with
their hunting parties, as did the Cherokees, Choctaws, Chickasaws, Shawnees, Delawares, and many
others. Yet the Creeks and other Indians had the
effrontery afterwards to assert that the Cumberland
Country had never been ceded at all, and that as the
settlers in it were thus outside of the territory prop-

[1] Blount MSS., Hawkins to Blount, March 10, 1791.

erly belonging to the United States, they were not entitled to protection under the treaty entered into with the latter.

Blount was vigilant and active in seeing that none of the frontiersmen trespassed on the Indian lands, and when a party of men, claiming authority under Georgia, started to settle at the Muscle Shoals, he co-operated actively with the Indians in having them brought back, and did his best, though in vain, to persuade the Grand Jury to indict the offenders.[1]

Blount's Good Faith with the Indians. He was explicit in his orders to Sevier, to Robertson, and to District Attorney Jackson that they should promptly punish any white man who violated the provisions of the treaty; and over a year after it had been entered into he was able to write in explicit terms that "not a single settler had built a house, or made a settlement of any kind, on the Cherokee lands, and that no Indians had been killed by the whites excepting in defence of their lives and property."[2] Robertson heartily co-operated with Blount, as did Sevier, in the effort to keep peace, Robertson showing much good sense and self-control, and acquiescing in Blount's desire that nothing should be done "inconsistent with the good of the nation as a whole," and that "the faith of the nation should be kept."[3]

The Indians as a body showed no appreciation whatever of these efforts to keep the peace, and plundered and murdered quite as freely as before the

[1] Robertson MSS., Blount to Robertson, Sept. 3, 1791.
[2] *Do.*, Blount to Robertson, Jan. 2, 1792; to Bloody Fellow, Sept. 13, 1792.
[3] Blount MSS., Robertson to Blount, Jan. 17, 1793.

treaties, or as when the whites themselves were the aggressors. The Creek Confederacy was in a condition of utter disorganization, McGillivray's **Bad Faith** authority was repudiated, and most of **of the** the towns scornfully refused to obey the **Indians.** treaty into which their representatives had entered at New York. A tory adventurer named Bowles, who claimed to have the backing of the English Government, landed in the nation and set himself in opposition to McGillivray. The latter, who was no fighter, and whose tools were treachery and craft, fled to the protection of the Spaniards. Bowles, among other feats, plundered the stores of Panton, a white trader in the Spanish interest, and for a moment his authority seemed supreme ; but the Spaniards, by a trick, got possession of him and put him in prison.

The Spaniards still claimed as their own the Southwestern country, and were untiring in their efforts to keep the Indians united among **Intrigues** themselves and hostile to the Americans. **of the** They concluded a formal treaty of friend- **Spaniards.** ship and of reciprocal guarantee with the Choctaws, Chickasaws, Creeks, and Cherokees at Nogales, in the Choctaw country, on May 14, 1792.[1] The Indians entered into this treaty at the very time they had concluded wholly inconsistent treaties with the Americans. On the place of the treaty the Spaniards built a fort, which they named Fort Confederation, to perpetuate, as they hoped, the memory of the

[1] Draper MSS., Spanish Documents ; Letter of Carondelet to Duke of Alcudia, Nov. 24, 1794.

confederation they had thus established among the Southern Indians. By means of this fort they intended to control all the territory enclosed between the rivers Mississippi, Yazoo, Chickasaw, and Mobile. The Spaniards also expended large sums of money in arming the Creeks, and in bribing them to do, what they were quite willing to do of their own accord,— that is, to prevent the demarkation of the boundary line as provided in the New York treaty; a treaty which Carondelet reported to his Court as "insulting and pernicious to Spain, the abrogation of which has lately been brought about by the intrigues with the Indians."[1]

At the same time that the bill for these expenses was submitted for audit to the home government the Spanish Governor also submitted his accounts for the expenses in organizing the expedition against the "English adventurer Bowles," and in negotiating with Wilkinson and the other Kentucky Separatists, and also in establishing a Spanish post at the Chickasaw Bluffs, for which he had finally obtained the permission of the Chickasaws. The Americans of course regarded the establishment both of the fort at the Chickasaw Bluffs and the fort at Nogales as direct challenges; and Carondelet's accounts show that the frontiersmen were entirely justified in their belief that the Spaniards not only supplied the Creeks with arms and munitions of war, but actively interfered to prevent them from keeping faith and carrying out the treaties which they had signed. The Spaniards did not wish the Indians to go to war

[1] Draper MSS., Letter of Carondelet, New Orleans, Sept. 25, 1795.

unless it was necessary as a last resort. They preferred that they should be peaceful, provided always
they could prevent the intrusion of the   Caronde-
Americans. Carondelet wrote: "We have   let's
inspired the Creeks with pacific intentions   Policy.
towards the United States, but with the precise re-
striction that there shall be no change of the boundaries," [1] and he added that "to sustain our allied
nations [of Indians] in the possession of their lands
becomes therefore indispensable, both to preserve
Louisiana to Spain, and in order to keep the Americans from the navigation of the Gulf." He expressed
great uneasiness at the efforts of Robertson to foment
war between the Chickasaws and Choctaws and the
Creeks, and exerted all his powers to keep the Indian
nations at peace with one another and united against
the settler-folk.[2]

The Spaniards, though with far more infamous
and deliberate deceit and far grosser treachery, were
pursuing towards the United States and   The
the Southwestern Indians the policy pur-   Spaniards
sued by the British towards the United   far more
States and the Northwestern Indians; with   Treach-
the difference that the Spanish Governor   erous
and his agents acted under the orders of   than the
the Court of Spain, while the English authorities   British.
connived at and profited by, rather than directly
commanded, what was done by their subordinates.
Carondelet expressly states that Colonel Gayoso and

---

[1] Draper MSS., Spanish Docs.; Carondelet's Report, Oct. 23, 1793.

[2] *Do.*, Carondelet to Don Louis De Las Casas, June 13, 1795, enclosing
letter from Don M. G. De Lemos, Governor of Natchez.

his other subordinates had been directed to unite the
Indian nations in a defensive alliance, under the protection of Spain, with the object of opposing Blount,
Robertson, and the frontiersmen, and of establishing
the Cumberland River as the boundary between the
Americans and the Indians.   The reciprocal guarantee of their lands by the Creeks, Cherokees, Choctaws,
and Chickasaws was, said Carondelet, the only way
by which the Americans could be retained within
their own boundaries.[1]   The Spaniards devoted
much attention to supporting those traders among
the Indians who were faithful to the cause of Spain
and could be relied upon to intrigue against the
Americans.[2]

The divided condition of the Creeks, some of
whom wished to carry out in good faith the treaty
of New York, while the others threatened
to attack whoever made any move towards
putting the treaty into effect, puzzled
Carondelet nearly as much as it did the
United States authorities ; and he endeavored to
force the Creeks to abstain from warfare with the
Chickasaws by refusing to supply them with munitions of war for any such purpose, or for any other
except to oppose the frontiersmen.   He put great
faith in the endeavor to treat the Americans not as
one nation, but as an assemblage of different communities.   The Spaniards sought to placate the
Kentuckians by promising to reduce the duties on
the goods that came down stream to New Orleans

*Caronde-
let's
Tortuous
Intrigues.*

---

[1] Carondelet to Alcudia, Aug. 17, 1793.

[2] *Do.*, Manuel Gayoso De Lemos to Carondelet, Nogales, July 25, 1793.

by six per cent., and thus to prevent an outbreak on
their part; at the same time the United States
Government was kept occupied by idle negotiations.
Carondelet further hoped to restrain the Cumberland
people by fear of the Creek and Cherokee nations,
who, he remarked, "had never ceased to commit
hostilities upon them and to profess implacable
hatred for them."[1] He reported to the Spanish
Court that Spain had no means of molesting the
Americans save through the Indians, as it would
not be possible with an army to make a serious impression on the "ferocious and well-armed" frontier
people, favored as they would be by their knowledge of the country; whereas the Indians, if properly
supported, offered an excellent defence, supplying
from the Southwestern tribes fifteen thousand warriors, whose keep in time of peace cost Spain not
more than fifty thousand dollars a year, and even
in time of war not more than a hundred and fifty
thousand.[2]

The Spaniards in this manner actively fomented
hostilities among the Creeks and Cherokees.   Their
support explained much in the attitude of
these peoples, but doubtless the war would **He Continu-**
have gone on anyhow until the savages **ally Incites**
were thoroughly cowed by force of arms. **the Indians to War.**
The chief causes for the incessantly renewed hostilities were the desire of the young braves for blood
and glory, a vague but well-founded belief among
the Indians that the white advance meant their ruin

[1] Carondelet to De Lemos, Aug. 15, 1793.
[2] Carondelet to Alcudia, Sept. 27, 1793.

unless stayed by an appeal to arms, and, more important still, the absolute lack of any central authority among the tribesmen which could compel them
all to war together effectively on the one hand, or
all to make peace on the other.

Blount was Superintendent of Indian Affairs for
the Southern Indians as well as Governor of the
Seagrove   Territory; and in addition the Federal
the Indian authorities established an Indian agent,
Agent.   directly responsible to themselves, among
the Creeks. His name was James Seagrove. He
did his best to bring about a peace, and, like all
Indian agents, he was apt to take an unduly harsh
view of the deeds of the frontiersmen, and to consider them the real aggressors in any trouble. Of
necessity his point of view was wholly different
from that of the border settlers. He was promptly
informed of all the outrages and aggressions committed by the whites, while he heard little or nothing
of the parties of young braves, bent on rapine, who
continually fell on the frontiers; whereas the frontiersmen came in contact only with these war bands,
and when their kinsfolk had been murdered and
their cattle driven off, they were generally ready to
take vengeance on the first Indians they could find.
Even Seagrove, however, was at times hopelessly
puzzled by the attitude of the Indians. He was
obliged to admit that they were the first offenders,
after the conclusion of the treaties of New York and
Holston, and that for a long time the settlers behaved with great moderation in refraining from
revenging the outrages committed on them by the

Indians, which, he remarked, would have to be stopped if peace was to be preserved.[1]

As the Government took no efficient steps to preserve the peace, either by chastising the Indians or by bridling the ill-judged vengeance of the frontier inhabitants, many of the latter soon grew to hate and despise those by whom they were neither protected nor restrained. The disorderly element got the upper hand on the Georgia frontier, where the backwoodsmen did all they could to involve the nation in a general Indian war; and displayed the most defiant and mutinous spirit toward the officers, civil and military, of the United States Government.[2] As for the Creeks, Seagrove found it exceedingly hard to tell who of them were traitors and who were not; and indeed the chiefs would probably themselves have found the task difficult, for they were obliged to waver more or less in their course as the fickle tribesmen were swayed by impulses towards peace or war. One of the men whom Seagrove finally grew to regard as a confirmed traitor was the chief, McGillivray. He was probably quite right in his estimate of the half-breed's character; and, on the other hand, McGillivray doubtless had as an excuse the fact that the perpetual intrigues of Spanish officers, American traders, British adventurers, Creek chiefs who wished peace, and Creek warriors who

Disorder among the Frontiersmen.

---

[1] American State Papers, IV., Seagrove to the Secretary of War, St. Mary's, June 14, 1792.

[2] *Do.*, Seagrove to the President, Rock Landing, on the Oconee, in Georgia, July 17, 1792.

wished war, made it out of the question for him to
follow any settled policy. He wrote to Seagrove:
McGillivray "It is no wonder the Indians are distracted,
Bewildered. when they are tampered with on every side.
I am myself in the situation of a keeper of Bedlam,
and nearly fit for an inhabitant."[1] However, what
he did amounted to but little, for his influence had
greatly waned, and in 1793 he died.

On the Georgia frontier the backwoodsmen were
very rough and lawless, and were always prone to
The   make aggressions on the red men; never-
Indians the theless, even in the case of Georgia in
Aggressors. 1791 and '92, the chief fault lay with
the Indians. They refused to make good the land
cession which they had solemnly guaranteed at the
treaty of New York, and which certain of their
towns had previously covenanted to make in the
various more or less fraudulent treaties entered into
with the State of Georgia separately. In addition
to this their plundering parties continually went
among the Georgians. The latter, in their efforts to
retaliate, struck the hostile and the peaceful alike;
and as time went on they made ready to take forci-
ble possession of the lands they coveted, without
regard to whether or not these lands had been ceded
in fair treaty.

In the Tennessee country the wrong was wholly
with the Indians. Some of the chiefs of the Cherokees went to Philadelphia at the beginning of the
year 1792 to request certain modifications of the
treaty of Holston, notably an increase in their annu-

[1] American State Papers, IV., McGillivray to Seagrove, May 18, 1793.

ity, which was granted.[1]   The General Government had conducted the treaties in good faith and had given the Indians what they asked.   The frontiersmen did not molest them in any way or trespass upon their lands; yet their ravages continued without cessation.   The authorities at Washington made but feeble efforts to check these outrages, and protect the southwestern settlers.   Yet at this time Tennessee was doing her full part in sustaining the National Government in the war against the Northwestern tribes; a company of Tennessee militia, under Captain Jacob Tipton, joined St. Clair's army, and Tipton was slain at the defeat, where he fought with the utmost bravery.[2]   Not unnaturally the Tennesseeans, and especially the settlers on the far-off Cumberland, felt it a hardship for the United States to neglect their defence at the very time that they were furnishing their quota of soldiers for an offensive war against nations in whose subdual they had but an indirect interest.   Robertson wrote to Blount that their silence and remoteness was the cause why the interests of the Cumberland settlers were thus neglected, while the Kentuckians were amply protected.[3]

Naturally the Tennesseeans, conscious that they had not wronged the Indians, and had scrupulously observed the treaty, grew imbittered over the wanton Indian outrages.   They were entirely at a loss to explain the reason why

Their Outrages on the Tennesseeans.

Anger of the Tennesseeans.

[1] *Do.*, Secretary of War to Governor Blount, Jan. 31, 1792.

[2] *Knoxville Gazette*, Dec. 17, 1791.   I use the word "Tennessee" for convenience; it was not at this time used in this sense.

[3] Robertson MSS., Robertson's letter, Nashville, Aug. 25, 1791.

the warfare against them was waged with such ferocity. Sevier wrote to Madison, with whom he
frequently corresponded : "This country is wholly
involved in a war with the Creek and Cherokee
Indians, and I am not able to suggest the reasons or
the pretended cause of their depredations. The suc-
cesses of the Northern tribes over our late unfortunate armies have created great exultation throughout
the whole Southern Indians, and the probabilities
may be they expect to be equally successful. The
Spaniards are making use of all their art to draw
over the Southern tribes, and I fear may have stimulated them to commence their hostilities. Governor
Blount has indefatigably labored to keep these people in a pacific humor, but in vain. War is una-
voidable, however ruinous and calamitous it may
be."[1] The Federal Government was most reluctant
to look facts in the face and acknowledge
that the hostilities were serious, and that
they were unprovoked by the whites. The
Secretary of War reported to the President
that the offenders were doubtless merely a
small banditti of Creeks and Cherokees, with a few
Shawnees who possessed no fixed residence ; and in
groping for a remedy he weakly suggested that inasmuch as many of the Cherokees seemed to be dis-
satisfied with the boundary line they had established
by treaty it would perhaps be well to alter it.[2]
Of course the adoption of such a measure would

Blindness
of the
Federal
Govern-
ment.

[1] State Dep. MSS., Madison Papers, Sevier's letter, Oct. 30, 1792.
[2] State Dep. MSS., Washington Papers, Secretary of War to the President, July 28, and Aug. 5, 1792.

have amounted to putting a premium on murder and treachery.

If the Easterners were insensible to the Western need for a vigorous Indian war, many of the Westerners showed as little appreciation of the necessity for any Indian war which did not immediately concern themselves. Individual Kentuckians, individual colonels and captains of the Kentucky militia, were always ready to march to the help of the Tennesseeans against the Southern Indians; but the highest officials of Kentucky were almost as anxious as the Federal authorities to prevent any war save that with the tribes northwest of the Ohio. One of the Kentucky senators, Brown, in writing to the Governor, Isaac Shelby, laid particular stress upon the fact that nothing but the most urgent necessity could justify a war with the Southern Indians.[1] Shelby himself sympathized with this feeling. He knew what an Indian war was, for he had owed his election largely to his record as an Indian fighter and to the confidence the Kentuckians felt in his power to protect them from their red foes.[2] His correspondence is filled with letters in relation to Indian affairs, requests to authorize the use of spies, requests to establish guards along the wilderness road and to garrison blockhouses on the frontier; and sometimes there are more pathetic letters, from a husband who had lost a wife, or from an "old, frail woman," who wished to know if the Governor could

Odd Manifestations of Particularistic Feeling.

[1] Shelby MSS., J. Brown to Isaac Shelby, Philadelphia, June 2, 1793.
[2] *Do.*, M. D. Hardin to Isaac Shelby, April 10, 1792, etc., etc.

not by some means get news of her little grand-
daughter who had been captured in the wilderness
two years before by a party of Indians.[1] He realized
fully what hostilities meant, and had no desire to
see his State plunged into any Indian war which
could be avoided.

Yet, in spite of this cautious attitude, Shelby had
much influence with the people of the Tennessee territory. They confided to him their indignation with
Blount for stopping Logan's march to the aid of
Robertson; while on the other hand the Virginians,
when anxious to prevent the Cumberland settlers
from breaking the peace, besought him to use his
influence with them in order to make them do what
was right.[2] When such a man as Shelby was reluctant to see the United States enter into open hostilities with the Southern Indians, there is small cause
for wonder in the fact that the authorities at the
National capital did their best to deceive themselves
into the belief that there was no real cause for war.

Inability to look facts in the face did not alter the
facts. The Indian ravages in the Southern Territory
grew steadily more and more serious. The
difficulties of the settlers were enormously
increased because the United States strictly
forbade any offensive measures. The militia
were allowed to drive off any war bands found among
the settlements with evidently hostile intent; but, acting under the explicit, often repeated, and emphatic

Intolerable
Hardships
of the
Settlers.

---

[1] *Do.*, Letter of Mary Mitchell to Isaac Shelby, May 1, 1793.

[2] Shelby MSS., Arthur Campbell to Shelby, January 6, 1890 ; letter from
Cumberland to Shelby, May 11, 1793 ; John Logan to Shelby, June 19,
1794 ; petition of inhabitants of Nelson County, May 9, 1793.

commands of the General Government, Blount was obliged to order the militia under no circumstances to assume the offensive, or to cross into the Indian hunting grounds beyond the boundaries established by the treaty of Holston.[1] The inhabitants of the Cumberland region, and of the frontier counties generally, petitioned strongly against this, stating that "the frontiers will break if the inroads of the savages are not checked by counter expeditions." [2]   It was a very disagreeable situation for Blount, who, in carrying out the orders of the Federal authorities, had to incur the ill-will of the people whom he had been appointed to govern; but even at the cost of being supposed to be lukewarm in the cause of the settlers, he loyally endeavored to execute the commands of his superiors.   Yet like every other man acquainted by actual experience with frontier life and Indian warfare, he knew the folly of defensive war against Indians.   At this very time the officers on the frontier of South Carolina, which was not a State that was at all inclined to unjust aggression against the Indians, notified the Governor that the defensive war was "expensive, hazardous, and distressing" to the settlers, because the Indians "had such advantages, being so wolfish in their manner and so savage in their nature," that it was impossible to make war upon them on equal terms if the settlers were confined to defending themselves in their own country, whereas a speedy and spirited counter-attack upon

Blount's Good Conduct.

---

[1] Robertson MSS., Blount to Robertson, April 1, 1792.

[2] *Do.*, Feb. 1, 1792.

them in their homes would probably reduce them to peace, as their mode of warfare fitted them much less to oppose such an attack than to "take skulking, wolfish advantages of the defenceless" settlers.[1]

The difficulties of Blount and the Tennessee frontiersmen were increased by the very fact that the Cherokees and Creeks still nominally remained at peace. The Indian towns nearest the frontier knew that they were jeopardized by the acts of their wilder brethren, and generally strove to avoid committing any offense themselves. The war parties from the remote towns were the chief offenders. Band after band came up from among the Creeks or from among the lower Cherokees, and, passing through the peaceful villages of the upper Cherokees, fell on the frontier, stole horses, ambushed men, killed or captured women and children, and returned whence they had come. In most cases it was quite impossible to determine even the tribe of the offenders with any certainty; and all that the frontiersmen knew was that their bloody trails led back towards the very villages where the Indians loudly professed that they were at peace. They soon grew to regard all the Indians with equal suspicion, and they were so goaded by the blows which they could not return that they were ready to take vengeance upon any one with a red skin, or at least to condone such vengeance when taken. The peaceful Cherokees, though they regretted these

Double-faced Conduct of the Creeks and Cherokees.

[1] American State Papers, IV., Robert Anderson to the Governor of South Carolina, Sep. 20, 1792.

actions and were alarmed and disquieted at the prob-able consequences, were unwilling or unable to punish the aggressors.

Blount was soon at his wits' ends to prevent the outbreak of a general war. In November, 1792, he furnished the War Department with a list of scores of people—men, women, and children—who had been killed in Tennessee, chiefly in the Cumberland district, since the signing of the treaty of Holston. Many others had been carried off, and were kept in slavery. Among the wounded were General Robertson and one of his sons, who were shot, although not fatally, in May, 1792, while working on their farm. Both Creeks and Cherokees took part in the outrages, and the Chickamauga towns on the Tennessee, at Running Water, Nickajack, and in the neighborhood, ultimately supplied the most persistent wrongdoers.[1]

Blount Warns the Federal Government.

As Sevier remarked, the Southern, no less than the Northern Indians were much excited and encouraged by the defeat of St. Clair, coming as it did so close upon the defeat of Harmar. The double disaster to the American arms made the young braves very bold, and it became impossible for the elder men to restrain them.[2] The Creeks harassed the frontiers of Georgia somewhat, but devoted their main attention to the Tennesseeans, and especially to the isolated settlements on the

Effect of the Defeat of Harmar and St. Clair.

[1] American State Papers, IV., Blount to Secretary of War, Nov. 8, 1792 ; also page 330, etc. Many of these facts will be found recited, not only in the correspondence of Blount, but in the Robertson MSS., in the *Knoxville Gazette*, and in Haywood, Ramsey, and Putman.

[2] American State Papers, IV., pp. 263, 439, etc.

Cumberland. The Chickamauga towns were right at the crossing place both for the Northern Indians when they came south and for the Creeks when they went north. Bands of Shawnees, who were at this time the most inveterate of the enemies of the frontiersmen, passed much time among them; and the Creek war parties, when they journeyed north to steal horses and get scalps, invariably stopped among them, and on their return stopped again to exhibit their trophies and hold scalp dances. The natural

Growth of the War Spirit.

effect was that the Chickamaugas, who were mainly Lower Town Cherokees, seeing the impunity with which the ravages were committed, and appreciating the fact that under the orders of the Government they could not be molested in their own homes by the whites, began to join in the raids; and their nearness to the settlements soon made them the worst offenders. One of their leading chiefs was John Watts, who was of mixed blood. Among all these Southern Indians, half-breeds were far more numerous than among the Northerners, and when the half-breeds lived with their mothers' people they usually became the deadliest enemies of their fathers' race. Yet, they generally preserved the father's name. In consequence, among the extraordinary Indian titles borne by the chiefs of the Creeks, Cherokees, and Choctaws—the Bloody Fellow, the Middle Striker, the Mad Dog, the Glass, the Breath—there were also many names like John Watts, Alexander Cornell, and James Colbert, which were common among the frontiersmen themselves.

These Chickamaugas, and Lower Cherokees, had solemnly entered into treaties of peace, and Blount had been taken in by their professions of friendship, and for some time was loath to believe that their warriors were among the war parties who ravaged the settlements. By the spring of 1792, however, the fact of their hostility could no longer be concealed. Nevertheless, in May of that year the chiefs of the Lower Cherokee Towns, joined with those of the Upper Towns in pressing Governor Blount to come to a council at Coyatee, where he was met by two thousand Cherokees, including all their principal chiefs and warriors.[1] The head men, not only from the Upper Towns, but from Nickajack and Running Water, including John Watts, solemnly assured Blount of their peaceful intentions, and expressed their regret at the outrages which they admitted had been committed by their young men. Blount told them plainly that he had the utmost difficulty in restraining the whites from taking vengeance for the numerous murders committed on the settlers, and warned them that if they wished to avert a war which would fall upon both the innocent and the guilty they must themselves keep the peace. The chiefs answered, with seeming earnestness, that they were most desirous of being at peace, and would certainly restrain their men; and they begged for the treaty goods which Blount had in his possession. So sincere did they seem that he gave them the goods.[2]

Fruitless Peace Negotiations.

[1] Robertson's MSS., Blount to Robertson, May 20, 1792.

[2] *Knoxville Gazette*, March 24, 1792 ; American State Papers, IV., Blount to Secretary of War, June 2, 1792, with minutes of conference at Coyatee.

This meeting began on the 17th of May, yet on the 16th, within twelve miles of Knoxville, two boys were killed and scalped while picking strawberries, and on the 13th a girl had been scalped within four miles of Nashville; and on the 17th itself, while Judge Campbell of the Territorial Court was returning from the Cumberland Circuit his party was attacked, and one killed.[1]

When such outrages were committed at the very time the treaty was being held, it was hopeless to expect peace. In September the Chickamaugas threw off the mask and made open war. When the news was received Blount called out the militia and sent word to Robertson that some friendly Cherokees had given warning that a big war party was about to fall on the settlements round Nashville.[2] Finding that the warning had been given, the Chickamauga chiefs sought to lull their foes into security by a rather adroit peace of treachery. Two of their chiefs, The Glass and The Bloody Fellow, wrote to Blount complaining that they had assembled their warriors because they were alarmed over rumors of a desire on the part of the whites to maltreat them; and on the receipt of assurances from Blount that they were mistaken, they announced their pleasure and stated that no hostilities would be undertaken. Blount was much relieved at this, and thought that the danger of an outbreak was past. Accordingly he wrote to Robertson

Chickamaugas Make Open War.

Try to Deceive Blount.

[1] *Knoxville Gazette*, June 2, 1792.
[2] American State Papers, IV., Blount to Secretary of War, Sept. 11, 1792.

telling him that he could disband his troops, as there was no longer need of them. Robertson, however, knew the Indian character as few men did know it, and, morever, he had received confidential information about the impending raid from a half-breed and a Frenchman who were among the Indians. He did not disband his troops, and wrote to Blount that The Glass and The Bloody Fellow had undoubtedly written as they did simply to deceive him and to secure their villages from a counter-attack while they were off on their raid against the Cumberland people. Accordingly three hundred militia were put under arms.[1]

It was well that the whites were on their guard. Towards the end of September a big war party, under the command of John Watts and including some two hundred Cherokees, eighty Creeks, and some Shawnees, left the Chickamauga Towns and marched swiftly and silently to the Cumberland district. They attempted to surprise one of the more considerable of the lonely little forted towns. It was known as Buchanan's Station, and in it there were several families, including fifteen "gun-men." Two spies went out from it to scour the country and give warning of any Indian advance; but with the Cherokees were two very white half-breeds, whose Indian blood was scarcely noticeable, and these two men met the spies and decoyed them to their death. The Indians

[1] Robertson MSS., Blount to Robertson, Sept. 6, 1792; Blount to The Bloody Fellow, Sept. 10, 1792; to Robertson, Sept. 12; to The Glass, Sept. 13; to The Bloody Fellow, Sept. 13; to Robertson, Sept. 14; Robertson to Blount, Sept. 26, 1792.

then, soon after midnight on the 30th of September, sought to rush the station by surprise. The alarm was given by the running of the frightened cattle, and when the sentinel fired at the assailants they were not ten yards from the gate of the blockhouse, The barred door withstood the shock and the flame-flashes lit up the night as the gun-men fired through the loop-holes. The Indians tried to burn the fort, one of the chiefs, a half-breed, leaping on the roof; he was shot through the thigh and rolled off; but he stayed close to the logs trying to light them with his torch, alternately blowing it into a blaze and halloing to the Indians to keep on with the attack. **Failure of the Attack.** However, he was slain, as was the Shawnee head chief, and several warriors, while John Watts, leader of the expedition, was shot through both thighs. The log walls of the grim little blockhouse stood out black in the fitful glare of the cane torches; and tongues of red fire streamed into the night as the rifles rang. The attack had failed, and the throng of dark, flitting forms faded into the gloom as the baffled Indians retreated. So disheartened were they by the check, and by the loss they had suffered, that they did not further molest the settlements, but fell back to their strongholds across the Tennessee. Among the Cherokee chiefs who led the raid were two signers of the treaty of Holston.[1]

After this the war was open, so far as the Indians of the Lower Cherokee Towns and of many of the

---

[1] Robertson MSS., Blount to Robertson, Oct. 17, 1792; *Knoxville Gazette*, Oct. 10, and Oct. 20, 1792; Brown's Narrative, in *Southwestern Monthly*.

Creek Towns were concerned; but the whites were still restrained by strict orders from the United States authorities, who refused to allow them to retaliate. Outrage followed outrage in monotonously bloody succession. The Creeks were the worst offenders in point of numbers, but the Lower Cherokees from the Chickamauga towns did most harm according to their power. Sometimes the bands that entered the settlements were several hundred strong; but their chief object was plunder, and they rarely attacked the strong places of the white frontiersmen, though they forced them to keep huddled in the stockaded stations; nor did they often fight a pitched battle with the larger bodies of militia. There is no reason for reciting in full the countless deeds of rapine and murder. The incidents, though with infinite variety of detail, were in substance the same as in all the Indian wars of the backwoods. Men, women, and children were killed or captured; outlying cabins were attacked and burned; the husbandman was shot as he worked in the field, and the housewife as she went for water. The victim was now a militiaman on his way to join his company, now one of a party of immigrants, now a settler on his lonely farm, and now a justice of the peace going to Court, or a Baptist preacher striving to reach the Cumberland country that he might preach the word of God to the people who had among them no religious instructor. The express messengers and post riders, who went through the wilderness from one commander to the other, always rode at hazard of

Monotony of the Indian Outrages.

their lives.   In one of Blount's letters to Robertson he remarks: "Your letter of the 6th of February sent express by James Russell was handed to me, much stained with his blood, by Mr. Shannon, who accompanied him." Russell had been wounded in an ambuscade, and his fifty dollars were dearly earned.[1]

The Indians were even more fond of horse-stealing than of murder, and they found a ready market for Horse-stealing. their horses not only in their own nations and among the Spaniards, but among the American frontiersmen themselves.   Many of the unscrupulous white scoundrels who lived on the borders of the Indian country made a regular practice of receiving the stolen horses.   As soon as a horse was driven from the Tennessee or Cumberland it was hurried through the Indian country to the Carolina or Georgia frontiers, where the red thieves delivered it to the foul white receivers, who took it to some town on the seaboard, so as effectually to prevent a recovery. At Swannanoa in North Carolina, among the lawless settlements at the foot of the Oconee Mountain in South Carolina, and at Tugaloo in Georgia, there were regular markets for these stolen horses.[2]   There were then, and continued to exist as long as the frontier lasted, plenty of white men who, though

[1] Robertson MSS., Blount to Robertson, March 8, 1794. The files of the *Knoxville Gazette* are full of details of these outrages, and so are the letters of Blount to the Secretary of War given in the American State Papers, as well as the letters of Blount and Robertson in the two bound volumes of Robertson MSS.   Many of them are quoted in more accessible form in Haywood.

[2] Blount to the Secretary of War, May 5, 1792, and Nov. 10, 1794. As before, I use the word "Tennessee" instead of "Southwestern Territory" for convenience; it was not regularly employed until 1796.

ready enough to wrong the Indians, were equally
ready to profit by the wrongs they inflicted on the
white settlers, and to encourage their mis-   Brutal
deeds if profit was thereby to be made.   White
Very little evildoing of this kind took place   Ruffians.
in Tennessee, for Blount, backed by Sevier and Robertson, was vigilant to put it down; but as yet the
Federal Government was not firm in its seat, and its
arm was not long enough to reach into the remote
frontier districts, where lawlessness of every kind
throve, and the whites wronged one another as
recklessly as they wronged the Indians.

The white scoundrels throve in the confusion of a
nominal peace which the savages broke at will; but
the honest frontiersmen really suffered more   Sufferings
than if there had been open war, as the   of the
Federal Government refused to allow raids   Honest
to be carried into the Indian territory, and   Settlers.
in consequence the marauding Indians could at any
time reach a place of safety. The blockhouses were
of little consequence in putting a stop to Indian
attacks. The most efficient means of defence was
the employment of the hardiest and best hunters as
scouts or spies, for they travelled hither and thither
through the woods and continually harried the war
parties.[1] The militia bands also travelled to and
fro, marching to the rescue of some threatened settlement, or seeking to intercept the attacking bands or
to overtake those who had delivered their stroke and
were returning to the Indian country. Generally

[1] American State Papers, IV., p. 364; letter of Secretary of War, May
30, 1793.

they failed in the pursuit. Occasionally they were themselves ambushed, attacked, and dispersed; sometimes they overtook and scattered their foes. In such a case they were as little apt to show mercy to the defeated as were the Indians themselves. Blount issued strict orders that squaws and children were not to be slain, and the frontiersmen did generally refuse to copy their antagonists in butchering the women

Blount's Efforts to Prevent Brutality.
and children in cold blood. When an attack was made on a camp, however, it was no uncommon thing to have the squaws killed while the fight was hot.
Blount, in one of his letters to Robertson, after the Cumberland militia had attacked and destroyed a Creek war party which had murdered a settler, expressed his pleasure at the perseverance with which the militia captain had followed the Indians to the banks of the Tennessee, where he had been lucky enough to overtake them in a position where not one was able to escape. Blount especially complimented him upon having spared the two squaws, " as all civilized people should "; and he added that in so doing the captain's conduct offered a most agreeable contrast to the behavior of some of his fellow citizens under like circumstances.[1]

Repeated efforts were made to secure peace with the Indians. Andrew Pickens, of South Carolina,

Repeated Failures to Secure Peace.
was sent to the exposed frontier in 1792 to act as Peace Commissioner. Pickens was a high-minded and honorable man, who never hesitated to condemn the frontiers-

[1] Robertson MSS., Blount's letter, March 8, 1794.

men when they wronged the Indians, and he was a champion of the latter wherever possible. He came out with every hope and belief that he could make a permanent treaty; but after having been some time on the border he was obliged to admit that there was no chance of bringing about even a truce, and that the nominal peace that obtained was worse for the settlers than actual war. He wrote to Blount that though he earnestly hoped the people of the border would observe the treaty, yet that the Cherokees had done more damage, especially in the way of horse stealing, since the treaty was signed than ever before, and that it was not possible to say what the frontier inhabitants might be provoked to do. He continued: "While a part, and that the ostensible ruling part, of a nation affect to be at, and I believe really are for, peace, and the more active young men are frequently killing people and stealing horses, it is extremely difficult to know how to act. The people, even the most exposed, would prefer an open war to such a situation. The reason is obvious. A man would then know when he saw an Indian he saw an enemy, and would be prepared and act accordingly."

The people of Tennessee were the wronged, and not the wrongdoers, and it was upon them that the heaviest strokes of the Indians fell. The Georgia frontiers were also harried continually, although much less severely; but the Georgians were themselves far from blameless. Georgia was the youngest, weakest, and most lawless

The Georgia Frontier.

[1] American State Papers, Pickens to Blount, Hopewell, April 28, 1792.

of the original thirteen States, and on the whole her dealings with the Indians were far from creditable, More than once she inflicted shameful wrong on the Cherokees. The Creeks, however, generally wronged her more than she wronged them, and at this particular period even the Georgia frontiersmen were much less to blame than were their Indian foes. By fair treaty the Indians had agreed to cede to the whites lands upon which they now refused to allow them to settle. They continually plundered and murdered the outlying Georgia settlers; and the militia, in their retaliatory expeditions, having no knowledge of who the murderers actually were, quite as often killed the innocent as the guilty. One of the complaints of the Indians was that the Georgians came in parties to hunt on the neutral ground, and slew quantities of deer and turkeys by fire hunting at night and by still hunting with the rifle in the daytime, while they killed many bears by the aid of their " great gangs of dogs." [1] This could hardly be called a legitimate objection on the part of the Creeks, however, for their own hunting parties ranged freely through the lands they had ceded to the whites and killed game wherever they could find it.

Evil and fearful deeds were done by both sides. Peaceful Indians, even envoys, going to the treaty grounds were slain in cold blood; and all that the Georgians could allege by way of offset was that the savages themselves had killed many peaceful whites.

[1] American State Papers, Timothy Barnard to James Seagrove, March 26, 1793.

The Georgia frontiersmen openly showed their sullen hatred of the United States authorities. The Georgia State government was too weak to enforce order. It could neither keep the peace among its own frontiersmen, nor wage effective war on the Indians; for when the militia did gather to invade the Creek country they were so mutinous and disorderly that the expeditions generally broke up without accomplishing anything. At one period a militia general, Elijah Clark, actually led a large party of frontiersmen into the unceded Creek hunting grounds with the purpose of setting up an independent government; but the Georgia authorities for once summoned energy sufficient to break up this lawless community.[1]

Brutal Nature of the Contest in Georgia.

The Georgians were thus far from guiltless themselves, though at this time they were more sinned against than sinning; but in the Tennessee Territory the white settlers behaved very well throughout these years, and showed both patience and fairness in their treatment of the Indians. Blount did his best to prevent outrages, and Sevier and Robertson heartily seconded him. In spite of the grumbling of the frontiersmen, and in spite of repeated and almost intolerable provocation in the way of Indian forays, Blount steadily refused to allow counter-expeditions into the Indian territory, and stopped both the Tennesseeans and

Blount's Faithful Efforts to Preserve the Peace.

[1] American State Papers, IV., pp. 260, 295, 365, 394, 397, 410, 412, 417, 427, 473, etc. ; *Knoxville Gazette*, Sept. 26, 1794. For further allusion to Clark's settlement, see next chapter.

Kentuckians when they prepared to make such expeditions.[1] Judge Campbell, the same man who was himself attacked by the Indians when returning from his circuit, in his charge to the Grand Jury at the end of 1791, particularly warned them to stop any lawless attack upon the Indians. In November, 1792, when five Creeks, headed by a Scotch half-breed, retreated to the Cherokee town of Chiloa with stolen horses, a band of fifty whites gathered to march after them and destroy the Cherokee town; but Sevier dispersed them and made them go to their own homes. The following February a still larger band gathered to attack the Cherokee towns and were dispersed by Blount himself. Robertson, in the summer of 1793, prevented militia parties from crossing the Tennessee in retaliation. In October, 1794, the Grand Jury of Hamilton County entreated and adjured the people, in spite of the Indian outrages to stand firmly by the law, and not to try to be their own avengers; and when some whites settled in Powell's Valley, on Cherokee lands, Governor Blount promptly turned them off.[2]

The unfortunate Indian agent among the Creeks, Seagrove, speedily became an object of special detestation to the frontiersmen generally, and the inhabitants of the Tennessee country in particular, because he persistently reported that he thought the Creeks peaceable, and deemed their behavior less blameable than that of the

Seagrove's Difficulties.

[1] Robertson MSS., Blount to Robertson, Jan. 8, 1793 ; to Benjamin Logan, Nov. 1, 1794, etc.

[2] *Knoxville Gazette*, Dec. 31, 1791 ; Nov. 17, 1792 ; Jan. 25, 1793 ; Feb. 9, Mar. 23, July 13, Sept. 14, 1793 ; Nov. 1 and 15, 1794 ; May 8, 1795.

whites. His attitude was natural, for probably most of the Creek chiefs with whom he came in contact were friendly, and many of those who were not professed to be so when in his company, if only for the sake of getting the goods he had to distribute; and of course they brought him word whenever the Georgians killed a Creek, either innocent or guilty, without telling him of the offence which the Georgians were blindly trying to revenge. Seagrove himself had some rude awakenings. After reporting to the Central Government at Philadelphia that the Creeks were warm in professing the most sincere friendship, he would suddenly find, to his horror, that they were sending off war parties and acting in concert with the Shawnees; and at one time they actually, without any provocation, attacked a trading store kept by his own brother, and killed the two men who were managing it.[1] Most of the Creeks, however, professed, and doubtless felt, regret at these outrages, and Seagrove continued to represent their conduct in a favorable light to the Central Government, though he was forced to admit that certain of the towns were undoubtedly hostile and could not be controlled by the party which was for peace.

Blount calls Seagrove to Account.

Blount was much put out at the fact that Seagrove was believed at Philadelphia when he reported the Creeks to be at peace. In a letter to Seagrove, at the beginning of 1794, Blount told him sharply that as far as the Cumberland district was concerned the Creeks had been

[1] American State Papers, Seagrove to James Holmes, Feb. 24, 1793; to Mr. Payne, April 14, 1793.

the only ones to blame since the treaty of New York, for they had killed or enslaved over two hundred whites, attacking them in their houses, fields, or on the public roads, and had driven off over a thousand horses, while the Americans had done the Creeks no injuries whatever except in defence of their homes and lives, or in pursuing war parties. It was possible of course that occasionally an innocent hunter suffered with the guilty marauders, but this was because he was off his own hunting grounds; and the treaty explicitly showed that the Creeks had no claim to the Cumberland region, while there was not a particle of truth in their assertion that since the treaty had been entered into there had been intrusion on their hunting grounds. Seagrove, in response, wrote that he believed the Creeks and Cherokees sincerely desired peace. This was followed forthwith by new outrages, and Blount wrote to Robertson: "It does really seem as if assurances from Mr. Seagrove of the peaceful disposition of the Creeks was the prelude to their murdering and plundering the inhabitants of your district."[1] The *Knoxville Gazette* called attention to the fact that Seagrove had written a letter to the effect that the Creeks were well disposed, just four days before the attack on Buchanan Station. On September 22d Seagrove wrote stating that the Creeks were peaceable, that all their chief men ardently wished for the cessation of hostilities, and that they had refused

---

[1] Robertson MSS., Blount to Robertson, Feb. 13, 1793 ; Blount to James Seagrove, Jan. 9, 1794 ; Seagrove to Blount, Feb. 10, 1794 ; Blount to Robertson, March 8, 1794.

the request of the Cherokees to go to war with the
United States; and his deputy agent, Barnard, re-
iterated the assertions and stated that the Upper
Creeks had remained quiet, although six of their
people had been killed at the mouth of the Tennessee. The *Gazette* thereupon published a list of
twenty-one men, women, and children who at that
very time were held in slavery in the Creek towns,
and enumerated scores of murders which had been
committed by the Creeks during precisely the period
when Seagrove and Barnard described them as so
desirous of peace.[1]

Under such circumstances the settlers naturally
grew indignant with the United States because they
were not protected, and were not even
allowed to defend themselves by punish-
ing their foes. The Creeks and Cherokees
were receiving their annuities regularly,
and many presents in addition, while their outrages
continued unceasingly. The Nashville people complained that the Creeks were " as busy in killing and
scalping as if they had been paid three thousand
dollars for so doing, in the room of fifteen hundred
dollars to keep the peace.[2] A public address was
issued in the *Knoxville Gazette* by the Tennesseeans
on the subjects of their wrongs. In respectful and
loyal language, but firmly, the Tennesseeans called
the attention of the Government authorities to their
sufferings. They avowed the utmost devotion to
the Union and a determination to stand by the

Increasing Indigna-tion of the Settlers.

[1] *Knoxville Gazette*, Dec. 29, 1792 ; Dec. 19, 1793.
[2] *Knoxville Gazette*, March 23, 1793.

laws, but insisted that it would be absolutely necessary for them to take measures to defend themselves
by retaliating on the Indians.

A feature of the address was its vivid picture of
the nature of the ordinary Indian inroad and of the
Nature of lack of any definite system of defence on
the Indian the frontier. It stated that the Indian raid
Inroads. or outbreak was usually first made known
either by the murder of some defenceless farmer, the
escape of some Indian trader, or the warning of some
friendly Indian who wished to avoid mischief. The
first man who received the news, not having made
any agreement with the other members of the community as to his course in such an emergency, ran
away to his kinsfolk as fast as he could. Every
neighbor caught the alarm, thought himself the only
person left to fight, and got off on the same route as
speedily as possible, until, luckily for all, the meeting of the roads on the general retreat, the difficulty
of the way, the straying of horses, and sometimes
the halting to drink whiskey, put a stop to "the
hurly-burly of the flight" and reminded the fugitives that by this time they were in sufficient force
to rally; and then they would return " to explore
the plundered country and to bury the unfortunate
scalped heads in the fag-end of the retreat";
whereas if there had been an appointed rendez-
vous where all could rally it would have prevented
such a flight from what might possibly have been a
body of Indians far inferior in numbers to the armed
men of the settlements attacked.[1]

[1] *Knoxville Gazette*, April 6, 1793.

The convention of Mero district early petitioned Congress for the right to retaliate on the Indians and to follow them to their towns, stating that they had refrained from doing so hitherto not from cowardice, but only from regard to Government, and that they regretted that their "rulers" (the Federal authorities at Philadelphia) did not enter into their feelings or seem to sympathize with them.[1] When the Territorial Legislature met in 1794 it petitioned Congress for war against the Creeks and Cherokees, reciting the numerous outrages committed by them upon the whites; stating that since 1792 the frontiersmen had been huddled together two or three hundred to the station, anxiously expecting peace, or a legally authorized war from which they would soon wring peace; and adding that they were afraid of war in no shape, but that they asked that their hands be unbound and they be allowed to defend themselves in the only possible manner, by offensive war. They went on to say that, as members of the Nation, they heartily approved of the hostilities which were then being carried on against the Algerines for the protection of the seafaring men of the coast-towns, and concluded: "The citizens who live in poverty on the extreme frontier are as much entitled to be protected in their lives, their families, and their little properties, as those who roll in luxury, ease, and affluence in the great and opulent Atlantic cities," —for in frontier eyes the little seaboard trading-towns assumed a rather comical aspect of magnifi-

The Frontiersmen Ask Permission to Retaliate.

---

[1] *Knoxville Gazette*, August 13, 1792.

cence. The address was on the whole dignified in tone, and it undoubtedly set forth both the wrong and the remedy with entire accuracy. The Tennesseeans felt bitterly that the Federal Government did everything for Kentucky and nothing for themselves, and they were rather inclined to sneer at the difficulty experienced by the Kentuckians and the Federal army in subduing the Northwestern Indians, while they themselves were left single-handed to contend with the more numerous tribes of the South. They were also inclined to laugh at the continual complaints the Georgians made over the comparatively trivial wrongs they suffered from the Indians, and at their inability either to control their own people or to make war effectively.[1]

Such a state of things as that which existed in the Tennessee territory could not endure. The failure The Situation Grows Intolerable. of the United States authorities to undertake active offensive warfare and to protect the frontiersmen rendered it inevitable that the frontiersmen should protect themselves; and under the circumstances, when retaliation began it was certain sometimes to fall upon the blameless. The rude militia officers began to lead their retaliatory parties into the Indian lands, and soon the innocent Indians suffered with the guilty, for the frontiersmen had no means of distinguishing between them. The Indians who visited the settlements with peaceful intent were of course at any time liable to be mistaken for their brethren who were hostile, or else to be attacked by scoundrels who were bent

[1] *Knoxville Gazette*, Feb. 26, 1794, March 27, 1794, etc., etc.

upon killing all red men alike. Thus, on one day, as Blount reported, a friendly Indian passing the home of one of the settlers was fired upon and wounded; while in the same region five hostile Indians killed the wife and three children of a settler in his sight; and another party stole a number of horses from a station; and yet another party, composed of peaceful Indian hunters, was attacked at night by some white militia, one man being killed and another wounded.[1]

One of the firm friends of the whites was Scolacutta, the chief of the Upper Cherokees. He tried to keep his people at peace, and repeatedly warned the whites of impending attacks. Nevertheless, he was unwilling or unable to stop by force the war parties of Creeks and Lower Cherokees who came through his towns to raid against the settlements and who retreated to them again when the raids were ended. Many of his young men joined the bands of horse-thieves and scalp-hunters. The marauders wished to embroil him with the whites, and were glad that the latter should see the bloody trails leading back to his towns. For two years after the signing of the treaty of Holston the war parties thus passed and repassed through his country, and received aid and comfort from his people, and yet the whites refrained from taking vengeance; but the vengeance was certain to come in the end.

Scolacutta, the Friendly Cherokee.

In March, 1793, Scolacutta's nearest neighbor, an

---

[1] State Department MSS., Washington Papers, War Department, Ex. C., page 19, extract of letter from Blount to Williamson, April 14, 1792.

Indian living next door to him in his own town, and
other Indians of the nearest towns, joined one of the
war parties which attacked the settlements and
killed two unarmed lads.[1] The Indians did nothing
to the murderers, and the whites forbore to attack
them; but their patience was nearly exhausted. In
His Village June following a captain, John Beard, with
Attacked. fifty mounted riflemen, fell in with a small
party of Indians who had killed several settlers. He
followed their trail to Scolacutta's town, where he
slew eight or nine Indians, most of whom were
friendly.[2] The Indians clamored for justice and the
surrender of the militia who had attacked them.
Blount warmly sympathized with them, but when he
summoned a court-martial to try Beard it promptly
acquitted him, and the general frontier feeling was
strongly in his favor. Other militia commanders
followed his example. Again and again they trailed
the war parties, laden with scalps and plunder, and
attacked the towns to which they went, killing the
warriors and capturing squaws and children.[3]

The following January another party of red marauders was tracked by a band of riflemen to Scolacutta's camp. The militia promptly fell on the camp
and killed several Indians, both the hostile and the
friendly. Other Cherokee towns were attacked and
partially destroyed. In but one instance were the
whites beaten off. When once the whites fairly began

[1] American State Papers, Blount's letter, March 20, 1793. Scolacutta was
usually known to the whites as Hanging Maw.
[2] Robertson MSS., Smith to Robertson, June 19, 1793, etc. ; *Knoxville
Gazette*, June 15 and July 13, 1793, etc.
[3] *Knoxville Gazette*, July 13, July 27, 1793, etc., etc.

to make retaliatory inroads they troubled themselves but little as to whether the Indians they assailed were or were not those who had wronged them. In one case, four frontiersmen dressed and painted themselves like Indians prior to starting on a foray to avenge the murder of a neighbor. They could not find the trail of the murderers, and so went at random to a Cherokee town, killed four Revengeful warriors who were asleep on the ground, Forays. and returned to the settlements. Scolacutta at first was very angry with Blount, and taunted him with his inability to punish the whites, asserting that the frontiersmen were "making fun" of their well-meaning governor; but the old chief soon made up his mind that as long as he allowed the war parties to go through his towns he would have to expect to suffer at the hands of the injured settlers. He wrote to Blount enumerating the different murders that had been committed by both sides, and stating that his people were willing to let the misdeeds stand as off-setting one another. He closed his letter by stating that the Upper Towns were for peace, and added: "I want my mate, General Sevier, to see my talk . . . We have often told lies, but now you may depend on hearing the truth," which was a refreshingly frank admission.[1]

When, towards the close of 1792, the ravages became very serious, Sevier, the man whom the Indians feared more than any other, was called to take command of the militia. For a year he confined

---

[1] American State Papers, iv., pp. 459, 460, etc. ; *Knoxville Gazette*, Jan. 16, and June 5, 1794.

himself to acting on the defensive, and even thus he was able to give much protection to the settlements.

Sevier Takes Command. In September, 1793, however, several hundred Indians, mostly Cherokees, crossed the Tennessee not thirty miles from Knoxville. They attacked a small station, within which there were but thirteen souls, who, after some resistance, surrendered on condition that their lives should be spared ; but they were butchered with obscene cruelty. Sevier immediately marched toward the assailants, who fled back to the Cherokee towns. Thither Sevier followed them, and went entirely He makes a Brilliant Raid. through the Cherokee country to the land of the Creeks, burning the towns and destroying the stores of provisions. He marched with his usual quickness, and the Indians were never able to get together in sufficient numbers to oppose him. When he crossed High Tower River there was a skirmish, but he soon routed the Indians, killing several of their warriors, and losing himself but three men killed and three wounded. He utterly destroyed a hostile Creek town, the chief of which was named Buffalo Horn. He returned late in October, and after his return the frontiers of Eastern Tennessee had a respite from the Indian ravages. Yet Congress refused to pay his militia for the time they were out, because they had invaded the Indian country instead of acting on the defensive.[1]

To chastise the Upper Cherokee Towns gave relief

[1] Robertson MSS., Blount to Robertson, Oct. 29, 1793 ; *Knoxville Gazette*, Oct. 12, and Nov. 23, 1793.

to the settlements on the Holston, but the chief sinners were the Chickamaugas of the Lower Cherokee towns, and the chief sufferers were the Cumberland settlers. The Cumberland people were irritated beyond endurance, alike by the ravages of these Indians and by the conduct of the United States in forbidding them to retaliate. In September, 1794, they acted for themselves. Early in the month Robertson received certain information that a large body of Creeks and Lower Cherokees had gathered at the towns and were preparing to invade the Cumberland settlements. The best way to meet them was by a stroke in advance, and he determined to send an expedition against them in their strongholds. There was no question whatever as to the hostility of the Indians, for at this very time settlers were being killed by war parties throughout the Cumberland country. Some Kentuckians, under Colonel Whitley, had joined the Tennesseeans, who were nominally led by a Major Ore; but various frontier fighters, including Kaspar Mansker, were really as much in command as was Ore. Over five hundred mounted riflemen, bold of heart and strong of hand, marched toward the Chickamauga towns, which contained some three hundred warriors. When they came to the Tennessee they spent the entire night in ferrying the arms across and swimming the horses; they used bundles of dry cane for rafts, and made four "bull-boats" out of the hides of steers. They passed over unobserved and fell on the towns of Nickajack and Running Water, taking the Indians

Destruction of Nickajack and Running Water.

completely by surprise; they killed fifty-five warriors and captured nineteen squaws and children. In the entire expedition but one white man was killed and three wounded.[1]

Not only the Federal authorities, but Blount himself, very much disapproved of this expedition; nevertheless, it was right and proper, and produced excellent effects. In no other way could the hostile towns have been brought to reason. It was followed by a general conference with the Cherokees at Tellico Blockhouse. Scolacutta appeared for the Upper, and Watts for the Lower Cherokee Towns. Watts admitted that "for their folly" the Lower Cherokees had hitherto refused to make peace, and remarked frankly, "I do not say they did not deserve the chastisement they received." Scolacutta stated that he could not sympathize much with the Lower Towns, saying, "their own conduct brought destruction upon them. The trails of murderers and thieves was followed to those towns . . . Their bad conduct drew the white people on me, who injured me nearly unto death. . . . All last winter I was compelled to lay in the woods by the bad conduct of my own people drawing war on me." At last the Cherokees seemed sincere in their desire for peace.[2]

This Brings the Cherokees to Terms.

---

[1] Robertson MSS., Robertson to Blount, Oct. 8, 1794; Blount to Robertson, Oct. 1, 1794, Sept. 9, 1794 (in which Blount expresses the utmost disapproval of Robertson's conduct, and says he will not send on Robertson's original letter to Philadelphia, for fear it will get him into a scrape; and requests him to send a formal report which can be forwarded); *Knoxville Gazette*, Sept. 26, 1794; Brown's Narrative.

[2] Robertson MSS., Blount's Minutes of Conference held with Cherokees, Nov. 7 and 8, 1794, at Tellico Blockhouse.

These counter-attacks served a double purpose. They awed the hostile Cherokees; and they forced the friendly Cherokees, for the sake of their own safety, actively to interfere against the bands of hostile Creeks. A Cherokee chief, The Stallion, and a number of warriors, joined with the Federal soldiers and Tennessee militia in repulsing the Creek war parties. They acted under Blount's directions, and put a complete stop to the passage of hostile Indians through their towns.[1] The Chickasaws also had become embroiled with the Creeks.[2] For over three years they carried on an intermittent warfare with them, and were heartily supported by the frontiersmen, who were prompt to recognize the value of their services. At the same time the hostile Indians were much cowed at the news of Wayne's victory in the North.

Cherokees and Chickasaws Restrain Creeks.

All these causes combined to make the Creeks sue for peace. To its shame and discredit the United States Government at first proposed to repeat towards the Chickasaws the treachery of which the British had just been guilty to the Northern Indians; for it refused to defend them from the Creeks, against whom they had been acting, partly, it is true, for their own ends, but partly in the interest of the settlers. The frontiersmen, however, took a much more just and generous view of the affair. Mansker and a number of the best fighters in the

Treachery of the United States Government to the Chickasaws.

---

[1] Robertson MSS., Ecooe to John McKee, Tellico, Feb. 1, 1795, etc.
[2] Blount MSS., James Colbert to Robertson, Feb. 10, 1792.

Cumberland district marched to the assistance of
the Chickasaws; and the frontier militia generally
The Fron- showed grateful appreciation of the way
tiersmen both the Upper Cherokees and the Chicka-
Stand by saws helped them put a stop to the hostili-
the Chicka-
saws. ties of the Chickamaugas and Creeks.
Robertson got the Choctaws to interfere on behalf
of the Chickasaws and to threaten war with the
Creeks if the latter persisted in their hostilities.
Moreover, the United States agents, when the treaty
was actually made, behaved better than their superiors had promised, for they persuaded the Creeks
to declare peace with the Chickasaws as well as with
the whites.[1] Many of the peaceful Creeks had become so alarmed at the outlook that they began to
exert pressure on their warlike brethren; and at last
the hostile element yielded, though not until bitter
feeling had arisen between the factions. The fact
was, that the Creeks were divided much as they
were twenty years later, when the Red Sticks went
to war under the inspiration of the Prophet; and it
would have been well if Wayne had been sent South,
to invade their country and anticipate by twenty
years Jackson's feats. But the nation was not yet
ready for such strong measures. The Creeks were
met half way in their desire for peace; and the
entire tribe concluded a treaty the provisions of
which were substantially those of the treaty of New

[1] Robertson MSS., Robertson to Blount, Jan. 13, 1795; Blount to
Robertson, Jan. 20, 1795, and April 26, 1795; Robertson to Blount, April
20, 1795; *Knoxville Gazette*, Aug. 25, 1792, Oct. 12, 1793, June 19, 1794,
July 17, Aug. 4 and Aug. 15, 1794; American State Papers, pp. 284, 285,
etc., etc.

York. They ceased all hostilities, together with the Cherokees.

The concluding stage of the negotiations was marked by an incident which plainly betrayed the faulty attitude of the National Government towards Southwestern frontiersmen. With incredible folly, Timothy Pickering, at this time Secretary of War, blindly refused to see the necessity of what had been done by Blount and the Tennessee frontiersmen. In behalf of the administration he wrote a letter to Blount which was as offensive as it was fatuous. In it he actually blamed Blount for getting the Cherokees and Chickasaws to help protect the **Fatuity of** frontier against the hostile Indians. He **Timothy** forbade him to give any assistance to the **Pickering.** Chickasaws. He announced that he disapproved of The Stallion's deeds, and that the Cherokees must not destroy Creeks passing through their country on the way to the frontier. He even intimated that the surrender of The Stallion to the Creeks would be a good thing. As for protecting the frontier from the ravages of the Creeks, he merely vouchsafed the statement that he would instruct Seagrove to make "some pointed declarations" to the Creeks on the subject! He explained that the United States Government was resolved not to have a direct or indirect war with the Creeks; and he closed by reiterating, with futile insistency, that the instruction to the Cherokees not to permit Creek war parties against the whites to come through their country, did not warrant their using force to stop them.[1] He

---

[1] Robertson MSS., Pickering to Blount, March 23, 1795.

failed to point out how it was possible, without force, to carry out these instructions.

A more shameful letter was never written, and it was sufficient of itself to show Pickering's conspicuous incapacity for the position he held. The trouble was that he represented not very unfairly the sentiment of a large portion of the Eastern, and especially the Northeastern, people. When Blount visited Philadelphia in the summer of 1793 to urge a vigorous national war as the only thing which could bring the Indians to behave themselves,[1] he reported that Washington had an entirely just idea of the whole Indian business, but that Congress generally knew little of the matter and was not disposed to act.[2] His report was correct; and he might have added that the congressmen were no more ignorant, and no more reluctant to do right, than their constituents.

The truth is that the United States Government during the six years from 1791 to 1796 behaved Misconduct shamefully to the people who were settled of the along the Cumberland and Holston. This Federal was the more inexcusable in view of the Government. fact that, thanks to the example of Blount, Sevier, and Robertson, the Tennesseeans, alone among the frontiersmen, showed an intelligent appreciation of the benefits of the Union and a readiness to render it loyal support. The Kentuckians acted far less rationally; yet the Government tolerated

[1] Blount MSS., Blount to Smith, June 17, 1793.
[2] Robertson MSS., Blount to gentleman in Cumberland, Philadelphia, Aug. 28, 1793.

much misconduct on their part, and largely for their benefit carried on a great national war against the Northwestern Indians. In the Southwest almost all that the Administration did was to prohibit the frontiersmen from protecting themselves. Peace was finally brought about largely through the effect of Wayne's victory, and the knowledge of the Creeks that they would have to stand alone in any further warfare; but it would not have been obtained at all if Sevier and the other frontier leaders had not carried on their destructive counter-inroads into the Cherokee and Upper Creek country, and if under Robertson's orders Nickajack and Running Water had not been destroyed; while the support of the Chickasaws and friendly Cherokees in stopping the Creek war parties was essential. The Southwesterners owed thanks to General Wayne and his army and to their own strong right hands; but they had small cause for gratitude to the Federal Government. They owed still less to the Northeasterners, or indeed to any of the men of the eastern seaboard; the benefits arising from Pinckney's treaty form the only exception. This neglect brought its own punishment. Blount and Sevier were naturally inclined to Federalism, and it was probably only the supineness of the Federal Government in failing to support the Southwesterners against the Indians which threw Tennessee, when it became a State, into the arms of the Democratic party.

However, peace was finally wrung from the Indians, and by the beginning of 1796 the outrages

ceased. The frontiers, north and south alike, enjoyed a respite from Indian warfare for the first

Peace.   time in a generation; nor was the peace
interrupted until fifteen years afterwards.

Throngs of emigrants had come into Tennessee.
A wagon road had been chopped to the Cumberland
Growth of District, and as the Indians gradually
Tennessee. ceased their ravages, the settlements about
Nashville began to grow as rapidly as the settlements along the Holston. In 1796 the required
limit of population had been reached, and Tennessee with over seventy-six thousand inhabitants was
formally admitted as a State of the Federal Union;
Sevier was elected Governor, Blount was made one
of the Senators, and Andrew Jackson was chosen
Representative in Congress. In their State Constitu-
The Ten- tion the hard-working backwoods farmers
nessee Con- showed a conservative spirit which would
stitution. seem strange to the radical democracy of
new Western States to-day. An elective Governor
and two legislative houses were provided; and the
representation was proportioned, not to the population at large, but to the citizen who paid taxes; for
persons with some little property were still considered to be the rightful depositaries of political
power. The Constitution established freedom of the
press, and complete religious liberty—a liberty then
denied in the parent State of North Carolina; but it
contained some unwise and unjust provisions. The
Judges were appointed by the Legislature, and were
completely subservient to it; and, through the influence of the land speculators all lands except town

lots were taxed alike, so that the men who had obtained possession of the best tracts shifted to other
shoulders much of their own proper burden.[1]

---

[1] " Constitutional History of Tennessee," by Joshua W. Caldwell, p. 101,
another of Robert Clark's publications ; an admirable study of institutional
development in Tennessee.

CHAPTER IV.

INTRIGUES AND LAND SPECULATIONS—THE TREATIES OF JAY AND PINCK-NEY, 1793-1797.

THROUGHOUT the history of the winning of the West what is noteworthy is the current of tendency The Current rather than the mere succession of indi-of Tendency. vidual events. The general movement, and the general spirit behind the movement, became evident in many different forms, and if attention is paid only to some particular manifestation we lose sight of its true import and of its explanation. Particular obstacles retarded or diverted, particular causes accelerated, the current; but the set was always in one direction. The peculiar circumstances of each case must always be taken into account, but it is also necessary to understand that it was but one link in the chain of causation.

Such events as Burr's conspiracy or the conquest of Texas cannot be properly understood if we fail to remember that they were but the most spectacular or most important manifestations of what occurred many times. The Texans won a striking victory and performed a feat of the utmost importance in our history; and, moreover, it happened that at the moment the accession of Texas was warmly favored by the party of the slave-holders. Burr had been Vice-President of the United States, and was a brilliant and able man, of imposing personality, whose intrigues in the West attracted an attention altogether disproportionate to their real weight. In consequence each event is often treated as if it were isolated and stood apart from the general current of Western history; whereas in truth each was but the most striking or important among a host of others. The feats performed by Austin and Houston and the other founders of the Texan Republic were identical in kind with the feats merely attempted, or but partially performed, by the men who, like Morgan, Elijah Clark, and George Rogers Clark, at different times either sought to found colonies in the Spanish-speaking lands under Spanish authority, or else strove to conquer these lands outright by force of arms. Boone settled in Missouri when it was still under the Spanish Government, and himself accepted a Spanish commission. Whether Missouri had or had not been ceded first by Spain to France and then by France to the United States early in the present century, really would not have altered its final destiny, so far at least as concerns the fact that it would ultimately have been independent of both France and Spain, and would have been dominated by an English-speaking people; for when once the backwoodsmen, of whom Boone was the forerunner, became sufficiently numerous in the land they were certain to throw off the yoke of the foreigner; and the fact

The Causes of the Various Separatist and Filibustering Movements.

that they had voluntarily entered the land and put themselves under this yoke would have made no more difference to them than it afterwards made to the Texans. So it was with Aaron Burr. His conspiracy was merely one, and by no means the most dangerous, of the various conspiracies in which men like Wilkinson, Sebastian, and many of the members of the early Democratic societies in Kentucky, bore a part. It was rendered possible only by the temper of the people and by the peculiar circumstances which also rendered the earlier conspiracies possible; and it came to naught for the same reasons that they came to naught, and was even more hopeless, because it was undertaken later, when the conditions were less favorable.

The movement deliberately entered into by many of the Kentuckians in the years 1793 and 1794, to conquer Louisiana on behalf of France, must be treated in this way. The leader in this movement was George Rogers Clark. His chance of success arose from the fact that there were on the frontier many men of restless, adventurous, warlike type, who felt a spirit of unruly defiance toward the home government and who greedily eyed the rich Spanish lands. Whether they got the lands by conquest or by colonization, and whether they warred under one flag or another, was to them a matter of little moment. Clark's career is of itself sufficient to prove the truth of this. He had already been at the head of a movement to make war against the Spaniards, in defiance of the Central Government, on

Clark's Part in the Proposed French Attack on Spain.

behalf of the Western settlements. On another
occasion he had offered his sword to the Spanish
Government, and had requested permission to found
in Spanish territory a State which should be tribu-
tary to Spain and a barrier against the American
advance. He had thus already sought to lead the
Westerners against Spain in a warfare undertaken
purely by themselves and for their own objects, and
had also offered to form by the help of some of
these Westerners a State which should be a constit-
uent portion of the Spanish dominion. He now
readily undertook the task of raising an army of
Westerners to overrun Louisiana in the interests of
the French Republic. The conditions which rendered possible these various movements were substantially the same, although the immediate causes,
or occasions, were different. In any event the result
would ultimately have been the conquest of the
Spanish dominions by the armed frontiersmen, and
the upbuilding of English-speaking States on Spanish
territory.

The expedition which at the moment Clark proposed to head took its peculiar shape from outside
causes. At this period Genet was in the
midst of his preposterous career as Minister from the French Republic to the
United States. The various bodies of
men who afterwards coalesced into the
Democratic-Republican party were frantically in
favor of the French Revolution, regarding it with a
fatuous admiration quite as foolish as the horror
with which it affected most of the Federalists.

The Ameri-
can Sympa-
thizers with
the French
Revolution.

They were already looking to Jefferson as their leader, and Jefferson, though at the time Secretary of State under Washington, was secretly encouraging them, and was playing a very discreditable part toward his chief. The ultra admirers of the French Revolution not only lost their own heads, but turned Genet's as well, and persuaded him that the people were with him and were ready to oppose Washington and the Central Government in the interests of revolutionary France. Genet wished to embroil America with England, and sought to fit out American privateers on the seacoast towns to prey on the English commerce, and to organize on the Ohio River an armed expedition to conquer Louisiana, as Spain was then an ally of England and at war with France. All over the country Genet's admirers formed Democratic societies on the model of the Jacobin Clubs of France. They were of course either useless or noxious in such a country and under such a government as that of the United States, and exercised a very mischievous effect. Kentucky was already under the influence of the same forces that were at work in Virginia and elsewhere, and the classes of her people who were politically dominant were saturated with the ideas of those doctrinaire politicians of whom Jefferson was chief. These Jeffersonian doctrinaires were men who at certain crises, in certain countries, might have rendered great service to the cause of liberty and humanity; but their influence in America was on the whole distinctly evil, save

The Jeffersonians' Western Policy.

that, by a series of accidents, they became the especial champions of the westward extension of the nation, and in consequence were identified with a movement which was all-essential to the national well-being.

Kentucky was ripe for Genet's intrigues, and he found the available leader for the movement in the person of George Rogers Clark. Clark was deeply imbittered, not only with the United States Government but with Virginia, for the Virginia assembly had refused to pay any of the debts he had contracted on account of the State, and had not even reimbursed him for what he had spent.[1] He had a right to feel aggrieved at the State's penuriousness and her indifference to her moral obligations ; and just at the time when he was most angered came the news that Genet was agitating throughout the United States for a war with England, in open defiance of Washington, and that among his plans he included a Western movement against Louisiana. Clark at once wrote to him expressing intense sympathy with the French objects and offering to undertake an expedition for the conquest of St. Louis and upper Louisiana if he was provided with the means to obtain provisions and stores. Clark further informed Genet that his country had been utterly ungrateful to him, and that as soon as he received Genet's approbation of what he proposed to do he would get himself "expatriated." He asked for commissions for officers, and stated his belief that

Kentucky
Ripe for
Genet's
Intrigues.

[1] Draper MSS., J. Clark to G. R. Clark, Dec. 27, 1792.

the Creoles would rise, that the adventurous Westerners would gladly throng to the contest, and that
the army would soon be at the gates of New
Orleans.[1]

Genet immediately commissioned Clark as a Major
General in the service of the French Republic, and
sent out various Frenchmen—Michaux, La
Chaise, and others—with civil and military
titles, to co-operate with him, to fit out his
force as well as possible, and to promise
him pay for his expenses.   Brown, now
one of Kentucky's representatives at Philadelphia,
gave these men letters of introduction to merchants
in Lexington and elsewhere, from whom they got
some supplies; but they found they would have to
get most from Philadelphia.[2]   Michaux was the
agent for the French Minister, though nominally his
visit was undertaken on purely scientific grounds.
Jefferson's course in the matter was characteristic.
Openly, he was endeavoring in a perfunctory manner to carry out Washington's policy of strict neu-
trality in the contest between France and England,
but secretly he was engaged in tortuous intrigues
against Washington and was thwarting his wishes,
so far as he dared, in regard to Genet.   It is impossible that he could have been really misled
as to Michaux's character and the object of
his visits; nevertheless, he actually gave
him a letter of introduction to the Kentucky Gover-

*Clark Com-
missioned
as a French
Major
General.*

*Jefferson's
Double-
dealing.*

---

[1] *Do.*, Letter of George Rogers Clark, Feb. 5, 1793; also Feb. 2d and
Feb. 3d.

[2] Draper MSS., Michaux to George Rogers Clark, undated, but early in
1793.

nor, Isaac Shelby[1]. Shelby had shown himself a gallant and capable officer in warfare against both the Indians and the Tories, but he possessed no marked political ability, and was entirely lacking in the strength of character which would have fitted him to put a stop to rebellion and lawlessness. He hated England, sympathized with France, and did not possess sufficient political good sense to appreciate either the benefits of the Central Government or the need of preserving order.

Clark at once proceeded to raise what troops he could, and issued a proclamation signed by himself as Major General of the Armies of France, Commander in Chief of the French Revolutionary Legions on the Mississippi. He announced that he proposed to raise volunteers for the reduction of the Spanish posts on the Mississippi and to open the trade of that river, and promised all who would join him from one to three thousand acres of any unappropriated land in the conquered regions, the officers to receive proportionately more. All lawful plunder was to be equally divided according to the customs of war.[2] The proclamation thus frankly put the revolutionary legions on the footing of a gang of freebooters. Each man was to receive a commission proportioned in grade to the number of soldiers he brought to Clark's band. In short, it was a piece of sheer filibustering, not differing materially from one of Walker's filibustering attempts in Central America sixty years later, save that at this

[1] State Department MSS., Jefferson Papers, Series I., Vol. V., p. 163.

[2] Marshall, II., page 103.

time Clark had utterly lost his splendid vigor of
body and mind and was unfit for the task he had
set himself. At first, however, he met with promises
of support from various Kentuckians of prominence,
including Benjamin Logan.[1] His agents gathered
flat-boats and pirogues for the troops and laid in
stores of powder, lead, and beef. The nature of
some of the provisions shows what a characteristic
backwoods expedition it was; for Clark's agent
notified him that he had ready " upwards of eleven
hundred weight of Bear Meat and about seventy or
seventy-four pair of Veneson Hams." [2]

The Democratic Societies in Kentucky entered
into Clark's plans with the utmost enthusiasm, and
issued manifestoes against the Central Government which were, in style, of hysterical
violence, and, in matter, treasonable. The
preparations were made openly, and
speedily attracted the attention of the
Spanish agents, besides giving alarm to the representatives of the Federal Government and to all sober
citizens who had sense enough to see that the proposed expedition was merely another step toward
anarchy. St. Clair, the Governor of the Northwestern Territory, wrote to Shelby to warn him of
what was being done, and Wayne, who was a much
more formidable person than Shelby or Clark or any
of their backers, took prompt steps to prevent the
expedition from starting, by building a fort near the
mouth of the Ohio, and ordering his lieutenants to

The Democratic Societies Support Clark.

[1] Draper MSS., Benjamin Logan to George Rogers Clark, Dec. 31, 1793.
[2] Draper MSS., John Montgomery to Geo. Rogers Clark, Jan. 12, 1794.

hold themselves in readiness for any action he might direct. At the same time the Administration wrote to Shelby telling him what was on foot, and requesting him to see that no expedition of the kind was allowed to march against the domains of a friendly power. Shelby, in response, entered into a long argument to show that he could not interfere Shelby's with the expedition, and that he doubted Vacillation. his constitutional power to do anything in the matter; his reasons being of the familiar kind usually advanced in such cases, where a government officer, from timidity or any other cause, refuses to do his duty. If his contention as to his own powers and the powers of the General Government had been sound, it would logically have followed that there was no power anywhere to back up the law. Innes, the Federal Judge, showed himself equally lukewarm in obeying the Federal authorities.[1]

Blount, the Governor of the Southwestern Territory, acted as vigorously and patriotically as St. Clair and Wayne, and his conduct showed in marked contrast to Shelby's. He possessed far too much political good sense not to be disgusted with the conduct of Genet, Blount's Decision and Patriotism. which he denounced in unmeasured terms. He expressed great pleasure when Washington summarily rebuked the blatant French envoy. He explained to the Tennesseeans that Genet had as his chief backers the disappointed office-hunters and other unsavory characters in New York and in the sea-

[1] American State Papers, Foreign Relations, I., pp. 454, 460 ; Marshall, II., 93.

coast cities, but that the people at large were beginning to realize what the truth was, and to show a
proper feeling for the President and his government.[1]
Some of the Cumberland people, becoming excited
by the news of Clark's preparation, prepared to join
him, or to undertake a separate filibustering attack
on their own account.   Blount immediately wrote
to Robertson directing him to explain to these "in-
considerate persons" that all they could possibly do
was to attempt the conquest of West Florida, and
that they would "lay themselves liable to heavy
Pains and Penalties, both pecuniary and corporal in
case they ever returned to their injured country."
He warned Robertson that it was his duty to prevent the attempt, and that the legal officers of the
district must proceed against any of the men having
French commissions, and must do their best to stop
the movement; which, he said, proceeded "from the
Machenations no doubt of that Jacobin Incendiary,
Genet, which is reason sufficient to make every
honest mind revolt at the Idea."   Robertson warmly
supported him, and notified the Spanish commander
at New Madrid of the steps which he was taking;
at which the Spaniards expressed great gratification.[2]

However, the whole movement collapsed when
Genet was recalled early in 1794, Clark being forced
Collapse   at once to abandon his expedition.[3]   Clark
of the   found himself out of pocket as the result
Movement.   of what he had done; and as there was no

[1] Robertson MSS., Blount's letter, Philadelphia, Aug. 28, 1793.

[2] Robertson MSS., Blount to Robertson, Jan. 18, 1794; letter from
Portello, New Madrid, Jan. 17, 1794.

[3] Blount MSS., Blount to Smith, April 3, 1794.

hope of reimbursing himself by Spanish plunder, he sought to obtain from the French Government re-imbursement for the expenses, forwarding to the French Assembly, through an agent in France, his bill for the "Expenses of Expedition ordered by Citizen Genet." The agent answered that he would try to secure the payment; and after he got to Paris he first announced himself as hopeful; but later he wrote that he had discovered that the French agents were really engaged in a dangerous conspiracy against the Western country, and he finally had to admit that the claim was disallowed.[1] With this squabble between the French and Americans the history of the abortive expedition ends.

The attempt, of course, excited and alarmed the Spaniards, and gave a new turn to their tortuous diplomacy. In reading the correspondence of the Spanish Governor, Baron Caronde-let, both with his subordinates and with his superiors, it is almost amusing to note the frankness with which he avows his treachery. It evidently did not occur to him that there was such a thing as national good faith, or that there was the slightest impropriety in any form of men-dacity when exercised in dealing with the ministers or inhabitants of a foreign State. In this he was a faithful reflex of his superiors at the Spanish Court. At the same time that they were solemnly cove-nanting for a definite treaty of peace with the United States they were secretly intriguing to bring

Tortuous Diplomacy of the Spaniards.

[1] Draper MSS., Clark's accounts, Aug. 23, 1794; Fulton to Clark, Nantes, Nov. 16, 1794; *Do.*, Paris, April 9 and 12, 1795.

about a rebellion in the western States; and while they were assuring the Americans that they were trying their best to keep the Indians peaceful, they were urging the savages to war.

As for any gratitude to the National Government for stopping the piratical expeditions of the West- **Their Alarm** erners, the Spaniards did not feel a trace. **at Clark's** They had early received news of Clark's **Movements.** projected expedition through a Frenchman who came to the Spanish agents at Philadelphia;[1] and when the army began to gather they received from time to time from their agents in Kentucky reports which, though exaggerated, gave them a fairly accurate view of what was happening. No overt act of hostility was committed by Clark's people, except by some of those who started to join him from the Cumberland district, under the lead of a man named Montgomery. These men built a wooden fort at the mouth of the Cumberland River, and held the boats that passed to trade with Spain; one of the boats that they took being a scow loaded with flour and biscuit sent up stream by the Spanish Government itself. When Wayne heard of the founding of this fort he acted with his usual **Good Con-** promptness, and sent an expedition which **duct of the** broke it up and released the various boats. **United** **States Gov-** Then, to stop any repetition of the offence, **ernment.** and more effectually to curb the overbearing truculence of the frontiersmen, he himself built, as already mentioned, a fort at Massac, not far from

---

[1] Draper MSS., Spanish Documents, Carondelet to Alcudia, March 20, 1794.

the Mississippi. All this of course was done in the interests of the Spaniards themselves and in accordance with the earnest desire of the United States authorities to prevent any unlawful attack on Louisiana; yet Carondelet actually sent word to Gayoso de Lemos, the Governor of Natchez and the upper part of the river, to persuade the Chicka- **Ingratitude** saws secretly to attack this fort and **of the** destroy it. Carondelet always had an **Spaniards.** exaggerated idea of the warlike capacity of the Indian nations, and never understood the power of the Americans, nor appreciated the desire of their Government to act in good faith. Gayoso was in this respect a much more intelligent man, and he positively refused to carry out the orders of his superior, remonstrating directly to the Court of Spain, by which he was sustained. He pointed out that the destruction of the fort would merely encourage the worst enemies of the Spaniards, even if accomplished; and he further pointed out that it was quite impossible to destroy it; for he understood fully the difference between a fort garrisoned by Wayne's regulars and one held by a mob of buccaneering militia.[1]

It was not the first time that Gayoso's superior knowledge of the Indians and of their American foes had prevented his carrying out the **Gayoso and** orders of his superior officer. On one **Carondelet.** occasion Carondelet had directed Gayoso to convene the Southern Indians, and to persuade them to send

[1] Draper MSS., Spanish Documents, Manuel Gayoso de Lemos to the Duke de Alcudia, Natchez, Sept. 19, 1794.

deputies to the United States authorities with proposals to settle the boundaries in accordance with the wishes of Spain, and to threaten open war as an alternative. Gayoso refused to adopt this policy, and persuaded Carondelet to alter it, showing that it was necessary above all things to temporize, that such a course as the one proposed would provoke immediate hostilities, and that the worst possible line for the Spaniards to follow would be one of open war with the entire power of the United States.[1]

Of course the action of the American Government in procuring the recall of Genet and putting a stop **Pressure of** to Clark's operations lightened for a mo-**the West-** ment the pressure of the backwoodsmen **erners on** upon the Spanish dominions; but it was **the Span-** **ish Domain.** only for a moment. The Westerners were bent on seizing the Spanish territory; and they were certain to persist in their efforts until they were either successful or were definitely beaten in actual war. The acts of aggression were sure to recur; it was only the form that varied. When the chance of armed conquest under the banner of the French Republic vanished, there was an immediate revival of plans for getting possession of some part of the Spanish domain through the instrumentality of the great land companies.

These land companies possessed on paper a weight which they did not have in actual history. **The Land** They occasionally enriched, and more often **Companies.** impoverished, the individual speculators; but in the actual peopling of the waste lands they

---

[1] *Do.*, De Lemos to Carondelet, Dec. 6, 1793.

counted for little in comparison with the steady
stream of pioneer farmers who poured in, each to
hold and till the ground he in fact occupied. However, the contemporary documents of the day were
full of details concerning the companies; and they
did possess considerable importance at certain times
in the settlement of the West, both because they in
places stimulated that settlement, and because in
other places they retarded it, inasmuch as they kept
out actual settlers, who could not pre-empt land
which had been purchased at low rates from some
legislative body by the speculators. The companies
were sometimes formed by men who wished themselves to lead emigrants into the longed-for region,
but more often they were purely speculative in character, and those who founded them wished only to
dispose of them at an advantage to third parties.
Their history is inextricably mixed with the history
of the intrigues with and against the Spaniards and
British in the West. The men who organized them
wished to make money. Their object was to obtain
title to or possession of the lands, and it was quite
a secondary matter with them whether their title
came from the United States, England, or Spain.
They were willing to form colonies on Spanish or
British territory, and they were even willing to work
for the dismemberment of the Western Territory
from the Union, if by so doing they could increase
the value of the lands which they sought to acquire.
American adventurers had been in correspondence
with Lord Dorchester, the Governor General of
Canada, looking to the possibility of securing British

aid for those desirous of embarking in great land speculations in the West. These men proposed to try to get the Westerners to join with the British in an attack upon Louisiana, or even to conduct this attack themselves in the British interests, believing that with New Orleans in British hands the entire province would be thrown open to trade with the outside world and to settlement; with the result that the lands would increase enormously in value, and the speculators and organizers of the companies, and of the movements generally, grow rich in consequence.[1] They assured the British agents that the Western country would speedily separate from the eastern States, and would have to put itself under the protection of some foreign state. Dorchester considered these plans of sufficient weight to warrant inquiry by his agents, but nothing ever came of them.

Much the most famous, or, it would be more correct to say, infamous, of these companies were those **The Yazoo** organized in connection with the Yazoo **Land** lands.[2] The country in what is now **Companies.** middle and northern Mississippi and Alabama possessed, from its great fertility, peculiar fascinations in the eyes of the adventurous land speculators. It was unoccupied by settlers, because as a matter of fact it was held in adverse possession by the Indians, under Spanish protection. It was

[1] Canadian Archives, Dorchester to Sydney, June 7, 1789 ; Grenville to Dorchester, May 6, 1790 ; Dorchester to Beckwith, June 17, 1790 ; Dorchester to Grenville, Sept. 25, 1790. See Brown's " Political Beginnings," 187.

[2] The best and most thorough account of these is to be found in Charles H. Haskin's " The Yazoo Land Companies."

claimed by the Georgians, and its cession was sought by the United States Government, so that there was much uncertainty as to the title, which could in consequence be cheaply secured. Wilkinson, Brown, Innes, and other Kentuckians, had applied to the Spaniards to be allowed to take these lands and hold them, in their own interests, but on behalf of Spain, and against the United States. The application had not been granted, and the next effort was of a directly opposite character, the adventurers this time proposing, as they could not hold the territory as armed subjects of Spain, to wrest it from Spain by armed entry after getting title from Georgia. In other words, they were going to carry on war as a syndicate, the military operations for the occupation of the ceded territory being part of the business for which the company was organized. Their relations with the Union were doubtless to be determined by the course of events.

This company was the South Carolina Yazoo Company. In 1789 several companies were formed to obtain from the Georgia Legislature grants of the western territory which Georgia asserted to be hers. One, the Virginia Company, had among its incorporators Patrick Henry, and received a grant of nearly 20,000 square miles, but accomplished nothing. Another, the Tennessee Company, received a grant of what is now most of northern Alabama, and organized a body of men under the leadership of an adventurer named Zachariah Cox, who drifted down the Tennessee in flat-boats to take possession,

The South Carolina Yazoo Company.

and repeated the attempt more than once. They were, however, stopped, partly by Blount, and partly by the Indians. The South Carolina Yazoo Company made the most serious effort to get possession of the coveted territory. Its grant included about 15,000 square miles in what is now middle Missisippi and Alabama; the nominal price being 67,000 dollars. One of the prime movers in this company was a man named Walsh, who called himself Washington, a person of unsavory character, who, a couple of years later, was hung at Charleston for passing forged paper money in South Carolina. All these companies had hoped to pay the very small prices they were asked for the lands in the depreciated currency of Georgia; but they never did make the full payments or comply with the conditions of the grants, which therefore lapsed.

Before this occurred the South Carolina Yazoo Company had striven to take possession of its purchase by organizing a military expedition **Its Abortive Efforts in Kentucky.** to go down the Mississippi from Kentucky. For commander of this expedition choice was made of a Revolutionary soldier named James O'Fallon, who went to Kentucky, where he married Clark's sister. He entered into relations with Wilkinson, who drew him into the tangled web of Spanish intrigue. He raised soldiers, and drew up a formal contract, entered into between the South Carolina Yazoo Company and their troops of the Yazoo Battalion—over five hundred men in all, cavalry, artillery and infantry. Each private was to receive two hundred and fifty acres of "stipendiary" lands and the officers in proportion, up to the Lieutenant Colonel, who was to receive six thousand. Commissions were formally issued, and the positions of all the regular officers were filled, so that the invasion was on the point of taking place.[1] However, the Spanish authorities called the matter to the attention of the United States, and the Federal Government put a prompt stop to the movement.[2] O'Fallon was himself threatened with arrest by the Federal officers, and had to abandon his project.[3] He afterwards re-established his relations with the Government, and became one of Wayne's correspondents;[4] but he entered heartily into Clark's plans for the expedition under Genet, and, like all the other participators in that wretched affair, became involved in broils with Clark and every one else.[5]

In 1795 the land companies, encouraged by the certainty that the United States would speedily take possession of the Yazoo territory, again sprang into life. In that year four, the Georgia, the Georgia-Mississippi, the Tennessee, and the Upper Mississippi, companies obtained grants from the Georgia Legislature to a territory of over thirty millions of acres, for which they paid but five hundred thousand dollars, or less than two cents an acre. Among the grantees were many men

Revival of the Companies.

[1] American State Papers, Indian Affairs, I., James O'Fallon to the President of the United States, Lexington, Sept. 25, 1790, etc., etc.

[2] Draper MSS., Spanish Documents, Carondelet to Alcudia, Jan. 1, 1794, and May 31, 1794.

[3] Draper MSS., Clark and O'Fallon Papers, anonymous letter to James O'Fallon, Lexington, March 30, 1791, etc., etc.

[4] Draper MSS., Wayne to O'Fallon, Sept. 16, 1793.

[5] Draper MSS., De Lemos to Carondelet, Dec. 23, 1793.

of note, congressmen, senators, even judges. The grants were secured by the grossest corruption, every member of the Legislature who voted for them, with one exception, being a stockholder in some one of the companies, while the procuring of the cessions was undertaken by James Gunn, one of the two Georgia Senators. The outcry against the transaction was so universal throughout the State that at the next session of the Legislature, in 1796, the acts were repealed and the grants rescinded. This caused great confusion, as most of the original grantees had hastily sold out to third parties; the purchases being largely made in South Carolina and Massachusetts. Efforts were made by the original South Carolina Yazoo Company to sue Georgia in the Federal Courts, which led to the adoption of the Constitutional provision forbidding such action.

Their Failure.
When in 1802, Georgia ceded the territory in question, including all of what is now middle and northern Alabama and Mississippi, to the United States for the sum of twelve hundred and fifty thousand dollars, the National Government became heir to these Yazoo difficulties. It was not until 1814 that the matter was settled by a compromise, after interminable litigation and legislation.[1] The land companies were more important

[1] American State Papers, Public Lands, I., pp. 99, 101, 111, 165, 172, 178; Haskin's "Yazoo Land Companies." In Congress, Randolph, on behalf of the ultra states'-rights people led the opposition to the claimants, whose special champions were Madison and the northern democrats. Chief Justice Marshall in the case of Fletcher *vs*. Peck, decided that the rescinding act impaired the obligation of contracts, and was therefore in violation of the Constitution of the United States ; a decision further amplified in the Dartmouth case, which has determined the national policy in regard to

to the speculators than to the actual settlers of the Mississippi; nevertheless, they did stimulate settlement, in certain regions, and therefore increased by just so much the western pressure upon Spain.

Some of the aggressive movements undertaken by the Americans were of so loose a nature that it is hard to know what to call them. This was true of Elijah Clark's company of Georgia freebooters in 1794. Accompanied by large bodies of armed men, he on several occasions penetrated into the territory southwest of the Oconee. He asserted at one time that he was acting for Georgia and in defence of her rights to the lands which the Georgians claimed under the various State treaties with the Indians, but which by the treaty of New York had been confirmed to the Creeks by the United States. On another occasion he entitled his motley force the Sans Culottes, and masqueraded as a major general of the French army, though the French Consul denied having any connection with him. He established for the time being a little independent government, with block-houses and small wooden towns, in the middle of the unceded hunting grounds, and caused great alarm to the Spaniards. The frontiersmen sympathized with him, and when he was arrested in Wilkes County the Grand Jury of the county ordered his discharge, and solemnly declared that the treaty of New York was inoperative and the

Georgian Filibusterers.

public contracts. This decision was followed by the passage of the Compromise Act by Congress in 1814, which distributed a large sum of money obtained from the land sales in the territory, in specified proportions among the various claimants.

proclamation of the Governor of Georgia against Clark, illegal. This was too much for the patience of the Governor. He ordered out the State troops to co-operate with the small Federal force, and Clark and his men were ignominiously expelled from their new government and forced to return to Georgia.[1]

In such a welter of intrigue, of land speculation, and of more or less piratical aggression, there was Benefit of imminent danger that the West would re-
Washing- lapse into anarchy unless a firm government
ton's Ad- were established, and unless the bound-
ministra-
tion to the aries with England and Spain were
West. definitely established. As Washington's administration grew steadily in strength and in the confidence of the people the first condition was met. The necessary fixity of boundary was finally obtained by the treaties negotiated through John Jay with England, and through Thomas Pinckney with Spain.

Jay's treaty aroused a perfect torrent of wrath throughout the country, and nowhere more than in
Jay's the West. A few of the coolest and most
Treaty. intelligent men approved it, and rugged old Humphrey Marshall, the Federalist Senator from Kentucky, voted for its ratification; but the general feeling against it was intense. Even Blount, who by this time was pretty well disgusted with the way he had been treated by the Central Government, denounced it, and expressed his belief that Washington would have hard work to explain his conduct in procuring its ratification.[2]

[1] Steven's "Georgia," II., 401.
[2] Blount MSS., Blount to Smith, Aug. 24, 1795.

Yet the Westerners were the very people who had no cause whatever to complain of the treaty. It was not an entirely satisfactory treaty; perhaps a man like Hamilton might have procured rather better terms; but, taken as a whole, it worked an immense improvement upon the condition of things already existing. Washington's position was undoubtedly right. He would have preferred a better treaty, but he regarded the Jay treaty as very much better than none at all. Moreover, the last people who had a right to complain of it were those who were most vociferous in their opposition. The anti-Federalist party was on the whole the party of weakness and disorder, the party that was clamorous and unruly, but ineffective in carrying out a sustained policy, whether of offense or of defence, in foreign affairs. The people who afterwards became known as Jeffersonian Republicans numbered in their ranks the extremists who had been active as the founders of Democratic societies in the French interest, and they were ferocious in their wordy hostility to Great Britain; but they were not dangerous foes to any foreign government which did not fear words. Had they possessed the foresight and intelligence to strengthen the Federal Government the Jay treaty would not have been necessary. Only a strong, efficient central government, backed by a good fleet and a well organized army, could hope to wring from England what the French party, the forerunners of the Jeffersonian Democracy, demanded. But the Jeffersonians were separatists and

Folly of the Westerners.

Futility of the State's-Rights Men in Foreign Affairs.

State's-rights men. They believed in a government so weak as to be ineffective, and showed a folly literally astounding in their unwillingness to provide for the wars which they were ready to provoke. They resolutely refused to provide an army or a navy, or to give the Central Government the power necessary for waging war. They were quite right in their feeling of hostility to England, and one of the fundamental and fatal weaknesses of the Federalists was the Federalist willingness to submit to England's aggressions without retaliation; but the Jeffersonians had no gift for government, and were singularly deficient in masterful statesmen of the kind imperatively needed by any nation which wishes to hold an honorable place among other nations. They showed their governmental inaptitude clearly enough later on when they came into power, for they at once stopped building the fleet which the Federalists had begun, and allowed the military forces of the nation to fall into utter disorganization, with, as a consequence, the shameful humiliations of the War of 1812. This war was in itself eminently necessary and proper, and was excellent in its results, but it was attended by incidents of shame and disgrace to America for which Jefferson and Madison and their political friends and supporters among the politicians and the people have never received a sufficiently severe condemnation.

Jay's treaty was signed late in 1794 and was ratified in 1795.[1] The indignation of the Kentuck-

---

[1] American State Papers, Foreign Relations, I., pp. 479, 484, 489, 502, 519, etc.

ians almost amounted to mania. They denounced the treaty with frantic intemperance, and even threatened violence to those of their own number, headed by Humphrey Marshall, who sup- ported it; yet they benefited much by it, for it got them what they would have been absolutely powerless to obtain for themselves, that is, the possession of the British posts on the Lakes. In 1796 the Americans took formal possession of these posts, and the boundary line in the Northwest as nominally established by the treaty of Versailles became in fact the actual line of demarcation between the American and the British possessions. The work of Jay capped the work of Wayne. Federal garri- sons were established at Detroit and elsewhere, and the Indians, who had already entered into the treaty of Greeneville, were prevented from breaking it by this intervention of the American military posts between themselves and their British allies. Peace was firmly established for the time being in the Northwest, and our boundaries in that direction took the fixed form they still retain.[1]

Benefits of Jay's Treaty to the West.

In dealing with the British the Americans some- times had to encounter bad faith, but more often a mere rough disregard for the rights of others, of which they could themselves scarcely complain with a good grace, as they showed precisely the same quality in their own actions. In dealing with the Spaniards, on the other hand, they had to encounter deliberate

Systematic Treachery of the Spaniards.

---

[1] American State Papers, Indian Affairs, I., p. 573 ; Foreign Relations, I., *passim*, etc., etc.

and systematic treachery and intrigue. The open
negotiations between the two governments over the
boundary ran side by side with a current of muddy
intrigue between the Spanish Government on the
one hand, and certain traitorous Americans on the
other; the leader of these traitors being, as usual,
the arch scoundrel, Wilkinson.

The Spaniards trusted almost as much to Indian intrigue as to bribery of American leaders; indeed they trusted to it more for momentary
effect, though the far-sighted among them
realized that in the long run the safety of
the Spanish possessions depended upon
the growth of divisional jealousies among the Americans themselves. The Spanish forts were built as
much to keep the Indians under command as to
check the Americans. The Governor of Natchez, De
Lemos, had already established a fort at the Chickasaw Bluffs, where there was danger of armed
collision between the Spaniards and either the Cumberland settlers under Robertson or the Federal
troops. Among the latter, by the way, the officer for
whose ability the Spaniards seemed to feel an especial
respect was Lieutenant William Clark.[1]

The Chickasaws were nearly drawn into a war with
the Spaniards, who were intensely irritated over their
antagonism to the Creeks, for which the Spaniards insisted that the Americans were responsible.[2] The
Americans, however, were able to prove conclusively

*Their In-
trigues
with the
Indians.*

[1] Draper MSS., Spanish Documents, Carondelet to Don Louis de Las
Casas, June 13, 1795 ; De Lemos to Carondelet, July 25, 1793.

[2] American State Papers, Foreign Relations, I., p. 305, etc.

that the struggle was due, not to their advice, but to the outrages of marauders from the villages of the Muscogee confederacy. They showed by the letter of the Chickasaw chief, James Colbert, that the Creeks had themselves begun hostilities early in 1792 by killing a Chickasaw, and that the Chickasaws, because of this spilling of blood, made war on the Creeks, and sent word to the Americans to join in the war. The letter ran: " I hope you will exert yourselves and join us so that we might give the lads a Drubbeen for they have encroached on us this great while not us alone you likewise for you have suffered a good dale by them I hope you will think of your wounds." [1] The Americans had " thought of their wounds " and had aided the Chickasaws in every way, as was proper; but the original aggressors were the Creeks. The Chickasaws had entered into what was a mere war of retaliation; though when once in they had fought hard, under the lead of Opiamingo, their most noted war chief, who was always friendly to the Americans and hostile to the Spaniards.

The Chickasaws Befriend the Americans.

At the Chickasaw Bluffs, and at Natchez, there was always danger of a clash; for at these places the Spanish soldiers were in direct contact with the foremost of the restless backwoods host, and with the Indians who were most friendly or hostile to them. Open collision was averted, but the Spaniards were kept uneasy and alert. There were plenty of American

The Situation at Natchez.

[1] Blount MSS., James Colbert to Robertson, Feb. 10, 1792.

settlers around Natchez, who were naturally friendly
to the American Government; and an agent from
the State of Georgia, to the horror of the Spaniards,
came out to the country with the especial purpose
of looking over the Yazoo lands, at the time when
Georgia was about to grant them to the various land
companies.   What with the land speculators, the
frontiersmen, and the Federal troops, the situation
grew steadily more harassing for the Spaniards; and
Carondolet kept the advisors of the Spanish Crown
well informed of the growing stress.

The Spanish Government knew it would be beaten
if the issue once came to open war, and, true to the
The Sepa- instincts of a weak and corrupt power, it
ratists Play chose as its weapons delay, treachery, and
into the intrigue.   To individual Americans the
Hands of
the Span- Spaniards often behaved with arrogance
iards. and brutality; but they feared to give too
serious offence to the American people as a whole.
Like all other enemies of the American Republic,
from the days of the Revolution to those of the
Civil War, they saw clearly that their best allies
were the separatists, the disunionists, and they
sought to encourage in every way the party which,
in a spirit of sectionalism, wished to bring about a
secession of one part of the country and the erection
of a separate government.   The secessionists then,
as always, played into the hands of the men who
wished the new republic ill.   In the last decade of
the eighteenth century the acute friction was not
between North and South, but between East and
West.   The men who, from various motives, wished
to see a new republic created, hoped that this repub-

lic would take in all the people of the western waters. These men never actually succeeded in carrying the West with them. At the pinch the majority of the Westerners remained loyal to the idea of national unity; but there was a very strong separatist party, and there were very many men who, though not separatists, were disposed to grumble loudly about the shortcomings of the Federal government.

These men were especially numerous and powerful in Kentucky, and they had as their organ the sole newspaper of the State, the *Ken-* _Their Influ-_ *tucky Gazette.* It was filled with fierce _ence in_ attacks, not only upon the General Govern- _Kentucky._ ment, but upon Washington himself. Sometimes these attacks were made on the authority of the *Gazette;* at other times they appeared in the form of letters from outsiders, or of resolutions by the various Democratic societies and political clubs. They were written with a violence which, in striving after forcefulness, became feeble. They described the people of Kentucky as having been " degraded and insulted," and as having borne these insults with " submissive patience." The writers insisted that Kentucky had nothing to hope from the Federal Government, and that it was nonsense to chatter about the infraction of treaties, for it was necessary, at any cost, to take Louisiana, which was "groaning under tyranny." They threatened the United States with what the Kentuckians would do if _Their_ their wishes were not granted, announcing _Fatuity._ that they would make the conquest of Louisiana an ultimatum, and warning the Government that they owed no eternal allegiance to it and might have to separate, and that if they did there would be small reason to deplore the separation. The separatist agitators failed to see that they could obtain the objects they sought, the opening of the Mississippi and the acquisition of Louisiana, only through the Federal Government, and only by giving that Government full powers. Standing alone the Kentuckians would have been laughed to scorn not only by England and France, but even by Spain. Yet with silly fatuity they vigorously opposed every effort to make the Government stronger or to increase national feeling, railing even at the attempt to erect a great Federal city as "unwise, impolitic, unjust," and "a monument to American folly."[1] The men who wrote these articles, and the leaders of the societies and clubs which inspired them, certainly made a pitiable showing; they proved that they themselves were only learning, and had not yet completely mastered, the difficult art of self government.

It was the existence of these Western separatists, nominally the fiercest foes of Spain, that in reality gave

Negotiations of the Spanish and American Governments. Spain the one real hope of staying the western advance. In 1794 the American agents in Spain were carrying on an interminable correspondence with the Spanish Court in the effort to come to some understanding about the boundaries.[2] The Spanish authorities were solemnly corresponding with the American envoys, as if they meant peace; yet at the same time

---

[1] *Kentucky Gazette*, Feb. 8, 1794; Sept. 16, 1797, etc., etc.

[2] American State Papers, Foreign Relations, I., p. 443, etc.; letters of Carmichael and Short to Gardoqui, Oct. 1, 1793; to Alcudia, Jan. 7, 1794, etc., etc.

they had authorized Carondelet to do his best to treat directly with the American States of the West so as to bring about their separation from the Union. In 1794 Wilkinson, who was quite incapable of understanding that his infamy was heightened by the fact that he wore the uniform of a Brigadier General of the United States, entered into negotiations for a treaty, the base of which should be the separation of the Western States from the Atlantic States.[1] He had sent two confidential envoys to Carondelet. Carondelet jumped at the chance of once more trying to separate the west from the east; and under Wilkinson's directions he renewed his efforts to try by purchase and pension to attach some of the leading Kentuckians to Spain. As a beginning he decided to grant Wilkinson's request and send him twelve thousand dollars for himself.[2] De Lemos was sent to New Madrid in October to begin the direct negotiations with Wilkinson and his allies. The funds to further the treasonable conspiracy were also forwarded, as the need arose.

Wilkinson's Ineffectual Treason.

Carondelet was much encouraged as to the outcome by the fact that De Lemos had not been dispossessed by force from the Chickasaw Bluffs. This shows conclusively that Washington's administration was in error in not acting with greater decision about the Spanish posts. Wayne should have been ordered to use the sword, and to dispossess the Spaniards from the east bank of the Mis-

Failure of the American Government to Act with Proper Decision.

---

[1] Draper MSS., Spanish Documents, Carondelet to Alcudia, July 30, 1794.   [2] *Do.*, De Lemos to Alcudia, Sept. 19, 1794.

sissippi. As so often in our history, we erred, not
through a spirit of over-aggressiveness, but through
a willingness to trust to peaceful measures instead
of proceeding to assert our rights by force.

The first active step taken by Carondelet and De
Lemos was to send the twelve thousand dollars to
Wilkinson, as the foundation and earnest
of the bribery fund. But the effort mis-
carried. The money was sent by two
men, Collins and Owen, each of whom
bore cipher letters to Wilkinson, including some
that were sewed into the collars of their coats.
Collins reached Wilkinson in safety, but Owen was
murdered, for the sake of the money he bore, by his
boat's crew while on the Ohio river.[1] The murderers
were arrested and were brought before the Federal
judge, Harry Innes. Owen was a friend of Innes,
and had been by him recommended to Wilkinson as
a trustworthy man for any secret and perilous
service. Nevertheless, although it was his own
friend who had been murdered, Innes refused to try
the murderers, on the ground that they were Spanish
subjects; a reason which was simply nonsensical.
He forwarded them to Wilkinson at Fort Warren.
The latter sent them back to New Madrid. On
their way they were stopped by the officer at Fort
Massac, a thoroughly loyal man, who had not been
engaged in the intrigues of Wilkinson and Innes.
He sent to the Spanish commander at New Madrid
for an interpreter to interrogate the men. Of course

Murder of the Mes- sengers to Wilkinson.

---

[1] *Do.*, letters of Carondelet to Alcudia, Oct. 4, 1794, and of De Lemos
to Carondelet, Aug. 28, 1795.

the Spaniards were as reluctant as Wilkinson and Innes that the facts as to the relations between Carondelet and Wilkinson should be developed,   The Mur-
and, like Wilkinson and Innes, they pre-   derers
ferred that the murderers should escape   Shielded.
rather than that these facts should come to light.
Accordingly the interpreter did not divulge the con-
fession of the villains, all evidence as to their guilt
was withheld, and they were finally discharged. The
Spaniards were very nervous about the affair, and
were even afraid lest travellers might dig up Owen's
body and find the dispatches hidden in his collar;
which, said De Lemos, they might send to the President of the United States, who would of course take
measures to find out what the money and the ciphers
meant.[1]

Wilkinson's motives in acting as he did were of
course simple. He could not afford to have the
murderers of his friend and agent tried lest they
should disclose his own black infamy. The conduct
of Judge Innes is difficult to explain on any ground
consistent with his integrity and with the official
propriety of his actions. He may not have been a
party to Wilkinson's conspiracy, but he must certainly have known that Wilkinson was engaged in
negotiations with the Spaniards so corrupt that they
would not bear the light of exposure, or else he
would never have behaved toward the murderers in
the way that he did behave.[2]

[1] *Do.*, letter of De Lemos.

[2] Marshall, II., 155 ; Green, p. 328. Even recently defenders of Wilkinson and Innes have asserted, in accordance with Wilkinson's explanations,
that the money forwarded him was due him from tobacco contracts entered

Carondelet, through De Lemos, entered into correspondence with Wayne about the fort built by his orders at the Chickasaw Bluffs. He refused to give up this fort; and as Wayne became more urgent in his demands, he continually responded with new excuses for delay. He was enabled to tell exactly what Wayne was doing, as Wilkinson, who was serving under Wayne, punctually informed the Spaniard of all that took place in the American army.[1] Carondelet saw that the fate of the Spanish-American province which he ruled, hung on the separation of the Western States from the Union.[2] As long as he thought it possible to bring about the separation, he refused to pay heed even to the orders of the Court of Spain, or to the treaty engagements by which he was nominally bound. He was forced to make constant demands upon the Spanish Court for money to be used in the negotiations; that is, to bribe Wilkinson and his fellows in Kentucky. He succeeded in placating the Chickasaws, and got from them a formal cession of the Chickasaw Bluffs, which was a direct blow at the American pretensions. As with all Indian tribes, the Chickasaws were not capable of any settled policy, and were not under any responsible authority. While some of them were in close alliance with the Americans and were

Marginal note: Carondelet Refuses to Give up the Posts.

into some years previously with Miro.   Carondelet in his letters above quoted, however, declares outright that the money was advanced to begin negotiations in Kentucky, through Wilkinson and others, for the pensioning of Kentuckians in the interests of Spain and the severance of the Western States from the Union.

[1] Draper MSS., Spanish Documents, Carondelet to Alcudia, Nov. 1, 1793.
[2] *Do.*, Carondelet to Alcudia, Sept. 25, 1795.

warring on the Creeks, the others formed a treaty with the Spaniards and gave them the territory they so earnestly wished.[1]

However, neither Carondelet's energy and devotion to the Spanish government nor his unscrupulous intrigues were able for long to defer the fate which hung over the Spanish possessions. In 1795 Washington nominated as Minister to Spain Thomas Pinckney, a member of a distinguished family of South Carolina statesmen, and a man of the utmost energy and intelligence. Pinckney finally wrung from the Spaniards a treaty which was as beneficial to the West as Jay's treaty, and was attended by none of the drawbacks which marred Jay's work. The Spaniards at the outset met his demands by a policy of delay and evasion. Finally, he determined to stand this no longer, and, on October 24, 1795, demanded his passports, in a letter to Godoy, the "Prince of Peace." The demand came at an opportune moment; for Godoy had just heard of Jay's treaty. He misunderstood the way in which this was looked at in the United States, and feared lest, if not counteracted, it might throw the Americans into the arms of Great Britain, with which country Spain was on the verge of war. It is not a little singular that Jay should have thus rendered an involuntary but important additional service to the Westerners who so hated him.

The Spaniards now promptly came to terms.

[1] *Do.*, De Lemos to Carondelet, enclosed in Carondelet's letter of Sept. 26, 1795.

They were in no condition to fight the Americans;
He Nego-   they knew that war would be the result if
tiates a   the conflicting claims of the two peoples
Treaty.   were not at once definitely settled, one way
or the other; and they concluded the treaty forthwith.[1]   Its two most important provisions were the
settlement of the southern boundary on the lines
claimed by the United States, and the granting of
the right of deposit to the Westerners.   The boundary followed the thirty-first degree of latitude from
the Mississippi to the Chattahoochee, down it to the
Flint, thence to the head of the St. Mary's, and down
it to the ocean.   The Spanish troops were to be
withdrawn from this territory within the space of
six months.   The Westerners were granted for three
years the right of deposit at New Orleans; after three
years, either the right was to be continued, or another equivalent port of deposit was to be granted
somewhere on the banks of the Mississippi.   The
right of deposit carried with it the right to export
goods from the place of deposit free from any but
an inconsiderable duty.[2]

The treaty was ratified in 1796, but with astonish-
ing bad faith the Spaniards refused to carry out its
The   provisions.   At this time Carondelet was
Spaniards   in the midst of his negotiations with Wil-
Delay the   kinson for the secession of the West, and
Execution
of the   had high hopes that he could bring it
Treaty.   about.   He had chosen as his agent an

---

[1] Pinckney receives justice from Lodge, in his "Washington," II., 160.
For Pinckney's life, see the biography by Rev. C. C. Pinckney, p. 129, etc.

[2] American State Papers, Foreign Relations, I., p. 533, etc.; Pinckney to
Secretary of State, Aug. 11, 1795; to Godoy (Alcudia), Oct. 24, 1795;
copy of treaty, Oct. 27th, etc.

Englishman, named Thomas Power, who was a naturalized Spanish subject, and very zealous in the service of Spain.[1] Power went to Kentucky, where he communicated with Wilkinson, Sebastian, Innes, and one or two others, and submitted to them a letter from Carondelet. This letter proposed a treaty, of which the first article was that Wilkinson and his associates should exert themselves to bring about a separation of the Western country and its formation into an independent government wholly unconnected with that of the Atlantic States; and Carondelet in his letter assured the men to whom he was writing, that, because of what had occurred in Europe since Spain had ratified the treaty of October 27th, the treaty would not be executed by his Catholic Majesty. Promises of favor to the Western people were held out, and Wilkinson was given a more substantial bribe, in the shape of ten thousand dollars, by Power. Sebastian, Innes, and their friends were also promised a hundred thousand dollars for their good offices ; and Carondelet, who had no more hesitation in betraying red men than white, also offered to help the Westerners subdue their Indian foes; these Indian foes being at the moment the devoted allies of Spain.

They Again Try to Intrigue with the Westerners.

The time had gone by, however, when it was possible to hope for success in such an intrigue. The treaty with Spain had caused much satisfaction in the West, and the Kentuckians generally were growing more and more loyal to the Central Government. Innes and

Failure of their Efforts.

[1] Gayarré, III., 345. Wilkinson's Memoirs, II., 225.

his friends, in a written communication, rejected the offer of Carondelet. They declared that they were devoted to the Union and would not consent to break it up ; but they betrayed curiously little surprise or indignation at the offer, nor did they in rejecting it use the vigorous language which beseemed men who, while holding the commissions of a government, were proffered a hundred thousand dollars to betray that government.[1] Power, at the close of 1797, reported to his superiors that nothing could be done.

Meanwhile Carondelet and De Lemos had persisted in declining to surrender the posts at the Chickasaw Bluffs and Natchez, on pretexts **Confusion at Natchez.** which were utterly frivolous.[2] At this time the Spanish Court was completely subservient to France, which was hostile to the United States ; and the Spaniards would not carry out the treaty they had made until they had exhausted every device of delay and evasion. Andrew Ellicott was appointed by Washington Surveyor-General to run the boundary ; but when, early in 1797, he reached Natchez, the Spanish representative refused point blank to run the boundary or evacuate the territory. Meanwhile the Spanish Minister at Philadelphia, Yrujo, in his correspondence with the Secretary of State, was pursuing precisely the same course of subterfuge and delay. But these tactics could only avail for a time. Neither the Government of the United States, nor the Western people

[1] American State Papers, Miscellaneous, I., 928 ; deposition of Harry Innes, etc.

[2] American State Papers, Foreign Relations, II., pp. 20, 70, 78, 79 ; report of Timothy Pickering, January 22, 1798, etc.

would consent to be balked much longer. The negotiations with Wilkinson and his associates had come to nothing. A detachment of American regular soldiers came down the river to support Ellicott. The settlers around Natchez arose in revolt against the Spaniards and established a Committee of Safety, under protection of the Americans. The population of Mississippi was very mixed, including criminals fleeing from justice, land speculators, old settlers, well-to-do planters, small pioneer farmers, and adventurers of every kind; and, thanks to the large tory element, there was a British, and a smaller Spanish party; but the general feeling was overwhelmingly for the United States. The Spanish Government made a virtue of necessity and withdrew its garrison, after for some time preserving a kind of joint occupancy with the Americans.[1] Captain Isaac Guyon, with a body of United States troops, took formal possession of both the Chickasaw Bluffs and Natchez in 1797. In 1798 the Spaniards finally evacuated the country,[2] their course being due neither to the wisdom nor the good faith of their rulers, but to the fear and worry caused by the unceasing pressure of the Americans. Spain yielded, because she felt that not to do so would involve the loss of all Louisiana.[3] The country was organized as the Mississippi Territory in June, 1798.[4]

The Posts Surrendered.

[1] B. A. Hinsdale: "The Establishment of the First Southern Boundary of the United States." Largely based upon Ellicott's Journal. Both Ellicott, and the leaders among the settlers, were warned of Blount's scheme of conquest and land speculation, and were hostile to it.

[2] Claiborne's "Mississippi," p. 176. He is a writer of poor judgment; his verdicts on Ellicott and Wilkinson are astounding.

[3] Gayarré, 413, 418; Pontalba's Memoir, Sept. 15, 1800.

[4] American State Papers, Public Lands, I., p. 209.

There was one incident, curious rather than important, but characteristic in its way, which marked the close of the transactions of the Western Americans with Spain at this time. During the very years when Carondelet, under the orders of his Government, was seeking to delay the execution of the boundary treaty, and to seduce the Westerners from their allegiance to the United States, a Senator of the United States, entirely without the knowledge of his Government, was engaged in an intrigue for the conquest of a part of the Spanish dominion. This Senator was no less a person than William Blount. Enterprising and ambitious, he was even more deeply engaged in land speculations than were the other prominent men of his time.[1] He felt that he had not been well treated by the United States authorities, and, like all other Westerners, he also felt that the misconduct of the Spaniards had been so great that they were not entitled to the slightest consideration. Moreover, he feared lest the territory should be transferred to France, which would be a much more dangerous neighbor than Spain; and he had a strong liking for Great Britain. If he could not see the territory taken by the Americans under the flag of the United States, then he wished to see them enter into possession of it under the standard of the British King.

In 1797 he entered into a scheme which was in part one of land speculation and in part one of armed aggression against Spain. He tried to organize an association with the purpose of seizing

[1] Clay MSS., Blount to Hart, March 13, 1799, etc., etc.

the Spanish territory west of the Mississippi, and putting it under the control of Great Britain, in the interests of the seizers. The scheme came to nothing. No definite steps were taken, and the British Government refused to take any share in the movement. Finally the plot was discovered by the President, who brought it to the attention of the Senate, and Blount was properly expelled from the Upper House for entering into a conspiracy to conquer the lands of one neighboring power in the interest of another. The Tennesseeans, however, who cared little for the niceties of international law, and sympathized warmly with any act of territorial aggression against the Spaniards, were not in the least affected by his expulsion. They greeted him with enthusiasm, and elected him to high office, and he lived among them the remainder of his days, honored and respected.[1] Nevertheless, his conduct in this instance was indefensible. It was an unfortunate interlude in an otherwise honorable and useful public career.[2]

[1] Blount MSS., letter of Hugh Williamson, March 3, 1808, etc., etc.

[2] General Marcus J. Wright, in his "Life and Services of William Blount," gives the most favorable view possible of Blount's conduct.

CHAPTER V.

THE MEN OF THE WESTERN WATERS, 1798–1802.

THE growth of the West was very rapid in the years immediately succeeding the peace with the Indians and the treaties with England and Spain. As the settlers poured into what had been the Indian-haunted wilderness it speedily became necessary to cut it into political divisions. Kentucky had already been admitted as a State in 1792; Tennessee likewise became a State in 1796. The Territory of Mississippi was organized in 1798, to include the country west of Georgia and south of Tennessee, which had been ceded by the Spaniards under Pinckney's treaty.[1] In 1800 the Connecticut Reserve, in what is now northeastern Ohio, was taken by the United States. The Northwestern Territory was divided into two parts; the eastern was composed mainly of what is now the State of Ohio, while the western portion was called Indiana Territory, and was organized with W. H. Harrison as Governor, his capital being at Vincennes.[2] Harrison had been Wayne's aid-de-camp at

Rapid Growth of the West.

[1] Claiborne's "Mississippi," p. 220, etc.

[2] "Annals of the West," by Thomas H. Perkins, p. 473. A valuable book, showing much scholarship and research. The author has never received proper credit. Very few indeed of the Western historians of his date showed either his painstaking care or his breadth of view.

the fight of the Fallen Timbers, and had been singled out by Wayne for mention because of his coolness and gallantry. Afterwards he had succeeded Sargent as Secretary of the Northwestern Territory when Sargent had been made Governor of Mississippi, and he had gone as a Territorial delegate to Congress.[1]

In 1802 Ohio was admitted as a State. St. Clair, and St. Clair's supporters, struggled to keep the Territory from statehood, and proposed to cut it down in size, nominally because they deemed the extent of territory too great for governmental purposes, but really, doubtless, because they distrusted the people, and did not wish to see them take the government into their own hands. The effort failed, however, and the State was admitted by Congress, beginning its existence in 1803.[2] Congress made the proviso that the State Constitution should accord with the Constitution of the United States, and should embody the doctrines contained in the Ordinance of 1787.[3] The rapid settlement of southeastern Ohio was hindered by the fact that the speculative land companies, the Ohio and Scioto associations, held great tracts of territory which the pioneers passed by in their desire to get to lands which they could acquire in their own right. This was one of the many bad effects which resulted from the Government's policy

Ohio Becomes a State.

[1] Jacob Burnett in "Ohio Historical Transactions," Part II., Vol. I., p. 69.

[2] Atwater, "History of Ohio," p. 169.

[3] The question of the boundaries of the Northwestern States is well treated in "The Boundaries of Wisconsin," by Reuben G. Thwaites, the Secretary of the State Historical Society of Wisconsin.

of disposing of its land in large blocks to the highest bidder, instead of allotting it, as has since been done, in quarter sections to actual settlers.[1]

Harrison was thoroughly in sympathy with the Westerners. He had thrown in his lot with theirs;

Harrison, St. Clair, and Sargent. he deemed himself one of them, and was accepted by them as a fit representative. Accordingly he was very popular as Governor of Indiana. St. Clair in Ohio and Sargent in Mississippi were both extremely unpopular. They were appointed by Federalist administrations, and were entirely out of sympathy with the Western people among whom they lived. One was a Scotchman, and one a New Englander. They were both high-minded men, with sound ideas on governmental policy, though Sargent was the abler of the two; but they were out of touch with the Westerners. They distrusted the frontier folk, and were bitterly disliked in return. Each committed the fundamental fault of trying to govern the Territory over which he had been put in accordance with his own ideas, and heedless of the wishes and prejudices of those under him. Doubtless each was conscientious in what he did, and each of course considered the difficulties under which he labored to be due solely to the lawlessness and the many shortcomings of the settlers. But this was an error. The experience of Blount when he occupied the exceedingly difficult position of Territorial Governor of Tennessee showed that it was quite possible for a

[1] Mr. Eli Thayer, in his various writings, has rightly laid especial stress on this point.

man of firm belief in the Union to get into touch
with the frontiersmen and to be accepted by them as
a worthy representative; but the virtues   Lessons
of St. Clair and Sargent were so different Taught by
from the backwoods virtues, and their   Blount's
                                            Experience.
habits of thought were so alien, that they
could not possibly get on with the people among
whom their lot had been cast.   Neither of them in
the end took up his abode in the Territory of which
he had been Governor, both returning to the East.
The code of laws which they enacted prior to the
Territories possessing a sufficient number of inhabitants to become entitled to Territorial legislatures
were deemed by the settlers to be arbitrary and unsuited to their needs.   There was much popular
feeling against them.   On one occasion St. Clair
was mobbed in Chillicothe, the then capital of Ohio,
with no other effect than to procure a change of
capital to Cincinnati.   Finally both Sargent and St.
Clair were removed by Jefferson, early in his administration.

The Jeffersonian Republican party did very much
that was evil, and it advocated governmental principles of such utter folly that the party   The Jeffer-
itself was obliged immediately to aban-   sonians the
don them when it undertook to carry on   Champions
                                           of the West.
the government of the United States, and
only clung to them long enough to cause serious and
lasting damage to the country; but on the vital
question of the West, and its territorial expansion,
the Jeffersonian party was, on the whole, emphatically right, and its opponents, the Federalists, em-

phatically wrong.   The Jeffersonians believed in
the acquisition of territory in the West, and the
Federalists did not.   The Jeffersonians believed
that the Westerners should be allowed to govern
themselves precisely as other citizens of the United
States did, and should be given their full share in
the management of national affairs.   Too many Federalists failed to see that these positions were the
only proper ones to take.   In consequence, notwith-
standing all their manifold shortcomings, the Jeffersonians, and not the Federalists, were those to whom
the West owed most.

Whether the Westerners governed themselves as
wisely as they should have mattered little.   The
essential point was that they had to be
given the right of self-government.   They
could not be kept in pupilage.   Like other
Americans, they had to be left to strike out
for themselves and to sink or swim according to the measure of their own capacities.   When
this was done it was certain that they would commit
many blunders, and that some of these blunders
would work harm not only to themselves but to the
whole nation.   Nevertheless, all this had to be
accepted as part of the penalty paid for free government.   It was wise to accept it in the first place,
and in the second place, whether wise or not, it was
inevitable.   Many of the Federalists saw this ; and
to many of them, the Adamses, for instance, and Jay
and Pinckney, the West owed more than it did to
most of the Republican statesmen ; but as a whole,
the attitude of the Federalists, especially in the

Right of the West-erners to Self-Gov-ernment.

Northeast, toward the West was ungenerous and improper, while the Jeffersonians, with all their unwisdom and demagogy, were nevertheless the Western champions.

Mississippi and Ohio had squabbled with their Territorial governors much as the Old Thirteen Colonies had squabbled with the governors appointed by the Crown. One curious consequence of this was common to both cases. When the old Colonies became States, they in their constitutions usually imposed the same checks upon the executive they themselves elected as they had desired to see imposed upon the executive appointed by an outside power. The new Territories followed the same course. When Ohio became a State it adopted a very foolish constitution. This constitution deprived the executive of almost all power, and provided a feeble, short-term judiciary, throwing the control of affairs into the hands of the legislative body, in accordance with what were then deemed Democratic ideas. The people were entirely unable to realize that, so far as their discontent with the Governor's actions was reasonable, it arose from the fact that he was appointed, not by themselves, but by some body or person not in sympathy with them. They failed to grasp the seemingly self-evident truth that a governor, one man elected by the people, is just as much their representative and is just as certain to carry out their ideas as is a legislature, a body of men elected by the people. They provided a government which accentuated, instead of softening, the defects in

Vagaries of Western Constitution-Making.

their own social system. They were in no danger of suffering from tyranny; they were in no danger of losing the liberty which they so jealously guarded. The perils that threatened them were lawlessness, lack of order, and lack of capacity to concentrate their efforts in time of danger from within or from an external enemy; and against these perils they made no provision whatever.

The inhabitants of Ohio Territory were just as bitter against St. Clair as the inhabitants of Mississippi Territory were against Sargent. The **Western Feeling against the East.** Mississipians did not object to Sargent as a Northern man, but, in common with the men of Ohio, they objected to governors who were Eastern men and out of touch with the West. At the end of the eighteenth century, and during the early years of the nineteenth, the important fact to be remembered in treating of the Westerners was their fundamental unity, in blood, in ways of life, and in habits of thought.[1] They were predominantly of Southern, not of Northern blood; though it was the blood of the Southerners of the uplands, not of the low coast regions, so that they were far more closely kin to the Northerners than were the seaboard planters. In Kentucky and Tennessee, in Indiana and Mississippi, the settlers were of the same quality. They possessed the same virtues and the same shortcomings, the same ideals and the same practices. There was already a considerable Eastern emigration to the West, but it

[1] Prof. Frederick A. Turner, of the University of Michigan, deserves especial credit for the stress he has laid upon this point.

went as much to Kentucky as to Ohio, and almost as much to Tennessee and Mississippi as to Indiana. As yet the Northeasterners were chiefly engaged in filling the vacant spaces in New England, New York, and Pennsyl- vania. The great flood of Eastern emigra- tion to the West, the flood which followed the parallels of latitude, and made the Northwest like the Northeast, did not begin until after the War of 1812. It was no accident that made Harrison, the first governor of Indiana and long the typical repre- sentative of the Northwest, by birth a Virginian, and the son of one of the Virginian signers of the Declaration of Independence. The Northwest was at this time in closer touch with Virginia than with New England.

The West in Close Touch with the South.

There was as yet no hard and fast line drawn between North and South among the men of the Western waters. Their sense of political cohesion was not fully developed, and the same qualities that at times made them loose in their ideas of allegiance to the Union at times also prevented a vivid realization on their part of their own political and social solidarity ; but they were always more or less conscious of this solidarity, and, as a rule, they acted together.

Homogene- ity of the West.

Most important of all, the slavery question, which afterwards rived in sunder the men west of the Alleghanies as it rived in sunder those east of them, was of small importance in the early years. West of the Alleghanies slaves were still to be found almost everywhere, while almost

Slavery in the West.

everywhere there were also frequent and open expressions of hostility to slavery. The Southerners still rather disliked slavery, while the Northerners did not as yet feel any very violent antagonism to it. In the Indiana Territory there were hundreds of slaves, the property of the old French inhabitants and of the American settlers who had come there prior to 1787; and the majority of the population of this Territory actually wished to reintroduce slavery, and repeatedly petitioned Congress to be allowed the reintroduction. Congress, with equal patriotism and wisdom, always refused the petition; but it was not until the new century was well under way that the anti-slavery element obtained control in Indiana and Illinois. Even in Ohio there was a considerable party which favored the introduction of slavery, and though the majority was against this, the people had small sympathy with the negroes, and passed very severe laws against the introduction of free blacks into the State, and even against those already in residence therein.[1] On the other hand, when Kentucky's first constitutional convention sat, a resolute effort was made to abolish slavery within the State, and this effort was only defeated after a hard struggle and a close vote. To their honor be it said that all of the clergymen—three Baptists, one Methodist, one Dutch Reformed, and one Presbyterian—who were members of the constitutional convention voted in favor of the abolition of slavery.[2]

[1] " Ohio," by Rufus King, pp. 290, 364, etc.

[2] John Mason Brown, " Political Beginnings of Kentucky," 229. Among the men who deserve honor for thus voting against slavery was Harry Innes. One of the Baptist preachers, Gerrard, was elected Governor over

In Tennessee no such effort was made, but the leaders of thought did not hesitate to express their horror of slavery and their desire that it might be abolished. There was no sharp difference between the attitudes of the Northwestern and the Southwestern States towards slavery.

North and South alike, the ways of life were substantially the same; though there were differences, of course, and these differences tended to *Features of* become accentuated. Thus, in the Missis- *Western* sippi Territory the planters, in the closing *Life.* years of the century, began to turn their attention to cotton instead of devoting themselves to the crops of their brethren farther north; and cotton soon became their staple product. But as yet the typical settler everywhere was the man of the axe and rifle, the small pioneer farmer who lived by himself, with his wife and his swarming children, on a big tract of wooded land, perhaps three *The Far-* or four hundred acres in extent. Of this *mer the* three or four hundred acres he rarely *Typical* cleared more than eight or ten; and these *Westerner.* were cleared imperfectly. On this clearing he tilled the soil, and there he lived in his rough log house with but one room, or at most two and a loft.[1]

The man of the Western waters, was essentially a man who dwelt alone in the midst of the forest on his rude little farm, and who eked out his living by hunting. Game still abounded everywhere,

Logan, four years later; a proof that Kentucky sentiment was very tolerant of attacks on slavery. All the clergymen, by the way, also voted to disqualify clergymen for service in the legislatures.

[1] F. A. Michaux, "Voyages" (in 1802), pp. 132, 214, etc.

save in the immediate neighborhood of the towns; so that many of the inhabitants lived almost exclu-**Game Still** sively by hunting and fishing, and, with **Abundant.** their return to the pursuits of savagery, adopted not a little of the savage idleness and thriftlessness. Bear, deer, and turkey were staple foods. Elk had ceased to be common, though they hung on here and there in out of the way localities for many years; and by the close of the century the herds of bison had been driven west of the Mississippi.[1] Smaller forms of wild life swarmed. Gray squirrels existed in such incredible numbers that they caused very serious damage to the crops, and at one time the Kentucky Legislature passed a law imposing upon every male over sixteen years of age the duty of killing a certain number of squirrels and crows every year.[2] The settlers possessed horses and horned cattle, but only a few sheep, which were not fitted to fight for their own existence in the woods, as the stock had to. On the other hand, slab-sided, long-legged hogs were the most plentiful of domestic animals, ranging in great, half-wild droves through the forest.

All observers were struck by the intense fondness of the frontiersmen for the woods and for a restless, **Fondness** lonely life.[3] They pushed independence **of the** to an extreme; they did not wish to work **Westerners** for others or to rent land from others. **for the** **Lonely Life** Each was himself a small landed proprie-**of the** tor, who cleared only the ground that he **Woods.** could himself cultivate. Workmen were

---

[1] Henry Ker, "Travels," p. 22.   [2] Michaux, 215, 236; Collins, I., 24.

[3] Crèvecœur, "Voyage dans la Haute Pennsylvanie," etc., p. 265.

scarce and labor dear. It was almost impossible to get men fit to work as mill hands, or to do high-class labor in forges even by importing them from Pennsylvania or Maryland.[1] Even in the few towns the inhabitants preferred that their children should follow agriculture rather than become handicrafts-men; and skilled workmen such as carpenters and smiths made a great deal of money, so much so that they could live a week on one day's wage.[2]

In addition to farming there was a big trade along the river. Land transportation was very difficult in-deed, and the frontiersman's whole life was The River one long struggle with the forest and with Trade. poor roads. The waterways were consequently of very great importance, and the flatboatmen on the Mississippi and Ohio became a numerous and note-worthy class. The rivers were covered with their craft. There was a driving trade between Pitts-burgh and New Orleans, the goods being drawn to Pittsburgh from the seacoast cities by great four-horse wagons, and being exported in ships from New Orleans to all parts of the earth. Not only did the Westerners build river craft, but they even went into shipbuilding; and on the upper Ohio, at Pitts-burgh, and near Marietta, at the beginning of the present century, seagoing ships were built and launched to go down the Ohio and Mississippi, and thence across the ocean to any foreign port.[3] There was, however, much risk in this trade; for the de-mand for commodities at Natchez and New Orleans

[1] Clay MSS., Letter to George Nicholas, Baltimore, Sept. 3, 1796.

[2] Michaux, pp. 96, 152.

[3] Thompson Mason Harris, " Journal of Tour," etc., 1803, p. 140 ; Mi-chaux, p. 77.

was uncertain, while the waters of the Gulf swarmed with British and French cruisers, always ready to pounce like pirates on the ships of neutral powers.[1]

Yet the river trade was but the handmaid of frontier agriculture. The Westerners were a farmer folk who lived on the clearings their own hands had made in the great woods, and who owned the land they tilled. Towns were few and small. At the end of Small Size the century there were some four hundred of the thousand people in the West; yet the largest Towns. town was Lexington, which contained less than three thousand people.[2] Lexington was a neatly built little burg, with fine houses and good stores. The leading people lived well and possessed much cultivation. Louisville and Nashville were each about half its size. In Nashville, of the one hundred and twenty houses but eight were of brick, and most of them were mere log huts. Cincinnati was a poor little village. Cleveland consisted of but two or three log cabins, at a time when there were already a thousand settlers in its neighborhood on the Connecticut Reserve, scattered out on their farms.[3] Natchez was a very important town, nearly as large Natchez. as Lexington. It derived its importance from the river traffic on the Mississippi. All the boatmen stopped there, and sometimes as many as one hundred and fifty craft were moored to the bank at the same time. The men who did this

[1] Clay MSS., W. H. Turner to Thomas Hart, Natchez, May 27, 1797.
[2] Perrin Du Lac " Voyage," etc., 1801, 1803, p. 153 ; Michaux, 150.
[3] " Historical Collections of Ohio," p. 120.

laborious river work were rude, powerful, and law-less, and when they halted for a rest their idea of enjoyment was the coarsest and most savage dissipation. At Natchez there speedily gathered every species of purveyor to their vicious pleasures, and the part of the town known as "Natchez under the Hill" became a by-word for crime and debauchery.[1]

Kentucky had grown so in population, possessing over two hundred thousand inhabitants, that she had begun to resemble an Eastern State. When, Growth of in 1796, Benjamin Logan, the representa- Kentucky. tive of the old woodchoppers and Indian fighters, ran for governor and was beaten, it was evident that Kentucky had passed out of the mere pioneer days. It was more than a mere coincidence that in the following year Henry Clay should have taken up his residence in Lexington. It showed that the State was already attracting to live within her borders men like those who were fitted for social and political leadership in Virginia.

Though the typical inhabitant of Kentucky was still the small frontier farmer, the class of well-to-do gentry had already attained good propor- The tions. Elsewhere throughout the West, in Kentucky Tennessee, and even here and there in Gentry. Ohio and the Territories of Indiana and Mississippi, there were to be found occasional houses that were well built and well finished, and surrounded by pleasant grounds, fairly well kept; houses to which the owners had brought their stores of silver and

[1] Henry Ker, "Travels," p. 41.

linen and heavy, old-fashioned furniture from their homes in the Eastern States. Blount, for instance, had a handsome house in Knoxville, well fitted, as beseemed that of a man one of whose brothers still lived at Blount Hall, in the coast region of North Carolina, the ancestral seat of his forefathers for generations.[1] But by far the greatest number of these fine houses, and the largest class of gentry to dwell in them, were in Kentucky. Not only were Lexington and Louisville important towns, but Danville, the first capital of Kentucky, also possessed importance, and, indeed, had been the first of the Western towns to develop an active and distinctive social and political life. It was in Danville that, in the years immediately preceding Kentucky's admission as a State, the Political Club met. The membership of this club included many of the leaders of Kentucky's intellectual life, and the record of its debates shows the keenness with which they watched the course of social and political development not only in Kentucky but in the United States. They were men of good intelligence and trained minds, and their meetings and debates undoubtedly had a stimulating effect upon Kentucky life, though they were tainted, as were a very large number of the leading men of the same stamp elsewhere throughout the country, with the doctrinaire political notions common among those who followed the French political theorists of the day.[2]

The Danville Political Club.

---

[1] Clay MSS., Blount to Hart, Knoxville, Feb. 9, 1794.
[2] " The Political Club," by Thomas Speed, Filson Club Publications.

Of the gentry many were lawyers, and the law led naturally to political life; but even among the gentry the typical man was still emphatically the big landowner. The leaders of Kentucky life were men who owned large estates, on which they lived in their great roomy houses. Even when they practised law they also supervised their estates; and if they were not lawyers, in addition to tilling the land they were always ready to try their hand at some kind of manufacture. They were willing to turn their attention to any new business in which there was a chance to make money, whether it was to put up a mill, to build a forge, to undertake a contract for the delivery of wheat to some big flour merchant, or to build a flotilla of flatboats, and take the produce of a given neighborhood down to New Orleans for shipment to the West Indies.[1] They were also always engaged in efforts to improve the breed of their horses and cattle, and to introduce new kinds of agriculture, notably the culture of the vine.[2] They speedily settled themselves definitely in the new country, and began to make ready for their chil-

The Large Land-owners.

[1] Clay MSS., Seitz & Lowan to Garret Darling, Lexington, January 23, 1797; agreement of George Nicholas, October 10, 1796, etc. This was an agreement on the part of Nicholas to furnish Seitz & Lowan with all the flour manufactured at his mill during the season of 1797 for exportation, the flour to be delivered by him in Kentucky. He was to receive $5.50 a barrel up to the receipt of $1500; after that it was to depend upon the price of wheat. Six bushels of wheat were reckoned to a barrel of flour, and the price of a bushel was put at four shillings; in reality it ranged from three to six.

[2] *Do.*, "Minutes of meeting of the Directors of the Vineyard Society," June 27, 1800.

dren to inherit their homes after them ; though they retained enough of the restless spirit which had made them cross the Alleghanies to be always on the lookout for any fresh region of exceptional advantages, such as many of them considered the lands along the lower Mississippi.   They led a life which
Open-air Life. appealed to them strongly, for it was passed much in the open air, in a beautiful region and lovely climate, with horses and hounds, and the management of their estates and their interest in politics to occupy their time ; while their neighbors were men of cultivation, at least by their own standards, so that they had the society for which they most cared.[1] In spite of their willingness to embark in commercial ventures and to build mills, rope-walks, and similar manufactures,— for which they had the greatest difficulty in procuring skilled laborers, whether foreign or native, from the Northeastern States[2]—and in spite of their liking for the law, they retained the deep-settled belief that the cultivation of the earth was the best of all possible pursuits for men of every station, high or low.[3]

[1] *Do.*, James Brown to Thomas Hart, Lexington, April 3, 1804.

[2] *Do.*, J. Brown to Thomas Hart, Philadelphia, February 11, 1797. This letter was brought out to Hart by a workman, David Dodge, whom Brown had at last succeeded in engaging. Dodge had been working in New York at a rope-walk, where he received $500 a year without board. From Hart he bargained to receive $350 with board. It proved impossible to engage other journeymen workers, Brown expressing his belief that any whom he chose would desert a week after they got to Kentucky, and Dodge saying that he would rather take raw hands and train them to the business than take out such hands as offered to go.

[3] *Do.*, William Nelson to Col. George Nicholas, Caroline, Va., December 29, 1794.

In many ways the life of the Kentuckians was
most like that of the Virginia gentry, though it had
peculiar features of its own.   Judged by   Virginia
Puritan standards, it seemed free enough;   and
and it is rather curious to find Virginia   Kentucky.
fathers anxious to send their sons out to Kentucky
so that they could get away from what they termed
"the constant round of dissipation, the scenes of
idleness, which boys are perpetually engaged in" in
Virginia.   One Virginia gentleman of note, in writing to a prominent Kentuckian to whom he wished
to send his son, dwelt upon his desire to get him
away from a place where boys of his age spent most
of the time galloping wherever they wished, mounted
on blooded horses.   Kentucky hardly seemed a place
to which a parent would send a son if he wished
him to avoid the temptations of horse flesh; but this
particular Virginian at least tried to provide against
this, as he informed his correspondent that he should
send his son out to Kentucky mounted on an "indifferent Nag," which was to be used only as a means
of locomotion for the journey, and was then immediately to be sold.[1]

The gentry strove hard to secure a good education
for their children, and in Kentucky, as in Tennessee,
made every effort to bring about the building of academies where their boys and   Education.
girls could be well taught.   If this was not possible,
they strove to find some teacher capable of taking a
class to which he could teach Latin and mathe-
matics; a teacher who should also "prepare his

[1] *Do.*, William Nelson to Nicholas, November 9, 1792.

pupils for becoming useful members of society and patriotic citizens."[1]   Where possible the leading families sent their sons to some Eastern college, Princeton being naturally the favorite institution of learning with people who dwelt in communities where the Presbyterians took the lead in social standing and cultivation.[2]

All through the West there was much difficulty in getting money.   In Tennessee particularly money was so scarce that the only way to get cash in hand was by selling provisions to the few Federal garrisons.[3]   Credits were long, and payment made largely in kind; and the price at which an article could be sold under such conditions was twice as large as that which it would command for cash down.   In the accounts kept by the landowners with the merchants who sold them goods, and the artizans who worked for them, there usually appear credit accounts in which the amounts due on account of produce of various kinds are deducted from the debt, leaving a balance to be settled by cash and by orders.   Owing to the fluctuating currency, and to the wide difference in charges when immediate cash payments were received as compared with charges when the payments were made on

Currency.

[1] Shelby MSS., letter of Toulmin, January 7, 1794 ; Blount MSS., January 6, 1792, etc.

[2] Clay MSS., *passim ;* letter to Thomas Hart, October 19, 1794 ; October 13, 1797, etc.   In the last letter, by the way, written by one John Umstead, occurs the following sentence : "I have lately heard a piece of news, if true, must be a valuable acquisition to the Western World, viz. a boat of a considerable burden making four miles and a half an hour against the strongest current in the Mississippi river, and worked by horses."

[3] *Do.*, Blount to Hart, Knoxville, March 13, 1799.

credit and in kind, it is difficult to know exactly
what the prices represent.   In Kentucky currency
mutton and beef were fourpence a pound, in the
summer of 1796, while four beef tongues cost three
shillings, and a quarter of lamb three and a sixpence.
In 1798, on the same account, beef was
down to threepence a pound.[1]   Linen cost   **Prices of
Goods.**
two and fourpence, or three shillings a
yard; flannel, four to six shillings; calico and chintz
about the same; baize, three shillings and ninepence.
A dozen knives and forks were eighteen shillings,
and ten pocket handkerchiefs two pounds. Worsted
shoes were eight shillings a pair, and buttons were
a shilling a dozen.   A pair of gloves were three and
ninepence; a pair of kid slippers, thirteen and sixpence; ribbons were one and sixpence.[2] The blacksmith charged six shillings and ninepence for a new
pair of shoes, and a shilling and sixpence for taking
off an old pair; and he did all the iron work for the
farm and the house alike, from repairing bridle bits
and sharpening coulters to mounting " wafil irons "[3]
—for the housewives excelled in preparing delicious
waffles and hot cakes.

The gentry were fond of taking holidays, going to
some mountain resort, where they met friends from
other parts of Kentucky and Tennessee, **Holidays of**
and from Virginia and elsewhere.   They **the Gentry.**
carried their negro servants with them, and at a

---

[1] *Do.*, Account of James Morrison and Melchia Myer, October 12, 1798.

[2] *Do.*, Account of Mrs. Marion Nicholas with Tillford, 1802. On this bill
appears also a charge for Hyson tea, for straw bonnets, at eighteen shillings ;
for black silk gloves, and for one "Æsop's Fables," at a cost of three
shillings and ninepence.   [3] *Do.*, Account of Morrison and Hickey, 1798.

good tavern the board would be three shillings a
day for the master and a little over a shilling for
the man.   They lived in comfort and they enjoyed
themselves; but they did not have much ready
money.   From the sales of their crops and stock
and from their mercantile ventures they got enough
to pay the blacksmith and carpenter, who did odd
jobs for them, and the Eastern merchants from
whom they got gloves, bonnets, hats, and shoes,
and the cloth which was made into dresses by
the womankind on their plantations.   But most of
their wants were supplied on their own places.
Their abundant tables were furnished mainly with
what their own farms yielded.   When they travelled
they went in their own carriages.   The rich men,
whose wants were comparatively many, usually had
on their estates white hired men or black slaves
whose labor could gratify them; while the ordinary
farmer, of the class that formed the great majority of
the population, was capable of supplying almost all
his needs himself, or with the assistance of his family.

The immense preponderance of the agricultural,
land-holding, and land-tilling element, and the comparative utter insignificance of town development, was highly characteristic of the
Western settlement of this time, and offers
a very marked contrast to what goes on
to-day, in the settlement of new countries.   At the end of the eighteenth century the
population of the Western country was about as
great as the population of the State of Washington
at the end of the nineteenth, and Washington is dis-

*Contrast of
Old and
New
Methods of
Settlement.*

tinctly a pastoral and agricultural State, a State of men who chop trees, herd cattle, and till the soil, as well as trade; but in Washington great cities, like Tacoma, Seattle, and Spokane, have sprung up with a rapidity which was utterly unknown in the West a century ago. Nowadays when new States are formed the urban population in them tends to grow as rapidly as in the old. A hundred years ago there was practically no urban population at all in a new country. Colorado even during its first decade of statehood had a third of its population in its capital city. Kentucky during its first decade did not have much more than one per cent of its population in its capital city. Kentucky grew as rapidly as Colorado grew, a hundred years later; but Denver grew thirty or forty times as fast as Lexington had ever grown.

In the strongly marked frontier character no traits were more pronounced than the dislike of crowding and the tendency to roam to and fro, hither and thither, always with a westward trend. Boone, the typical frontiersman, embodied in his own person the spirit of loneliness and restlessness which marked the first venturers into the wilderness. He had wandered in his youth from Pennsylvania to Carolina, and, in the prime of his strength, from North Carolina to Kentucky. When Kentucky became well settled in the closing years of the century, he crossed into Missouri, that he might once more take up his life where he could see the game come out of the woods at nightfall, and could wander among trees

untouched by the axe of the pioneer. An English
traveller of note who happened to encounter him
about this time has left an interesting account of the
meeting. It was on the Ohio, and Boone was in a
canoe, alone with his dog and gun, setting forth on
a solitary trip into the wilderness to trap beaver.
He would not even join himself to the other travellers for a night, preferring to plunge at once into
the wild, lonely life he so loved. His strong character and keen mind struck the Englishman, who
yet saw that the old hunter belonged to the class of
pioneers who could never themselves civilize the
land, because they ever fled from the face of the
very civilization for which they had made ready
the land. In Boone's soul the fierce impatience of
all restraint burned like a fire. He told the Englishman that he no longer cared for Kentucky, because
its people had grown too easy of life; and that he
wished to move to some place where men still lived
untrammelled and unshackled, and enjoyed uncontrolled the free blessings of nature.[1] The isolation
of his life and the frequency with which he changed
his abode brought out the frontiersman's wonderful
capacity to shift for himself, but it hindered the
development of his power of acting in combination
with others of his kind. The first comers to the
new country were so restless and so intolerant of
the presence of their kind, that as neighbors came
in they moved ever westward. They could not act
with their fellows.

[1] Francis Bailey's "Journal of a Tour in Unsettled Parts of North
America in 1796 and 1797," p. 234.

Of course in the men who succeeded the first pioneers, and who were the first permanent settlers, the restlessness and the desire for a lonely life were much less developed. These men wandered only until they found a good piece of land, and took up claims on this land, not because the country was lonely, but because it was fertile. They hailed with joy the advent of new settlers and the upbuilding of a little market town in the neighborhood. They joined together eagerly in the effort to obtain schools for their children. As yet there were no public schools supported by government in any part of the West, but all the settlers of any pretension to respectability were anxious to give their children a decent education. Even the poorer people, who were still engaged in the hardest and roughest struggle for a livelihood, showed appreciation of the need of schooling for their children; and wherever the clearings of the settlers were within reasonable distance of one another a log school-house was sure to spring up. The school-teacher boarded around among the different families, and was quite as apt to be paid in produce as in cash. Sometimes he was a teacher by profession; more often he took up teaching simply as an interlude to some of his other occupations. School-books were more common than any others in the scanty libraries of the pioneers.

The settlers who became firmly established in the land gave definite shape to its political career. The county was throughout the West the unit of division,

though in the North it became somewhat mixed
with the township system. It is a pity that the town-

The
County-
System in
the West. ship could not have been the unit, as it
would have rendered the social and political development in many respects easier,
by giving to each little community responsibility for, and power in, matters concerning its own
welfare ; but the backwoodsmen lived so scattered
out, and the thinly-settled regions covered so large
an extent of territory, that the county was at first in
some ways more suited to their needs. Moreover,
it was the unit of organization in Virginia, to which
State more than to any other the pioneers owed
their social and governmental system. The people
were ordinarily brought but little in contact with
the Government. They were exceedingly jealous of
their individual liberty, and wished to be interfered
with as little as possible. Nevertheless, they were
fond of litigation. One observer remarks that
horses and lawsuits were their great subjects of
conversation.[1]

The vast extent of the territory and the scantiness
of the population forced the men of law, like the

The Law-
yers and
Clergymen
Forced to
Much
Travel. religious leaders, to travel about rather
than stay permanently fixed in any one
place. In the few towns there were lawyers and clergymen who had permanent
homes ; but as a rule both rode circuits.
The judges and the lawyers travelled together on the
circuits, to hold court. At the Shire-town all might
sleep in one room, or at least under one roof ; and it

[1] Michaux, p. 240.

was far from an unusual thing to see both the grand
and petty juries sitting under trees in the open.[1]

The fact that the Government did so little for the
individual and left so much to be done by him
rendered it necessary for the individuals   Power to
voluntarily to combine. Huskings and   Combine
house-raisings were times when all joined   among the
                                              Frontiers-
freely to work for the man whose corn   men.
was to be shucked or whose log cabin was to be
built, and turned their labor into a frolic and merry-
making, where the men drank much whiskey and
the young people danced vigorously to the sound of
the fiddle. Such merry-makings were attended from
far and near, offering a most welcome break to the
dreariness of life on the lonely clearings in the midst
of the forest. Ordinarily the frontiersman at his
home only drank milk or water; but at the taverns
and social gatherings there was much drunkenness,
for the men craved whiskey, drinking the fiery liquor
in huge draughts. Often the orgies ended with
brutal brawls. To outsiders the craving of the
backwoodsman for whiskey was one of his least attractive traits.[2] It must always be remembered,
however, that even the most friendly outsider is apt
to apply to others his own standards in matters of
judgment. The average traveller overstated the
drunkenness of the backwoodsman, exactly as he
overstated his misery.

The frontiersman was very poor. He worked
hard and lived roughly, and he and his family had

[1] Atwater, p. 177.
[2] Perrin Du Lac, p. 131 ; Michaux, 95, etc.

little beyond coarse food, coarse clothing, and a rude shelter. In the severe winters they suffered both

Roughness and Poverty of the Life.
from cold and hunger. In the summers there was sickness everywhere, fevers of various kinds scourging all the new settlements. The difficulty of communication was so great that it took three months for the emigrants to travel from Connecticut to the Western Reserve near Cleveland, and a journey from a clearing, over the forest roads, to a little town not fifty miles off was an affair of moment to be undertaken but once a year.[1] Yet to the frontiersmen themselves the life was far from unattractive. It gratified their intense

Its Attractiveness.
love of independence; the lack of refinement did not grate on their rough, bold natures; and they prized the entire equality of a life where there were no social distinctions, and few social restraints. Game was still a staple, being sought after for the flesh and the hide, and of course all the men and boys were enthralled by the delights of the chase. The life was as free as it was rude, and it possessed great fascinations, not only for the wilder spirits, but even for many men who, when they had the chance, showed that they possessed ability to acquire cultivation.

One old pioneer has left a pleasant account of the beginning of an ordinary day's work in a log cabin[2]:

---

[1] "Historical Collections of Ohio," p. 120; Perrin Du Lac, p. 143.

[2] Drake's "Pioneer Life in Kentucky." This gives an excellent description of life in a family of pioneers, representing what might be called the average frontiersman of the best type. Drake's father and mother were poor and illiterate, but hardworking, honest, God-fearing folk, with an earnest desire to do their duty by their neighbors and to see their children rise in the world.

" I know of no scene in civilized life more primitive than such a cabin hearth as that of my mother. In the morning, a buckeye back-log, a hickory Life in a forestick, resting on stone and irons, with Log Cabin. a johnny-cake, on a clean ash board, set before the fire to bake ; a frying pan, with its long handle resting on a split-bottom turner's chair, sending out its peculiar music, and the tea-kettle swung from a wooden lug pole, with myself setting the table or turning the meat, or watching the johnny-cake, while she sat nursing the baby in the corner and telling the little ones to hold still and let their sister Lizzie dress them. Then came blowing the conch-shell for father in the field, the howling of old Lion, the gathering round the table, the blessing, the dull clatter of pewter spoons and pewter basins, the talk about the crop and stock, the inquiry whether Dan'l (the boy) could be spared from the house, and the general arrangements for the day. Breakfast over, my function was to provide the sauce for dinner ; in winter, to open the potato or turnip hole, and wash what I took out ; in spring, to go into the field and collect the greens ; in summer and fall, to explore the truck patch, our little garden. If I afterwards went to the field my household labors ceased until night ; if not, they continued through the day. As often as possible mother would engage in making pumpkin pies, in which I generally bore a part, and one of these more commonly graced the supper than the dinner table. My pride was in the labors of the field. Mother did the spinning. The standing dye-stuff was the inner bark of the white walnut, from which we obtained that peculiar and permanent shade of dull yellow, the butternut [so common and typical in the clothing of the backwoods farmer]. Oak bark, with copperas as a mordant, when father had money to purchase it, supplied the ink with which I learned to write. I drove the horses to and from the range, and salted them. I tended the sheep, and hunted up the cattle in the woods."[1] This was the life of the thrifty pioneers, whose children more than held their own in the world. The shiftless men without ambition and without thrift, lived in laziness and filth; their eating and sleeping arrangements were as unattractive as those of an Indian wigwam.

The pleasures and the toils of the life were alike peculiar. In the wilder parts the loneliness and the

Peculiar Qualities of the Pioneers. fierce struggle with squalid poverty, and with the tendency to revert to savage conditions, inevitably produced for a generation or two a certain falling off from the standard of civilized communities. It needed peculiar qualities to insure success, and the pioneers were almost exclusively native Americans. The Germans

Native Americans did Best. were more thrifty and prosperous, but they could not go first into the wilderness.[2] Men fresh from England rarely succeeded.[3] The most pitiable group of emigrants that reached the West at this time was formed by the French

---

[1] *Do.*, pp. 90, 111, etc., condensed.

[2] Michaux, p. 63, etc.

[3] Parkinson's "Tour in America, 1798–1800," pp. 504, 588, etc. Parkinson loathed the Americans. A curious example of how differently the same facts will affect different observers may be gained by contrasting his

who came to found the town of Gallipolis, on the
Ohio. These were mostly refugees from the Revolution, who had been taken in by a swindling land
company. They were utterly unsuited to life in the
wilderness, being gentlemen, small tradesmen, lawyers, and the like. Unable to grapple with the wild
life into which they found themselves plunged, they
sank into shiftless poverty, not one in fifty showing
industry and capacity to succeed. Congress took
pity upon them and granted them twenty-four thousand acres in Scioto County, the tract being known
as the French grant; but no gift of wild land was
able to insure their prosperity. By degrees they were
absorbed into the neighboring communities, a few
succeeding, most ending their lives in abject failure.[1]

The trouble these poor French settlers had with
their lands was far from unique. The early system
of land sales in the West was most unwise. In Kentucky and Tennessee the grants were made
under the laws of Virginia and North Carolina, and each man purchased or pre-
empted whatever he could, and surveyed it where he
liked, with a consequent endless confusion of titles.
The National Government possessed the disposal of
the land in the Northwest and in Mississippi; and
it avoided the pitfall of unlimited private surveying;
but it made little effort to prevent swindling by land
companies, and none whatever to people the country

Trouble
with Land
Titles.

observations with those of his fellow Englishman, John Davis, whose trip
covered precisely the same period ; but Parkinson's observations as to the
extreme difficulty of an Old Country farmer getting on in the backwoods
regions are doubtless mainly true.

[1] Atwater, p. 159 ; Michaux, p. 122, etc.

with actual settlers. Congress granted great tracts of lands to companies and to individuals, selling to the highest bidder, whether or not he intended personally to occupy the country. Public sales were thus conducted by competition, and Congress even declined to grant to the men in actual possession the right of pre-emption at the average rate of sale, refusing the request of settlers in both Mississippi and Indiana that they should be given the first choice to the lands which they had already partially cleared.[1] It was not until many years later that we adopted the wise policy of selling the National domain in small lots to actual occupants.

The pioneer in his constant struggle with poverty was prone to look with puzzled anger at those who made more money than he did, and whose lives were easier. The backwoods farmer or planter of that day looked upon the merchant with much the same suspicion and hostility now felt by his successor for the banker or the railroad magnate. He did not quite understand how it was that the merchant, who seemed to work less hard than he did, should make more money; and being ignorant and suspicious, he usually followed some hopelessly wrong-headed course when he tried to remedy his wrongs. Sometimes these efforts to obtain relief took the form of resolutions not to purchase from merchants or traders such articles as woollens, linens, cottons, hats, or shoes, unless the same could be paid for in articles grown or manufactured

Sullen Jealousy of the Pioneers.

Clouded Economic Notions.

---

[1] American State Papers, Public Lands, I., 261 ; also pp. 71, 74, 99, etc.

by the farmers themselves.   This particular move
was taken because of the alarming scarcity of money,
and was aimed particularly at the inhabitants of the
Atlantic States.   It was of course utterly ineffective.[1]
A much less wise and less honest course was that
sometimes followed of refusing to pay debts when
the latter became inconvenient and pressing.[2]

The frontier virtue of independence and of impatience of outside direction found a particularly
vicious expression in the frontier abhor-   Vices of
rence of regular troops, and advocacy of a   the Militia
hopelessly feeble militia system. The people   System
were foolishly convinced of the efficacy of their
militia system, which they loudly proclaimed to be
the only proper mode of national defence.[3]   While
in the actual presence of the Indians the stern neces-
sities of border warfare forced the frontiersmen into
a certain semblance of discipline.   As soon as the
immediate pressure was relieved, however, the whole
militia system sank into a mere farce.   At certain
stated occasions there were musters for company or
regimental drill.   These training days were treated
as occasions for frolic and merry-making.   There
were pony races and wrestling matches, with unlimited fighting, drunkenness, and general uproar. Such
musters were often called, in derision, cornstalk
drills, because many of the men, either having no
guns or neglecting to bring them, drilled with corn-

---

[1] Marshall, II., p. 325.

[2] The inhabitants of Natchez, in the last days of the Spanish dominion,
became inflamed with hostility to their creditors, the merchants, and insisted upon what were practically stay laws being enacted in their favor.
Gayarré and Claiborne.   [3] Marshall, II., p. 279.

stalks instead.   The officers were elected by the men
and when there was no immediate danger of war
they were chosen purely for their social qualities.
For a few years after the close of the long Indian
struggle there were here and there officers who had
seen actual service and who knew the rudiments of
drill; but in the days of peace the men who had
taken part in Indian fighting cared but little to
attend the musters, and left them more and more to
be turned into mere scenes of horseplay.

The frontier people of the second generation in
the West thus had no military training whatever,
Lack of   and though they possessed a skeleton
Military   militia organization, they derived no benefit
Training.   from it, because their officers were worthless, and the men had no idea of practising self-restraint or of obeying orders longer than they saw
fit.   The frontiersmen were personally brave, but
their courage was entirely untrained, and being
unsupported by discipline, they were sure to be
disheartened at a repulse, to be distrustful of themselves and their leaders, and to be unwilling to per-
severe in the face of danger and discouragement.
They were hardy, and physically strong, and they
were good marksmen ; but here the list of their soldierly qualities was exhausted.   They had to be put
through a severe course of training by some man
like Jackson before they became fit to contend on
equal terms with regulars in the open or with
Indians in the woods.   Their utter lack of discipline
was decisive against them at first in any contest with
regulars.   In warfare with the Indians there were a

very few of their number, men of exceptional qualities as woodsmen, who could hold their own ; but the average frontiersman, though he did a good deal of hunting and possessed much knowledge of woodcraft, was primarily a tiller of the soil and a feller of trees, and he was necessarily at a disadvantage when pitted against an antagonist whose entire life was passed in woodland chase and woodland warfare. These facts must all be remembered if we wish to get an intelligent explanation of the utter failure of the frontiersmen when, in 1812, they were again pitted against the British and the forest tribes. They must also be taken into account when we seek to explain why it was possible but a little later to develop out of the frontiersmen fighting armies which under competent generals could overmatch the red coat and the Indian alike.

The extreme individualism of the frontier, which found expression for good and for evil both in its governmental system in time of peace and in its military system in time of war, was also shown in religious matters. In 1799 and 1800 a great revival of religion swept over the West. Up to that time the Presbyterian had been the leading creed beyond the mountains. There were a few Episcopalians here and there, and there were Lutherans, Catholics, and adherents of the Reformed Dutch and German churches ; but, aside from the Presbyterians, the Methodists and Baptists were the only sects powerfully represented. The great revival of 1799 was mainly carried on by Methodists and Baptists, and under their guidance the Methodist and Baptist churches at once sprang to the front and became the most important religious forces in the frontier communities.[1]   The Presbyterian church remained the most prominent as regards the wealth and social standing of its adherents, but the typical frontiersman who professed religion at all became either a Methodist or a Baptist, adopting a creed which was intensely democratic and individualistic, which made nothing of social distinctions, which distrusted educated preachers, and worked under a republican form of ecclesiastical government.

The great revival was accompanied by scenes of intense excitement.   Under the conditions of a vast

Camp-Meetings.   wooded wilderness and a scanty population the camp-meeting was evolved as the typical religious festival.   To the great camp-meetings the frontiersmen flocked from far and near, on foot, on horseback, and in wagons.   Every morning at daylight the multitude was summoned to prayer by sound of trumpet.   No preacher or exhorter was suffered to speak unless he had the power of stirring the souls of his hearers.   The preaching, the praying, and the singing went on without intermission, and under the tremendous emotional stress whole communities became fervent professors of religion.   Many of the scenes at these camp-meetings were very distasteful to men whose religion was not emotional and who shrank from the fury of excitement into which the great masses were thrown, for under the strain many indi-

[1] McFerrin's " History of Methodism in Tennessee," 338, etc.; Spencer's " History of Kentucky Baptists," 69, etc.

viduals literally became like men possessed, whether of good or of evil spirits, falling into ecstasies of joy or agony, dancing, shouting, jumping, fainting, while there were widespread and curious manifestations of a hysterical character, both among the believers and among the scoffers; but though this might seem distasteful to an observer of education and self-restraint, it thrilled the heart of the rude and simple backwoodsman and reached him as he could not possibly have been reached in any other manner. Often the preachers of the different denominations worked in hearty unison; but often they were sundered by bitter jealousy and distrust. The fiery zeal of the Methodists made them the leaders; and in their war on the forces of evil they at times showed a tendency to include all non-methodists—whether Baptists, Lutherans, Catholics, or infidels—in a common damnation. Of course, as always in such a movement, many even of the earnest leaders at times confounded the essential and the non-essential, and railed as bitterly against dancing as against drunkenness and lewdness, or anathematized the wearing of jewelry as fiercely as the commission of crime.[1] More than one hearty, rugged old preacher, who did stalwart service for decency and morality, hated Calvinism as heartily as Catholicism, and yet yielded to no Puritan in his austere condemnation of amusement and luxury.

Often men backslid, and to a period of intense emotional religion succeeded one of utter unbelief and of reversion to the worst practices which had been given up. Nevertheless, Good Accomplished.

---

[1] Autobiography of Peter Cartwright, the Backwoods Preacher.

on the whole there was an immense gain for good. The people received a new light, and were given a sense of moral responsibility such as they had not previously possessed. Much of the work was done badly or was afterwards undone, but very much was really accomplished. The whole West owes an immense debt to the hard-working frontier preachers, sometimes Presbyterian, generally Methodist or Baptist, who so gladly gave their lives to their labors and who struggled with such fiery zeal for the moral wellbeing of the communities to which they penetrated. Wherever there was a group of log cabins, thither some Methodist circuit-rider made his way or there some Baptist preacher took up his abode. Their prejudices and narrow dislikes, their raw vanity and sullen distrust of all who were better schooled than they, count for little when weighed against their intense earnestness and heroic self-sacrifice. They proved their truth by their endeavor. They yielded scores of martyrs, nameless and unknown men who perished at the hands of the savages, or by sickness or in flood or storm. They had to face no little danger from the white inhabitants themselves. In some of the communities most of the men might heartily support them, but in others, where the vicious and lawless elements were in control, they were in constant danger of mobs. The Godless and lawless people hated the religious with a bitter hatred, and gathered in great crowds to break up their meetings. On the other hand, those who had experienced religion were no believers in the doctrine of non-

Trials of the Frontier Preachers.

resistance. At the core, they were thoroughly healthy men, and they fought as valiantly against the powers of evil in matters physical as in matters moral. Some of the successful frontier preachers were men of weak frame, whose intensity of conviction and fervor of religious belief supplied the lack of bodily powers; but as a rule the preacher who did most was a stalwart man, as strong in body as in faith. One of the continually recurring incidents in the biographies of the famous frontier preachers is that of some particularly hardened sinner who was never converted until, tempted to assault the preacher of the Word, he was soundly thrashed by the latter, and his eyes thereby rudely opened through his sense of physical shortcoming to an appreciation of his moral iniquity.

Throughout these years, as the frontiersmen pressed into the West, they continued to fret and strain against the Spanish boundaries. There was no temptation to them to take possession of Canada. The lands south of the Lakes were more fertile than those north of the Lakes, and the climate *The Frontiersmen Threaten the Spanish Regions.* was better. The few American settlers who did care to go into Canada found people speaking their own tongue, and with much the same ways of life; so that they readily assimilated with them, as they could not assimilate with the French and Spanish creoles. Canada lay north, and the tendency of the backwoodsman was to thrust west; among the Southern backwoodsmen, the tendency was south and southwest. The Mississippi formed no natural barrier whatever. Boone, when he moved into Missouri, was but a forerunner among the pioneers; many others followed him. He himself became an official under the Spanish Government, and received a grant of lands. Of the other frontiersmen who went into the Spanish territory, some, like Boone, continued to live as hunters and backwoods farmers.[1] Others settled in St. Louis, or some other of the little creole towns, and joined the parties of French traders who ascended the Missouri and the Mississippi to barter paint, beads, powder, and blankets for the furs of the Indians.

The Spanish authorities were greatly alarmed at the incoming of the American settlers. Gayoso de **Uneasiness** Lemos had succeeded Carondelet as Gov-**of the** ernor, and he issued to the commandants **Spaniards.** of the different posts throughout the colonies a series of orders in reference to the terms on which land grants were to be given to immigrants; he particularly emphasized the fact that liberty of conscience was not to be extended beyond the first generation, and that the children of the immigrant would either have to become Catholics or else be expelled, and that this should be explained to settlers who did not profess the Catholic faith. He **Their** ordered, moreover, that no preacher of any **Religious** religion but the Catholic should be allowed **Intoler-** to come into the provinces.[2] The Bishop of **ance.** Louisiana complained bitterly of the American immigration and of the measure of religious tol-

---

[1] American State Papers, Public Lands, II., pp. 10, 872.
[2] Gayarré, III., p. 387.

eration accorded the settlers, which, he said, had introduced into the colony a gang of adventurers who acknowledged no religion. He stated that the Americans had scattered themselves over the country almost as far as Texas and corrupted the Indians and creoles by the example of their own restless and ambitious temper; for they came from among people who were in the habit of saying to their stalwart boys, "You will go to Mexico." Already the frontiersmen had penetrated even into New Mexico from the district round the mouth of the Missouri, in which they had become very numerous; and the Bishop earnestly advised that the places where the Americans were allowed to settle should be rigidly restricted.[1]

When the Spaniards held such views it was absolutely inevitable that a conflict should come. Whether the frontiersman did or did not A Conflict possess deep religious convictions, he was Inevitable. absolutely certain to refuse to be coerced into becoming a Catholic; and his children were sure to fight as soon as they were given the choice of changing their faith or abandoning their country. The minute that the American settlers were sufficiently numerous to stand a chance of success in the conflict it was certain that they would try to throw off the yoke of the fanatical and corrupt Spanish Government. As early as 1801 bands of armed Americans had penetrated here and there into the Spanish provinces in defiance of the commands of the authorities, and were striving to set up little bandit governments of their own.[2]

[1] *Do.*, p. 408.   [2] *Do.*, p. 447.

The frontiersmen possessed every advantage of position, of numbers, and of temper. In any contest **Advantages of the Frontiers- men.** that might arise with Spain they were sure to take possession at once of all of what was then called Upper Louisiana. The immediate object of interest to most of them was the commerce of the Mississippi River and the possession of New Orleans; but this was only part of what they wished, and were certain to get, for they demanded all the Spanish territory that lay across the line of their westward march. At the beginning of the nineteenth century the settlers on the Western waters recognized in Spain their natural enemy, because she was the power who held the mouth and the west bank of the Mississippi. They would have transferred their hostility to any other power which fell heir to her possessions, for these possessions they were bound one day to make their own.

A thin range of settlements extended from the shores of Lake Erie on the north to the boundary of **Predomi- nance of the Middle West.** Florida on the south; and there were out- posts here and there beyond this range, as at Fort Dearborn, on the site of what is now Chicago; but the only fairly well- settled regions were in Kentucky and Tennessee. These two States were the oldest, and long remained the most populous and influential, communities in the West. They shared qualities both of the Northerners and of the Southerners, and they gave the tone to the thought and the life in the settle- ments north of them no less than the settlements south of them. This fact of itself tended to make the West homogeneous and to keep it a unit with a peculiar character of its own, neither Northern nor Southern in political and social tendency. It was the middle West which was first settled, and the middle West stamped its peculiar characteristics on all the growing communities beyond the Alleghanies. Inasmuch as west of the mountains the Northern communities were less distinctively Northern and the Southern communities less distinctively Southern than was the case with the Eastern States on the seaboard, it followed naturally that, considered with reference to other sections of the Union, the West formed a unit, possessing marked characteristics of its own. A distinctive type of character was developed west of the Alleghanies, and for the first generation the typical representatives of this Western type were to be found in Kentucky and Tennessee.

The settlement of the Northwest had been begun under influences which in the end were to separate it radically from the Southwest. It was set- The tled under Governmental supervision, and Northwest. because of and in accordance with Governmental action ; and it was destined ultimately to receive the great mass of its immigrants from the Northeast; but as yet these two influences had not become strong enough to sunder the frontiersmen north of the Ohio by any sharp line from those south of the Ohio. The settlers on the Western waters were substantially the same in character North and South.

In sum, the western frontier folk, at the beginning of the nineteenth century, possessed in common
marked and peculiar characteristics, which
the people of the rest of the country shared
to a much less extent. They were backwoods farmers, each man preferring to live
alone on his own freehold, which he himself tilled
and from which he himself had cleared the timber.
The towns were few and small; the people were
poor, and often ignorant, but hardy in body and in
temper. They joined hospitality to strangers with
suspicion of them. They were essentially warlike
in spirit, and yet utterly unmilitary in all their
training and habits of thought. They prized beyond measure their individual liberty and their
collective freedom, and were so jealous of governmental control that they often, to their own great
harm, fatally weakened the very authorities whom
they chose to act over them. The peculiar circumstances of their lives forced them often to act in
advance of action by the law, and this bred a lawlessness in certain matters which their children
inherited for generations; yet they knew and
appreciated the need of obedience to the law, and
they thoroughly respected the law.

The Westerners Formed One People.

The separatist agitations had largely died out.
In 1798 and 1799 Kentucky divided with Virginia
the leadership of the attack on the Alien
and Sedition laws; but her extreme feelings were not shared by the other Westerners, and she acted not as a representative
of the West, but on a footing of equality with Vir-

Decadence of Separatist Feeling.

ginia. Tennessee sympathized as little with the nullification movement of these two States at this time as she sympathized with South Carolina in her nullification movement a generation later. With the election of Jefferson the dominant political party in the West became in sympathy with the party in control of the nation, and the West became stoutly loyal to the National Government.

The West had thus achieved a greater degree of political solidarity, both as within itself and with the nation as a whole, than ever before. Its wishes were more powerful with the East. The pioneers stood for an extreme Americanism, in social, political, and religious matters alike. The trend of American thought was toward them, not away from them. More than ever before, the Westerners were able to make their demands felt at home, and to make their force felt in the event of a struggle with a foreign power.

Importance of the West.

CHAPTER VI.

THE PURCHASE OF LOUISIANA; AND BURR'S CONSPIRACY, 1803–1807.

A GREAT and growing race may acquire vast stretches of scantily peopled territory in any one of several ways. Often the statesman, no less than the soldier, plays an all-important part in winning the new land; nevertheless, it is usually true that the diplomatists who by treaty ratify the acquisition usurp a prominence in history to which they are in no way entitled by the real worth of their labors.

The territory may be gained by the armed forces of the nation, and retained by treaty. It was in this Ways in way that England won the Cape of Good which Hope from Holland; it was in this way Territorial that the United States won New Mexico. Expansion may Take Such a conquest is due, not to the indi-Place. vidual action of members of the winning race, but to the nation as a whole, acting through her soldiers and statesmen. It was the English Navy which conquered the Cape of Good Hope for England; it was the English diplomats that secured its retention. So it was the American Army which added New Mexico to the United States; and its retention was due to the will of the politicians who had set that army in motion. In neither case was there any previous settlement of moment by the conquerors in the conquered territory. In neither case was there much direct pressure by the people of the conquering races upon the soil which was won for them by their soldiers and statesmen. The acquisition of the territory must be set down to the credit of these soldiers and statesmen, representing the nation in its collective capacity ; though in the case of New Mexico there would of course ultimately have been a direct pressure of rifle-bearing settlers upon the people of the ranches and the mud-walled towns.

In such cases it is the government itself, rather than any individual or aggregate of individuals, which wins the new land for the race. Diplomatic When it is won without appeal to arms, Victories. the credit, which would otherwise be divided between soldiers and statesmen, of course accrues solely to the latter. Alaska, for instance, was acquired by mere diplomacy. No American settlers were thronging into Alaska. The desire to acquire it among the people at large was vague, and was fanned into sluggish activity only by the genius of the far-seeing statesmen who purchased it. The credit of such an acquisition really does belong to the men who secured the adoption of the treaty by which it was acquired. The honor of adding Alaska to the national domain belongs to the statesmen who at the time controlled the Washington Government. They were not figure-heads in the transaction. They were the vital, moving forces.

Just the contrary is true of cases like that of the

conquest of Texas. The Government of the United
States had nothing to do with winning
Victories with Which Diplomats Have no Concern. Texas for the English-speaking people of
North America. The American frontiers-
men won Texas for themselves, unaided
either by the statesmen who controlled the
politics of the Republic, or by the soldiers
who took their orders from Washington.

In yet other cases the action is more mixed.
Statesmen and diplomats have some share in shap-
Victories of Mixed Nature. ing the conditions under which a country
is finally taken; in the eye of history they
often usurp much more than their proper
share; but in reality they are able to bring matters
to a conclusion only because adventurous settlers, in
defiance or disregard of governmental action, have
pressed forward into the longed-for land. In such
cases the function of the diplomats is one of some
importance, because they lay down the conditions
under which the land is taken; but the vital question as to whether the land shall be taken at all,
upon no matter what terms, is answered not by the
diplomats, but by the people themselves.

It was in this way that the Northwest was won
from the British, and the boundaries of the Southwest established by treaty with the Spaniards.
Adams, Jay, and Pinckney deserve much credit for
the way they conducted their several negotiations;
but there would have been nothing for them to
negotiate about had not the settlers already thronged
into the disputed territories or strenuously pressed
forward against their boundaries.

So it was with the acquisition of Louisiana. Jefferson, Livingston, and their fellow-statesmen and diplomats concluded the treaty which determined the manner in which it came into our possession; but they did not really have much to do with fixing the terms even of this treaty; and the part which they played in the acquisition of Louisiana *Louisiana Really Acquired by the Western Settlers.* in no way resembles, even remotely, the part which was played by Seward, for instance, in acquiring Alaska. If it had not been for Seward, and the political leaders who thought as he did, Alaska might never have been acquired at all; but the Americans would have won Louisiana in any event, even if the treaty of Livingston and Monroe had not been signed. The real history of the acquisition must tell of the great westward movement begun in 1769, and not merely of the feeble diplomacy of Jefferson's administration. In 1802 American settlers were already clustered here and there on the eastern fringe of the vast region which then went by the name of Louisiana. All the stalwart freemen who had made their rude clearings, and built their rude towns, on the hither side of the mighty Mississippi, were straining with eager desire against the forces which withheld them from seizing with strong hand the coveted province. They did not themselves know, and far less did the public men of the day realize, the full import and meaning of the conquest upon which they were about to enter. For the moment the navigation of the mouth of the Mississippi seemed to them of the first importance.

Even the frontiersmen themselves put second to this the right to people the vast continent which lay between the Pacific and the Mississippi. The statesmen at Washington viewed this last proposition with positive alarm, and cared only to acquire New Orleans. The winning of Louisiana was due to no one man, and least of all to any statesman or set of statesmen. It followed inevitably upon the great westward thrust of the settler-folk; a thrust which was delivered blindly, but which no rival race could parry, until it was stopped by the ocean itself.

Louisiana was added to the United States because the hardy backwoods settlers had swarmed into the Pressure valleys of the Tennessee, the Cumberland, of the Back- and the Ohio by hundreds of thousands; woodsmen and had already begun to build their raw on the Spanish hamlets on the banks of the Mississippi, Dominions. and to cover its waters with their flat-bottomed craft. Restless, adventurous, hardy, they looked eagerly across the Mississippi to the fertile solitudes where the Spaniard was the nominal, and the Indian the real, master; and with a more immediate longing they fiercely coveted the creole province at the mouth of the river.

The Mississippi formed no barrier whatsoever to the march of the backwoodsmen. It could be crossed at any point; and the same rapid current which made it a matter of extreme difficulty for any power at the mouth of the stream to send reinforcements up against the current would have greatly facilitated the movements of the Ohio, Kentucky,

and Tennessee levies down-stream to attack the
Spanish provinces. In the days of sails and oars a
great river with rapid current might vitally affect
military operations if these depended upon sending
flotillas up or down stream. But such a river has
never proved a serious barrier against a vigorous and
aggressive race, where it lies between two peoples,
so that the aggressors have merely to cross it. It
offers no such shield as is afforded by a high mountain range. The Mississippi served as a convenient
line of demarkation between the Americans and the
Spaniards; but it offered no protection whatever to
the Spaniards against the Americans.

Therefore the frontiersmen found nothing serious
to bar their farther march westward; the diminutive
Spanish garrisons in the little creole towns near the
Missouri were far less capable of effective resistance
than were most of the Indian tribes whom the Americans were brushing out of their path. Towards the
South the situation was different. The Floridas were
shielded by the great Indian confederacies of the
Creeks and Choctaws, whose strength was as yet unbroken. What was much more important, the mouth
of the Mississippi was commanded by the Importance
important seaport of New Orleans, which of New
was accessible to fleets, which could readily Orleans.
be garrisoned by water, and which was the capital
of a region that by backwoods standards passed for
well settled. New Orleans by its position was absolute master of the foreign trade of the Mississippi
valley; and any power in command of the seas could
easily keep it strongly garrisoned. The vast region

that was then known as Upper Louisiana—the territory stretching from the Mississippi to the Pacific—
was owned by the Spaniards, but only in shadowy
fashion, and could not have been held by any European power against the sturdy westward pressure of
the rifle-bearing settlers. But New Orleans and its
neighborhood were held even by the Spaniards in
good earnest; while a stronger power, once in possession, could with difficulty have been dislodged.

It naturally followed that for the moment the
attention of the backwoodsmen was directed much

Desire of the Settlers for it. more to New Orleans than to the trans-
Mississippi territory. A few wilderness
lovers like Boone, a few reckless adventurers of the type of Philip Nolan, were settling
around and beyond the creole towns of the North,
or were endeavoring to found small buccaneering
colonies in dangerous proximity to the Spanish com-
manderies in the Southwest. But the bulk of the
Western settlers as yet found all the vacant territory
they wished east of the Mississippi. What they
needed at the moment was, not more wild land, but
an outlet for the products yielded by the land they
already possessed. The vital importance to the Westerners of the free navigation of the Mississippi has
already been shown. Suffice it to say that the control of the mouth of the great Father of Waters was
of direct personal consequence to almost every tree
feller, every backwoods farmer, every land owner,
every townsman, who dwelt beyond the Alleghanies.
These men did not worry much over the fact that
the country on the farther bank of the Mississippi

was still under the Spanish Flag. For the moment
they did not need it, and when they did, they knew
they could take it without the smallest difficulty.
But the ownership of the mouth of the Mississippi
was a matter of immediate importance ; and though
none of the settlers doubted that it would ultimately
be theirs, it was yet a matter of much consequence
to them to get possession of it as quickly as possible,
and with as little trouble as possible, rather than to
see it held, perhaps for years, by a powerful hostile
nation, and then to see it acquired only at the cost
of bloody, and perchance checkered, warfare.

This was the attitude of the backwoods people as
with sinewy, strenuous shoulder they pressed against
the Spanish boundaries. The Spanish at- Terror of
titude on the other hand was one of appre- the Span-
hension so intense that it overcame even iards.
anger against the American nation. For mere diplomacy, the Spaniards cared little or nothing ; but they
feared the Westerners. Their surrender of Louisiana was due primarily to the steady pushing and
crowding of the frontiersmen, and the continuous
growth of the Western commonwealths. In spite
of Pinckney's treaty the Spaniards did not leave
Natchez until fairly drowned out by the American
settlers and soldiers. They now felt the same pressure upon them in New Orleans ; it was growing
steadily and was fast becoming intolerable. Year
by year, almost month by month, they saw the numbers of their foes increase, and saw them settle more
and more thickly in places from which it would be
easy to strike New Orleans. Year by year the offen-

sive power of the Americans increased in more than arithmetical ratio as against Louisiana.

The more reckless and lawless adventurers from time to time pushed southwest, even toward the borders of Texas and New Mexico, and strove to form little settlements, keeping the Spanish Governors and Intendants in a constant fume of anxiety. One of these settlements was founded by Philip Nolan, a man whom rumor had connected with Wilkinson's intrigues, and who, like many another lawless trader of the day, was always dreaming of empires to be carved from, or wealth to be won in, the golden Spanish realms. In the fall of 1800, he pushed beyond the Mississippi with a score or so of companions, and settled on the Brazos. The party built pens or corrals, and began to catch wild horses, for the neighborhood swarmed not only with game but with immense droves of mustangs. The handsomest animals they kept and trained, letting the others loose again. The following March these tamers of wild horses were suddenly set upon by a body of Spaniards, three hundred strong, with one field-piece. The assailants made their attack at daybreak, slew Nolan, and captured his comrades, who for many years afterwards lived as prisoners in the Mexican towns.[1] The menace of such buccaneering movements kept the Spaniards alive to the imminent danger of the general American attack which they heralded.

Spain watched her boundaries with the most

Incursions of American Adventurers.

[1] Pike's letter, July 22, 1807, in Natchez *Herald;* in Col. Durrett's collection; see Coue's edition of Pike's "Expedition," LII.; also Gayarré, III., 447.

jealous care.   Her colonial system was evil in its
suspicious exclusiveness towards strangers ;   **Spain's**
and her religious system was marked by an   **Colonial**
intolerance still almost as fierce as in the   **System.**
days of Torquemada. The Holy Inquisition was a
recognized feature of Spanish political life ; and
the rulers of the Spanish-American colonies put the
stranger and the heretic under a common ban.   The
reports of the Spanish ecclesiastics of Louisiana
dwelt continually upon the dangers with which
the oncoming of the backwoodsmen threatened the
Church no less than the State.[1]   All the men in
power, civil, military, and religious alike, showed
towards strangers, and especially towards American
strangers, a spirit which was doubly unwise ; for by
their jealousy they created the impression that the
lands they so carefully guarded must hold treasures
of great price ; and by their severity they created an
anger which when fully aroused they could not well
quell. The frontiersmen, as they tried to peer into
the Spanish dominions, were lured on by the attraction they felt for what was hidden and forbidden ;
and there was enough danger in the path to madden
them, while there was no exhibition of a strength
sufficient to cow them.

The Spanish rulers realized fully that they were
too weak effectively to cope with the Ameri-   **Spain**
cans, and as the pressure upon them grew   **Wishes a**
ever heavier and more menacing they   **Barrier**
    against
began to fear not only for Louisiana but   **American**
also for Mexico.   They clung tenacious-   **Advance·**
ly to all their possessions ; but they were willing

---

[1] Report of Bishop Peñalvert, Nov. 1, 1795, Gayarré.

to sacrifice a part, if by so doing they could erect a barrier for the defence of the remainder. Such a chance was now seemingly offered them by France.

At the beginning of the century Napoleon was First Consul; and the France over which he ruled was already the mightiest nation in Europe, and yet had not reached the zenith of her power. It was at this time that the French influence over Spain was most complete. Both the Spanish King and the Spanish people were dazzled and awed by the splendor of Napoleon's victories. Napoleon's magnificent and wayward genius was always striving after more than merely European empire. As throne after throne went down before him he planned conquests which should include the interminable wastes of snowy Russia, and the sea-girt fields of England; and he always dreamed of yet vaster, more shadowy triumphs, won in the realms lying eastward of the Mediterranean, or among the islands and along the coasts of the Spanish Main. In 1800 his dream of Eastern conquest was over, but his lofty ambition was planning for France the re-establishment in America of that colonial empire which a generation before had been wrested from her by England.

Napoleon's Dreams of Empire.

The need of the Spaniards seemed to Napoleon his opportunity. By the bribe of a petty Italian principality he persuaded the Bourbon King of Spain to cede Louisiana to the French, at the treaty of San Ildefonso, concluded in October, 1800. The cession was agreed to by the Spaniards on the express

The Treaty of San Ildefonso.

pledge that the territory should not be transferred to any other power; and chiefly for the purpose of erecting a barrier which might stay the American advance, and protect the rest of the Spanish possessions.

Every effort was made to keep the cession from being made public, and owing to various political complications it was not consummated for a couple of years; but meanwhile it was impossible to prevent rumors from going abroad, and the mere hint of such a project was enough to throw the West into a fever of excitement. Moreover, at this moment, before the treaty between France and Spain had been consummated, Morales, the Intendant of New Orleans, deliberately threw down the gage of battle to the Westerners.[1] On October 16, 1802, he proclaimed that the Americans had forfeited their right of deposit in New Orleans. By Pinckney's treaty this right had been granted for three years, with the stipulation that it should then be extended for a longer period, and that if the Spaniards chose to revoke the permit so far as New Orleans was concerned, they should make some other spot on the river a port of free entry. The Americans had taken for granted that the privilege when once conferred would never be withdrawn; but Morales, under pretence that the Americans had slept on their rights by failing to discover some other spot as a treaty port, declared that the right of deposit had lapsed, and would not be renewed. The Governor, Salcedo—who had suc-

The Right of Deposit Annulled.

[1] Gayarré, III., 456.

ceeded Gayoso, when the latter died of yellow fever, complicated by a drinking-bout with Wilkinson— was not in sympathy with the movement; but this mattered little. Under the cumbrous Spanish colonial system, the Governor, though he disapproved of the actions of the Intendant, could not reverse them, and Morales paid no heed to the angry protests of the Spanish Minister at Washington, who saw that the Americans were certain in the end to fight rather than to lose the only outlet for the commerce of the West.[1] It seems probable that the Intendant's action was due to the fact that he deemed the days of Spanish dominion numbered, and, in his jealousy of the Americans, wished to place the new French authorities in the strongest possible position; but the act was not done with the knowledge of France.

Of this, however, the Westerners were ignorant. They felt sure that any alteration in policy so fatal to their interests must be merely a fore-shadowing of the course the French intended thereafter to follow. They believed that their worst fears were justified. Kentucky and Tennessee clamored for instant action, and Claiborne offered to raise in the Mississippi territory alone a force of volunteer riflemen sufficient to seize New Orleans before its transfer into French hands could be effected.

Jefferson was President, and Madison Secretary of

---

[1] Gayarré, III., 576. The King of Spain, at the instigation of Godoy, disapproved the order of Morales, but so late that the news of the disapproval reached Louisiana only as the French were about to take possession. However, the reversal of the order rendered the course of the further negotiations easier.

State. Both were men of high and fine qualities who rendered, at one time or another, real Jefferson and great service to the country. Jeffer- Forced into son in particular played in our political *Action.* life a part of immense importance. But the country has never had two statesmen less capable of uphold- ing the honor and dignity of the nation, or even of preserving its material well-being, when menaced by foreign foes. They were peaceful men, quite unfitted to grapple with an enemy who expressed himself through deeds rather than words. When stunned by the din of arms they showed themselves utterly inefficient rulers.

It was these two timid, well-meaning statesmen who now found themselves pitted against Napoleon, and Napoleon's Minister, Talleyrand; against the greatest warrior and lawgiver, and against one of the greatest diplomats, of modern times; against two men, moreover, whose sodden lack of conscience was but heightened by the contrast with their brilliant genius and lofty force of character; two men who were unable to so much as appreciate that there was shame in the practice of venality, dishonesty, mendacity, cruelty, and treachery.

Jefferson was the least warlike of presidents, and he loved the French with a servile devotion. But his party was strongest in precisely those parts of the country where the mouth of the Mississippi was held to be of right the property of the United States; and the pressure of public opinion was too strong for Jefferson to think of resisting it. The South and the West were a unit in demanding that France should not be allowed to establish herself on the lower Mississippi. Jefferson was forced to tell his French friends that if their nation persisted in its purpose America would be obliged to marry itself to the navy and army of England. Even he could see that for the French to take Louisiana meant war with the United States sooner or later; and as above all things else he wished peace, he made every effort to secure the coveted territory by purchase.

Chancellor Robert R. Livingston of New York represented American interests in Paris; but at the

very close of the negotiation he was suc-
Beginning of Negotia- ceeded by Monroe, whom Jefferson sent
tions with over as a special envoy. The course of the
France. negotiations was at first most baffling to the Americans.[1] Talleyrand lied with such unmoved calm that it was impossible to put the least weight upon anything he said; moreover, the Americans soon found that Napoleon was the sole and absolute master, so that it was of no use attempting to influence any of his subordinates, save in so far as these subordinates might in their turn influence him. For some time it appeared that Napoleon was bent upon occupying Louisiana in force and using it as a basis for the rebuilding of the French colonial power. The time seemed ripe for such a project. After a decade of war with all the rest of Europe, France in 1802 concluded the Peace of Amiens,

---

[1] In Henry Adams' "History of the United States," the account of the diplomatic negotiations at this period, between France, Spain, and the United States, is the most brilliant piece of diplomatic history, so far as the doings of the diplomats themselves are concerned, that can be put to the credit of any American writer.

which left her absolutely free to do as she liked in the New World. Napoleon thoroughly despised a republic, and especially a republic without an army or navy. After the Peace of Amiens he began to treat the Americans with contemptuous disregard; and he planned to throw into Louisiana one of his generals with a force of veteran troops sufficient to hold the country against any attack.

His hopes were in reality chimerical. At the moment France was at peace with her European foes, and could send her ships of war and her transports across the ocean without fear of the British navy. It would there-fore have been possible for Napoleon with-out molestation to throw a large body of French soldiers into New Orleans. Had there been no European war such an army might have held New Orleans for some years against American attack, and might even have captured one or two of the American posts on the Mississippi, such as Natchez; but the instant it had landed in New Orleans the entire American people would have accepted France as their deadliest enemy, and all American foreign policy would have been determined by the one consideration of ousting the French from the mouth of the Mississippi. To the United States, France was by no means as formidable as Great Britain, because of her inferiority as a naval power. Even if unsup-ported by any outside alliance the Americans would doubtless in the end have driven a French army from New Orleans, though very probably at the cost of one or two preliminary rebuffs. The West was

stanch in support of Jefferson and Madison; but in
time of stress it was sure to develop leaders of more
congenial temper, exactly as it actually did develop
Andrew Jackson a few years later. At this very
time the French failed to conquer the negro republic
which Toussaint Louverture had founded in Hayti.
What they thus failed to accomplish in one island,
against insurgent negroes, it was folly to think
they could accomplish on the American continent,
against the power of the American people. This
struggle with the revolutionary slaves in Hayti
hindered Napoleon from immediately throwing an
army into Louisiana; but it did more, for it helped
to teach him the folly of trying to carry out such a
plan at all.

A very able and faithful French agent in the meanwhile sent a report to Napoleon plainly pointing
Report of   out the impossibility of permanently hold-
Pontalba.   ing Louisana against the Americans. He
showed that on the Western waters alone it would
be possible to gather armies amounting in the aggregate to twenty or thirty thousand men, all of them
inflamed with the eager desire to take New Orleans.[1]
The Mississippi ran so as to facilitate the movement
of any expedition against New Orleans, while it
offered formidable obstacles to counter-expeditions
from New Orleans against the American commonwealths lying farther up stream. An expeditionary
force sent from the mouth of the Mississippi, whether

[1] Pontalba's Memoir. He hoped that Louisiana might, in certain con-
tingencies, be preserved for the French, but he insisted that it could only be
by keeping peace with the American settlers, and by bringing about an
immense increase of population in the province.

to assail the towns and settlements along the Ohio, or to defend the creole villages near the Missouri, could at the utmost hope for only transient success, while its ultimate failure was certain. On the other hand, a backwoods army could move down stream with comparative ease ; and even though such an expedition were defeated, it was certain that the attempt would be repeated again and again, until by degrees the mob of hardy riflemen changed into a veteran army, and brought forth some general like " Old Hickory," able to lead to victory.

The most intelligent French agents on the ground saw this. Some of Napoleon's Ministers were equally far-sighted. One of them, Barbé Marbois, *Views of* represented to him in the strongest terms *Barbé* the hopelessness of the undertaking on *Marbois.* which he proposed to embark. He pointed out that the United States was sure to go to war with France if France took New Orleans, and that in the end such a war could only result in victory for the Americans.

We can now readily see that this victory was certain to come even had the Americans been left without allies. France could never have defended the vast region known as Upper Louisiana, and sooner or later New Orleans itself would have fallen, though it may well be only after humiliating defeats for the Americans and much expenditure of life and treasure. But as things actually were the Americans would have had plenty of powerful allies. The Peace of Ameins lasted but a couple of years before England again went to war. Napoleon knew, and the American statesmen knew, that the British intended to attack New Orleans upon the outbreak of hostilities, if it were in French hands. In such event Louisiana would have soon fallen; for any French force stationed there would have found its reinforcements cut off by the English navy, and would have dwindled away until unable to offer resistance.

Nevertheless, European wars, and the schemes and fancies of European statesmen, could determine merely the conditions under which the catastrophe was to take place, but not the catastrophe itself. The fate of Louisiana was already fixed. It was not the diplomats who decided its destiny, but the settlers of the Western states. The growth of the teeming folk who had crossed the Alleghanies and were building their rude, vigorous commonwealths in the northeastern portion of the Mississippi basin, decided the destiny of all the lands that were drained by that mighty river. The steady westward movement of the Americans was the all-important factor in determining the ultimate ownership of New Orleans. Livingston, the American minister, saw plainly the inevitable outcome of the struggle. He expressed his wonder that other Americans should be uneasy in the matter, saying that for his part it seemed as clear as day that no matter what trouble might temporarily be caused, in the end Louisiana was certain to fall into the grasp of the United States.[1]

Louisiana's Destiny Really Fixed by the Backwoodsmen.

[1] Livingston to Madison, Sept. 1, 1802. Later Livingston himself became uneasy, fearing lest Napoleon's wilfulness might plunge him into an undertaking which, though certain to end disastrously to the French, might meanwhile cause great trouble to the Americans.

There were many Americans and many Frenchmen of note who were less clear-sighted. Livingston encountered rebuff after rebuff, and delay after delay. Talleyrand met him with his usual front of impenetrable duplicity. He calmly denied everything connected with the cession of Louisiana until even the details became public property, and then admitted them with unblushing equanimity. His delays were so tantalizing that they might well have revived unpleasant memories of the famous X. Y. Z. negotiations, in which he tried in vain to extort bribe-money from the American negotiators [1]; but Livingston, and those he represented, soon realized that it was Napoleon himself who alone deserved serious consideration. Through Napoleon's character, and helping to make it great, there ran an imaginative vein which at times bordered on the fantastic; and this joined with his imperious self-will, brutality, and energy to make him eager to embark on a scheme which, when he had thought it over in cold blood, he was equally eager to abandon. For some time he seemed obstinately bent on taking possession of Louisiana, heedless of the attitude which this might cause the Americans to assume. He designated as commander of his army of occupation, Victor, a general as capable and brave as he was insolent, who took no pains to conceal from the American representatives his intention to treat their people with a high hand.

Tedious Course of the Negotiations.

[1] Jefferson was guilty of much weak and undignified conduct during these negotiations, but of nothing weaker and more petty than his attempt to flatter Talleyrand by pretending that the Americans disbelieved his admitted venality, and were indignant with those who had exposed it. See Adams.

Jefferson took various means, official and un-official, of impressing upon Napoleon the strength of the feeling in the United States over the matter ; and his utterances came as near menace as his pacific nature would permit. To the great French Conqueror however, accustomed to violence and to the strife of giants, Jefferson's somewhat vacillating attitude did not seem impressive ; and the one course which would have impressed Na-poleon was not followed by the American President. Jefferson refused to countenance any proposal to take prompt possession of Louisiana by force or to assemble an army which could act with immediate vigor in time of need ; and as he was the idol of the Southwesterners, who were bitterly anti-federalist in sympathy, he was able to prevent any violent action on their part until events rendered this violence un-necessary. At the same time, Jefferson himself never for a moment ceased to feel the strong pres-sure of Southern and Western public sentiment; and so he continued resolute in his purpose to obtain Louisiana.

It was no argument of Jefferson's or of the Ameri-can diplomats, but the inevitable trend of events that finally brought about a change in Napoleon's mind. The army he sent to Hayti wasted away by disease and in com-bat with the blacks, and thereby not only diminished the forces he intended to throw into Louisiana, but also gave him a terrible object lesson as to what the fate of these forces was certain ultimately to be. The attitude of England and Austria grew steadily more hostile, and his most

Napoleon Forced to Change his Purpose.

trustworthy advisers impressed on Napoleon's mind the steady growth of the Western-American communities, and the implacable hostility with which they were certain to regard any power that seized or attempted to hold New Orleans. Napoleon could not afford to hamper himself with the difficult defence of a distant province, and to incur the hostility of a new foe, at the very moment when he was entering on another struggle with his old European enemies. Moreover, he needed money in order to carry on the struggle. To be sure he had promised Spain not to turn over Louisiana to another power; but he was quite as incapable as any Spanish statesman, or as Talleyrand himself, of so much as considering the question of breach of faith or loss of honor, if he could gain any advantage by sacrificing either. Livingston was astonished to find that Napoleon had suddenly changed front, and that there was every prospect of gaining what for months had seemed impossible. For some time there was haggling over the terms. Napoleon at first demanded an exorbitant sum; but having once made up his mind to part with Louisiana his impatient disposition made him anxious to conclude the bargain. **Louisiana Ceded to the United States.** He rapidly abated his demands, and the cession was finally made for fifteen millions of dollars.

The treaty was signed in May, 1803. The definition of the exact boundaries of the ceded territory was purposely left very loose by Napoleon. On the east, the Spanish Government of the Floridas still kept possession of what **The Boundaries Undecided.** are now several parishes in the State of Louisiana.

In the far west the boundary lines which divided upper Louisiana from the possessions of Britain on the north and of Spain on the south led through a wilderness where no white man had ever trod, and they were of course unmapped, and only vaguely guessed at.

There was one singular feature of this bargain, which showed, as nothing else could have shown, how little American diplomacy had to do with obtaining Louisiana, and how impossible it was for any European power, even the greatest, to hold the territory in the face of the steady westward growth of the American people. Napoleon forced Livingston and Monroe to become the reluctant purchasers not merely of New Orleans, but of all the immense territory which stretched vaguely northwestward to the Pacific. Jefferson at moments felt a desire to get all this western territory; but he was too timid and too vacillating to insist strenuously upon anything which he feared Napoleon would not grant. Madison felt a strong disinclination to see the national domain extend west of the Mississippi; and he so instructed Monroe and Livingston. In their turn the American envoys, with solemn fatuity, believed it might impress Napoleon favorably if they made much show of moderation, and they spent no small part of their time in explaining that they only wished a little bit of Louisiana, including New Orleans and the east bank of the lower Mississippi. Livingston indeed went so far as to express a very positive disinclination to take the territory west of the Mississippi at any price, stating that he should much prefer to see it remain in the hands of France or Spain, and suggesting, by way of apology for its acquisition, that it might be re-sold to some European power! But Napoleon saw clearly that if the French ceded New Orleans it was a simple physical impossibility for them to hold the rest of the Louisiana territory. If his fierce and irritable vanity had been touched he might, through mere wayward anger, have dared the Americans to a contest which, however disastrous to them, would ultimately have been more so to him; but he was a great statesman, and a still greater soldier, and he did not need to be told that it would be worse than folly to try to keep a country when he had given up the key-position.

The region west of the Mississippi could become the heritage of no other people save that which had planted its populous communities along the eastern bank of the river. It was quite possible for a powerful European nation to hold New Orleans for some time, even though all upper Louisiana fell into the hands of the Americans; but it was entirely impossible for any European nation to hold upper Louisiana if New Orleans became a city of the United States. The Westerners, wiser than their rulers, but no wiser than Napoleon at the last, felt this, and were not in the least disturbed over the fate of Louisiana, provided they were given the control of the mouth of the Mississippi. As a matter of fact, it is improbable that the fate of the great territory lying west of the upper

The Great West Gained against the Wishes of the American Diplomats.

Mississippi would even have been seriously delayed
had it been nominally under the control of France or
Spain.   With the mouth of the Mississippi once in
American hands it was a physical impossibility in
any way to retard the westward movement of the men
who were settling Ohio, Kentucky, and Tennessee.

The ratification of the treaty brought on some
sharp debates in Congress. Jefferson had led his
Debates in party into power as the special champion
Congress. of States' Rights and the special opponent
of national sovereignty.   He and they rendered a
very great service to the nation by acquiring Louisiana ; but it was at the cost of violating every pre-
cept which they had professed to hold dear, and of
showing that their warfare on the Federalists had
been waged on behalf of principles which they were
obliged to confess were shams the moment they
were put to the test.   But the Federalists of the
Northeast, both in the Middle States and in New
England, at this juncture behaved far worse than
the Jeffersonian Republicans.   These Jeffersonian
Republicans did indeed by their performance give
the lie to their past promise, and thereby em-
phasize the unworthiness of their conduct in years
gone by; nevertheless, at this juncture they were
right, which was far more important than being
logical or consistent.   But the Northeastern Federalists, though with many exceptions, did as a whole
stand as the opponents of national growth.   They
had very properly, though vainly, urged Jefferson to
take prompt and effective steps to sustain the national honor, when it seemed probable that the

country could be won from France only at the cost
of war ; but when the time actually came to incor-
porate Louisiana into the national domain, Folly of the
they showed that jealous fear of Western Federalists.
growth which was the most marked defect in Northeastern public sentiment until past the middle of
the present century. It proved that the Federalists
were rightly distrusted by the West; and it proved
that at this crisis, the Jeffersonian Republicans, in
spite of their follies, weaknesses, and crimes, were
the safest guardians of the country, because they
believed in its future, and strove to make it
greater.

The Jeremiads of the Federalist leaders in Congress
were the same in kind as those in which many cultivated men of the East always indulged whenever we
enlarged our territory, and in which many persons
like them would now indulge were we at the present
day to make a similar extension. The people of the
United States were warned that they were incor-
porating into their number men who were wholly
alien in every respect, and who could never be
assimilated. They were warned that when they
thus added to their empire, they merely rendered it
unwieldy and assured its being split into two or
more confederacies at no distant day. Some of the
extremists, under the lead of Quincy, went so far
as to threaten dissolution of the Union because of
what was done, insisting that the Northeast ought
by rights to secede because of the injury done it by
adding strength to the South and West. Fortunately, however, talk of this kind did not affect the

majority; the treaty was ratified and Louisiana became part of the United States.

Meanwhile the Creoles themselves accepted their very rapidly changing fates with something much The French Prefect Laussat. like apathy. In March, 1803, the French Prefect Laussat arrived to make preparations to take possession of the country. He had no idea that Napoleon intended to cede it to the United States. On the contrary, he showed that he regarded the French as the heirs, not only to the Spanish territory, but of the Spanish hostility to the Americans. He openly regretted that the Spanish Government had reversed Morales' act taking away from the Americans the right of deposit; and he made all his preparations as if on the theory that New Orleans was to become the centre of an aggressive military government.

His dislikes, however, were broad, and included the Spaniards as well as the Americans. There was Corruption of the Spanish Government. much friction between him and the Spanish officials; he complained bitterly to the home government of the insolence and intrigues of the Spanish party. He also portrayed in scathing terms the gross corruption of the Spanish authorities. As to this corruption he was borne out by the American observers. Almost every high Spanish official was guilty of peculation at the expense of the government, and of bribe-taking at the expense of the citizens.

Nevertheless the Creoles were far from ill-satisfied with Spanish rule. They were not accustomed to self-government, and did not demand it; and they cared very little for the fact that their superiors made money improperly. If they paid due deference to their lay and clerical rulers they were little interfered with; and they were in full accord with the governing classes concerning most questions, both of principle or lack of principle, and of prejudice. The Creoles felt that they were protected, rather than oppressed, by people who shared their tastes, and who did not interfere with the things they held dear. On the whole they showed only a tepid joy at the prospect of again becoming French citizens.

The Creoles not Ill-Satisfied with it.

Laussat soon discovered that they were to remain French citizens for a very short time indeed; and he prepared faithfully to carry out his instructions, and to turn the country over to the Americans. The change in the French attitude greatly increased the friction with the Spaniards. The Spanish home government was furious with indignation at Napoleon for having violated his word, and only the weakness of Spain prevented war between it and France. The Spanish party in New Orleans muttered its discontent so loud that Laussat grew alarmed. He feared some outbreak on the part of the Spanish sympathizers, and, to prevent such a mischance, he not only embodied the comparatively small portion of the Creole militia whom he could trust, but also a number of American volunteers, concerning whose fidelity in such a crisis as that he anticipated there could be no question. It was not until December first, 1803, that he took final pos-

Preparations to Turn the Country Over to the United States.

session of the provinces. Twenty days afterwards
he turned it over to the American authorities.

Wilkinson, now commander of the American army,
—the most disgraceful head it has ever had—was
Claiborne entrusted with the governorship of all of
Made Upper Louisiana. Claiborne was made gov-
Governor. ernor of Lower Louisiana, officially styled
the Territory of Orleans. He was an honest man,
loyal to the Union, but had no special qualifications
for getting on well with the Creoles. He could not
speak French, and he regarded the people whom he
governed with a kindly contempt which they bitterly resented. The Americans, pushing and masterful, were inclined to look down on their neighbours,
and to treat them overbearingly ; while the Creoles
in their turn disliked the Americans as rude and un-
cultivated barbarians. For some time they felt
much discontent with the United States ; nor was
this discontent allayed when in 1804 the territory of
Orleans was reorganized with a government much
less liberal than that enjoyed by Indiana or Mississippi ; nor even when in 1805 an ordinary territorial
government was provided. A number of years were
to pass before Louisiana felt itself, in fact no less
than in name, part of the Union.

Naturally there was a fertile field for seditious
agitation in New Orleans, a city of mixed popula-
New Or- tion, where the numerically predominant
leans Offers race felt a puzzled distrust for the nation
a Field for of which it suddenly found itself an inte-
Sedition. gral part, and from past experience firmly
believed in the evanescent nature of any political

connection it might have, whether with Spain, France, or the United States. The Creoles murmured because they were not given the same privileges as American citizens in the old States, and yet showed themselves indifferent to such privileges as they were given. They were indignant because the National Government prohibited the importation of slaves into Louisiana, and for the moment even the transfer thither of slaves from the old States—a circumstance, by the way, which curiously illustrated the general dislike and disapproval of slavery then felt, even by an administration under Southern control. The Creoles further complained of Claiborne's indifference to their wishes ; and as he possessed little tact he also became embroiled with the American inhabitants, who were men of adventurous and often lawless temper, impatient of restraint. Representatives of the French and Spanish governments still remained in Louisiana, and by their presence and their words tended to keep alive a disaffection for the United States Government. It followed from these various causes that among all classes there was a willingness to talk freely of their wrongs and to hint at righting them by methods outlined with such looseness as to make it uncertain whether they did or did not comport with entire loyalty to the United States Government.

Furthermore, there already existed in New Orleans a very peculiar class, representatives of which are still to be found in almost every Gulf   The city of importance. There were in the city Filibusters. a number of men ready at any time to enter into any plot for armed conquest of one of the Spanish American countries.[1]   Spanish America was feeling the stir of unrest that preceded the revolutionary outbreak against Spain.   Already insurrectionary leaders like Miranda were seeking assistance from the Americans.   There were in New Orleans a number of exiled Mexicans who were very anxious to raise some force with which to invade Mexico, and there erect the banner of an independent sovereignty. The bolder spirits among the Creoles found much that was attractive in such a prospect; and reckless American adventurers by the score and the hundred were anxious to join in any filibustering expedition of the kind.   They did not care in the least what form the expedition took.   They were willing to join the Mexican exiles in an effort to rouse Mexico to throw off the yoke of Spain, or to aid any province of Mexico to revolt from the rest, or to help the leaders of any defeated faction who wished to try an appeal to arms, in which they should receive aid from the sword of the stranger.   Incidentally they were even more willing to attempt the conquest on their own account; but they did not find it necessary to dwell on this aspect of the case when nominally supporting some faction which chose to make use of such watchwords as liberty and independence.

Under such conditions New Orleans, even more than the rest of the West, seemed to offer an inviting Burr's Con- field for adventurers whose aim was both re- spiracy.   volutionary and piratical.   A particularly spectacular adventurer of this type now appeared

[1] Wilkinson's " Memoirs," II., 284.

in the person of Aaron Burr.   Burr's conspiracy attracted an amount of attention, both at home and in the pages of history, altogether disproportioned to its real consequence.   His career had been striking. He had been Vice-President of the United States.   He had lacked but one vote of being made President, when the election of 1800 was thrown into the House of Representatives.   As friend or as enemy he had been thrown intimately and on equal terms with the greatest political leaders of the day.   He had supplied almost the only feeling which Jefferson, the chief of the Democratic party, and Hamilton, the greatest Federalist, ever possessed in common; for bitterly though Hamilton and Jefferson had hated each other, there was one man whom each of them had hated more, and that was Aaron Burr.   There was not a man in the country who did not know about the brilliant and unscrupulous party leader who had killed Hamilton in the most famous duel that ever took place on American soil, and who by a nearly successful intrigue had come within one vote of supplanting Jefferson in the presidency.

In New York Aaron Burr had led a political career as stormy and chequered as the careers of New York politicians have generally been.   He had shown himself as adroit as he was unscrupulous in the use of all the arts of the machine manager.   The fitful and gusty breath of popular favor made him at one time the most prominent and successful politician in the State, and one of the two or three most prominent and successful in the nation.   In the State he was the leader of

Burr's Previous Career in New York.

the Democratic party, which under his lead crushed the Federalists ; and as a reward he was given the second highest office in the nation. Then his open enemies and secret rivals all combined against him. The other Democratic leaders in New York, and in the nation as well, turned upon the man whose brilliant abilities made them afraid, and whose utter untrustworthiness forbade their entering into alliance with him. Shifty and fertile in expedients, Burr made an obstinate fight to hold his own. Without hesitation, he turned for support to his old enemies, the Federalists ; but he was hopelessly beaten. Both his fortune and his local political prestige were ruined ; he realized that his chance for a career in New York was over.

He was no mere New York politician, however. He was a statesman of national reputation ; and he When turned his restless eyes toward the West, Beaten in which for a score of years had seethed in a New York he Turned turmoil out of which it seemed that a to the West. bold spirit might make its own profit. He had already been obscurely connected with sep- aratist intrigues in the Northeast; and he deter- mined to embark in similar intrigues on an infinitely grander scale in the West and Southwest. He was a cultivated man, of polished manners and pleas- ing address, and of great audacity and physical courage ; and he had shown himself skilled in all the baser arts of political management.

It is small wonder that the conspiracy of which such a man was head should make a noise out of all proportion to its real weight. The conditions were such that if Burr journied West he was certain to attract universal attention, and to be received with marked enthusiasm. No man of his prominence in national affairs had ever travelled through the wild new commonwealths on the Mississippi. The men who were founding states and building towns on the wreck of the conquered wilderness were sure to be flattered by the appearance of so notable a man among them, and to be impressed not only by his reputation, but by his charm of manner and brilliancy of intellect. Moreover they were quite ready to talk vaguely of all kinds of dubious plans for increasing the importance of the West. Very many, perhaps most, of them had dabbled at one time or another in the various separatist schemes of the preceding two decades; and they felt strongly that much of the Spanish domain would and should ultimately fall into their hands—and the sooner the better.

There was thus every chance that Burr would be favorably received by the West, and would find plenty of men of high standing who would profess friendship for him and would show **He Misun-** a cordial interest in his plans so long **derstands** as he refrained from making them too **the West-** definite; but there was in reality no **ern Situa-** **tion.** chance whatever for anything more than this to happen. In spite of Burr's personal courage he lacked entirely the great military qualities necessary to successful revolutionary leadership of the kind to which he aspired. Though in some ways the most practical of politicians he had a strong element of the visionary in his character; it was perhaps

this, joined to his striking moral defects, which
brought about and made complete his downfall in
New York.   Great political and revolutionary leaders may, and often must, have in them something of
the visionary; but it must never cause them to get
out of touch with the practical.   Burr was capable
of conceiving revolutionary plans on so vast a scale
as to be fairly appalling, not only from their daring
but from their magnitude.   But when he tried to
put his plans into practice, it at once became evident
that they were even more unsubstantial than they
were audacious.   His wild schemes had in them too
strong an element of the unreal and the grotesque to
be in very fact dangerous.

Besides, the time for separatist movements in the
West had passed, while the time for arousing the
The West
Had Grown
Loyal.
West to the conquest of part of Spanish-
America had hardly yet come.   A man
of Burr's character might perhaps have
accomplished something mischievous in Kentucky
when Wilkinson was in the first flush of his Spanish
intrigues; or when the political societies were raving
over Jay's treaty; or when the Kentucky legislature
was passing its nullification resolutions.   But the
West had grown loyal as the Nineteenth Century
came in.   The Westerners were hearty supporters of
the Jeffersonian democratic-republican party; Jefferson was their idol; they were strongly attached to
the Washington administration, and strongly opposed
to the chief opponents of that administration, the
Northeastern Federalists.   With the purchase of
Louisiana all deep-lying causes of Western discontent
had vanished.   The West was prosperous, and was

attached to the National Government. Its leaders might still enjoy a discussion with Burr or among themselves concerning separatist principles in the abstract, but such a discussion was at this time purely academic. Nobody of any weight in the community would allow such plans as those of Burr to be put into effect. There was, it is true, a strong buccaneering spirit, and there were plenty of men ready to enlist in an invasion of the Spanish dominions under no matter what pretext; but even those men of note who were willing to lead such a movement, were not willing to enter into it if it was complicated with open disloyalty to the United States.

Burr began his treasonable scheming before he ceased to be Vice-President. He was an old friend and crony of Wilkinson; and he knew much about the disloyal agitations which had convulsed the West during the previous two decades. These agitations always took one or the other of two forms that at first sight would seem diametrically opposed. Their end was always either to bring about a secession of the West from the East by the aid of Spain or some other foreign power; or else a conquest of the Spanish dominions by the West, in defiance of the wishes of the East and of the Central Government. Burr proposed to carry out both of these plans.

The exact shape which his proposals took would be difficult to tell. Seemingly they remained nebulous even in his own mind. They certainly so remained in the minds of those to whom he confided them. At any rate his scheme, though in reality less dangerous than those of his predecessors in Western treason, were in theory much more comprehensive. He planned the seizure of Washington, the kidnapping of the President, and the corruption of the United States Navy. He also endeavored to enlist foreign powers on his side. His first advances were made to the British. He proposed to put the new empire, no matter what shape it might assume, under British protection, in return for the assistance of the British fleet in taking New Orleans. He gave to the British ministers full—and false—accounts of the intended uprising, and besought the aid of the British Government on the ground that the secession of the West would so cripple the Union as to make it no longer a formidable enemy of Great Britain. Burr's audacity and plausibility were such that he quite dazzled the British minister, who detailed the plans at length to his home government, putting them in as favorable a light as he could. The statesmen at London, however, although at this time almost inconceivably stupid in their dealings with America, were not sunk in such abject folly as to think Burr's schemes practicable, and they refused to have anything to do with them.

He Endeavors to Enlist the Aid of Foreign Powers.

In April, 1805, Burr started on his tour to the West. One of his first stoppages was at an island on the Ohio near Parkersburg, where an Irish gentleman named Blennerhassett had built what was, for the West, an unusually fine house. Only Mrs. Blennerhassett was at home at the time; but Blennerhassett later became a mainstay of the "conspiracy." He

He Starts West and Stays with Blennerhassett.

was a warm-hearted man, with no judgment and a natural tendency toward sedition, who speedily fell under Burr's influence, and entered into his plans with eager zeal. With him Burr did not have to be on his guard, and to him he confided freely his plans; but elsewhere, and in dealing with less emotional people, he had to be more guarded.

It is always difficult to find out exactly what a conspirator of Burr's type really intended, aud exactly how guilty his various temporary friends and allies were. Part of the conspirator's business is to dissemble the truth, and in after-time it is nearly impossible to differentiate it from the false, **How Far Burr's Allies were Privy to his Treason.** even by the most elaborate sifting of the various untruths he has uttered. Burr told every kind of story, at one time or another, and to different classes of auditors. It would be unsafe to deny his having told a particular falsehood in any given case or to any given man. On the other hand when once the plot was unmasked those persons to whom he had confided his plans were certain to insist that he had really kept them in ignorance of his true intention. In consequence it is quite impossible to say exactly how much guilty knowledge his various companions possessed. When it comes to treating of his relationship with Wilkinson all that can be said is that no single statement ever made by either man, whether during the conspiracy or after it, whether to the other or to an outsider, can be considered as either presumptively true or presumptively false.

It is therefore impossible to say exactly how far

the Westerners with whom Burr was intimate were
privy to his plans. It is certain that the great mass
of the Westerners never seriously considered entering
into any seditious movement under him. It is equally
certain that a number of their leaders were more or
less compromised by their associations with him. It
seems probable that to each of these leaders he re-
vealed what he thought would most attract him in
the scheme; but that to very few did he reveal an
outright proposition to break up the Union. Many
of them were very willing to hear the distinguished
Easterner make vague proposals for increasing the
power of the West by means which were hinted at
with sinister elusiveness; and many others were delighted to go into any movement which promised an
attack upon the Spanish territory; but it seems
likely that there were only a few men—Wilkinson,
for instance, and Adair of Kentucky—who were
willing to discuss a proposition to commit down-
right treason.

Burr stopped at Cincinnati, in Ohio, and at one
or two places in Kentucky. In both States many
prominent politicians, even United States
Senators, received him with enthusiasm.
He then visited Nashville where he became
the guest of Andrew Jackson. Jackson was now
Major General of the Tennessee militia; and the
possibility of war, especially of war with the Spaniards, roused his hot nature to uncontrollable
eagerness.[1] Burr probably saw through Jackson's
character at once, and realized that with him it was

Burr and Andrew Jackson.

[1] Adams, III., 221.

important to dwell solely upon that part of the plan which contemplated an attack upon the Spaniards.

The United States was at this time on the verge of war with Spain. The Spanish Governor and Intendant remained in New Orleans after the Threatened cession, and by their conduct gave such Hostilities offence that it finally became necessary to with Spain. order them to leave. Jefferson claimed, as part of Louisiana, portions of both West Florida and Texas. The Spaniards refused to admit the justice of the claim and gathered in the disputed territories armies which, though small, outnumbered the few regular troops that Wilkinson had at his disposal. More than once a collision seemed imminent. The Westerners clamored for war, desiring above all things to drive the Spaniards by force from the debatable lands. For some time Jefferson showed symptoms of yielding to their wishes; but he was too timid and irresolute to play a high part, and in the end he simply did nothing. However, though he declined to make actual war on the Spaniards, he also refused to recognize their claims as just, and his peculiar, hesitating course, tended to inflame the Westerners, and to make them believe that their government would not call them to account for acts of aggression. To Jackson doubtless Burr's pro- Jackson's posals seemed quite in keeping with what Eagerness he hoped from the United States Govern- to Assail ment. He readily fell in with views so Spain. like his own, and began to make preparations for an expedition against the Spanish dominions; an expedition which in fact would not have differed essentially from the expeditions he actually did make into the Spanish Floridas six or eight years afterward, or from the movement which still later his fellow-Tennessean, Houston, headed in Texas.

From Nashville Burr drifted down the Cumberland, and at Fort Massac, on the Ohio, he met Wilkinson, a kindred spirit, who possessed neither honor nor conscience, and could not be shocked by any proposal. Moreover, Wilkinson much enjoyed the early stages of a seditious agitation, when the risk to himself seemed slight; and as he was at this time both the highest military officer of the United States, and also secretly in the pay of Spain, the chance to commit a double treachery gave an added zest to his action. He entered cordially into Burr's plans, and as soon as he returned to his headquarters, at St. Louis, he set about trying to corrupt his subordinates, and seduce them from their allegiance.

Meanwhile Burr passed down the Mississippi to New Orleans, where he found himself in the society of persons who seemed more willing than any others he had encountered to fall in with his plans. Even here he did not clearly specify his purposes, but he did say enough to show that they bordered on the treasonable; and he was much gratified at the acquiescence of his listeners. His gratification, however, was over-hasty. The Creoles, and some of the Americans, were delighted to talk of their wrongs and to threaten any course of action which they thought might yield vengeance; but they had little intention of proceeding from words to deeds. Claiborne, a straightforward and honest man, set his face like a flint against all of Burr's doings.

From New Orleans Burr retraced his steps and visited Wilkinson at St. Louis. But Wilkinson was no longer in the same frame of mind as at Fort Massac. He had tested his officers, to see if they could be drawn into any disloyal movement, and had found that they were honorable men, firm in their attachment to the Union ; and he was beginning to perceive that the people generally were quite unmoved by Burr's intrigues. Accordingly, when Burr reached him he threw cold water on his plans, and though he did not denounce or oppose them, he refrained from taking further active part in the seditious propaganda.

After visiting Harrison, the Governor of the Indiana territory, Burr returned to Washington. If he had possessed the type of character which would have made him really dangerous as a revolutionist, he would have seen how slight was his hope of stirring up revolt in the West ; but he would not face facts, and he still believed he could bring about an uprising against the Union in the Mississippi Valley. His immediate need was money. This he hoped to obtain from some foreign government. He found that nothing could be done with Great Britain ; and then, incredible though it may seem, he turned to Spain, and sought to obtain from the Spaniards themselves the funds with which to conquer their own territories.

This was the last touch necessary to complete the

grotesque fantasy which his brain had evolved.
He approached the Spanish Minister first
through one of his fellow conspirators and
then in his own person. At one time he
made his request on the pretence that he
wished to desert the other filibusterers, and save Spain
by committing a double treachery, and betraying the
treasonable movement into which he had entered ;
and again he asked funds on the ground that all he
wished to do was to establish a separate government
in the West, and thus destroy the power of the
United States to molest Spain. However, his efforts
came to naught, and he was obliged to try what
he could do unaided in the West.

*His Bur-
lesque Pro-
posals to
Spain.*

In August, 1806, he again crossed the Alleghenies.
His first stop of importance was at Blennerhassett's.
Blennerhassett was the one person of any importance who took his schemes so seriously
as to be willing to stake his fortune on
their success. Burr took with him to Blennerhassett's
his daughter, Theodosia, a charming woman, the wife
of a South Carolinian, Allston. The attractions of the
daughter, and Burr's own address and magnetism, completely overcame both Blennerhassett and his wife.
They gave the adventurer all the money they could
raise, with the understanding that they would receive
it back a hundred-fold as the result of a land speculation which was to go hand in hand with the
expected revolution. Then Blennerhassett began,
in a very noisy and ineffective way, to make what
preparations were possible in the way of rousing the
Ohio settlers, and of gathering a body of armed

*His Second
Trip to the
West.*

men to serve under Burr when the time came. It
was all done in a way that savored of farce rather
than of treason.

There was much less comedy however in what
went on in Kentucky and Tennessee where Burr next
went. At Nashville he was received with
open arms by Jackson and Jackson's
friends. This was not much to Jackson's
Again
Visits
Jackson.
credit, for by this time he should have known Burr's
character; but the temptation of an attack on the
Spaniards proved irresistible. As Major General, he
called out the militia of West Tennessee, and began
to make ready in good earnest to invade Florida or
Mexico. At public dinners he and his friends and
Burr made speeches in which they threatened immediate war against Spain, with which country the
United States was at peace; but they did not
threaten any attack on the Union, and indeed Jackson exacted from Burr a guarantee of his loyalty to
the Union.

From Nashville the restless conspirator returned
to Kentucky to see if he could persuade the most
powerful of the Western States to take
some decided step in his favor. Senator
John Adair, former companion-in-arms of
His Expe-
rience in
Kentucky.
Wilkinson in the wars against the Northwestern Indians, enlisted in support of Burr with heart and
soul. Kentucky society generally received him with
enthusiasm. But there was in the State a remnant
of the old Federalist party, which although not
formidable in numbers, possessed weight because of
the vigor and ability of its leaders. The chief

among them were Humphrey Marshall, former United States Senator, and Joseph H. Daveiss, who was still District Attorney, not having, as yet, been turned out by Jefferson.[1] These men saw—what Eastern politicians could not see—the connection between Burr's conspiracy and the former Spanish intrigues of men like Wilkinson, Sabastian, and Innes. They were loyal to the Union; and they felt a bitter factional hatred for their victorious foes in whose ranks were to be found all the old time offenders; so they attacked the new conspiracy with a double zest. They not only began a violent newspaper war upon Burr and all the former conspirators, but also proceeded to invoke the aid of the courts and the legislature against them. Their exposure of the former Spanish intrigues, as well as of Burr's plots, attracted widespread attention in the West, even at New Orleans[2]; but the Kentuckians, though angry and ashamed, were at first reluctant to be convinced. Twice Daveiss presented Burr for treason before the Grand Jury; twice the Grand Jury declared in his favor; and the leaders of the Kentucky Democracy gave him their countenance, while Henry Clay acted as his counsel. Daveiss, by a constant succession of letters, kept Jefferson fully informed of all that was done. Though his attacks on Burr for the moment seemed failures, they really accomplished their object. They created such uneasiness that the prominent

[1] For the Kentucky episode, see Marshall and Greene. Gayarré is the authority for what occurred in New Orleans. For the whole conspiracy, see Adams.

[2] Gayarré, IV., 180.

Kentuckians made haste to clear themselves of all possible connection with any treasonable scheme. Henry Clay demanded and received from Burr a formal pledge that his plans were in no wise hostile to the Union; and the other people upon whom Burr counted most, both in Ohio and Kentucky, hastily followed this example. This immediate defection showed how hopeless Burr's plans were. The moment he attempted to put them into execution, their utter futility was certain to be exposed.

Meanwhile Jefferson's policy with the Spaniards, which neither secured peace nor made ready for war, kept up constant irritation on the border. Both the Spanish Governor Folch, in West Florida, and the Spanish General Herrera, in Texas, menaced the Americans.[1] Wilkinson hurried with his little army towards Herrera, until the two stood face to face, each asserting that the other was on ground that belonged to his own nation. Just at this time Burr's envoys, containing his final propositions, reached Wilkinson. But Wilkinson now saw as clearly as any one that Burr's scheme was foredoomed to fail; and he at once determined to make use of the only weapon in which he was skilled,—treachery. At this very time he, the commander of the United States Army, was in the pay of Spain, and was in secret negotiation with the Spanish officials against whom he was supposed to be acting; he had striven to corrupt his own army and had failed; he had found out that the people of the West were not disloyal. He saw that

[1] Gayarré, IV., 137, 151, etc.

there was no hope of success for the conspirators;
Wilkinson and he resolved to play the part of de-
Resolves to fender of the nation, and to act with vigor
Desert Burr. against Burr. Having warned Jefferson,
in language of violent alarm, about Burr's plans, he
prepared to prevent their execution. He first made
a truce with Herrera in accordance with which each
was to retire to his former position, and then he
started for the Mississippi.

When Burr found that he could do nothing in
Kentucky and Tennessee, he prepared to go to New
Burr Flees Orleans. The few boats that Blennerhas-
Down the sett had been able to gather were sent hur-
Mississippi. riedly down stream lest they should be
interfered with by the Ohio authorities. Burr had
made another visit to Nashville. Slipping down the
Cumberland, he joined his little flotilla, passed Fort
Massac, and began the descent of the Mississippi.

The plot was probably most dangerous at New
Orleans, if it could be said to be dangerous any-
The Alarm where. Claiborne grew very much alarmed
at New about it, chiefly because of the elusive mys-
Orleans. tery in which it was shrouded. But when
the pinch came it proved as unsubstantial there as
elsewhere. The leaders who had talked most loosely
about revolutionary proceedings grew alarmed, as
the crisis approached, lest they might be called on to
make good their words ; and they hastened to repu-
diate all connection with Burr, and to avow themselves loyal to the Union. Even the Creole militia,
—a body which Claiborne regarded with just suspicion,—volunteered to come to the defence of the

Government when it was thought that Burr might actually attack the city.

But Burr's career was already ruined. Jefferson, goaded into action, had issued a proclamation for his arrest; and even before this proclama- Collapse
tion was issued, the fabric of the con- of the
spiracy had crumbled into shifting dust. Conspiracy.
The Ohio Legislature passed resolutions demanding prompt action against the conspirators; and the other Western communities followed suit. There was no real support for Burr anywhere. All his plot had been but a dream; at the last he could not do anything which justified, in even the smallest degree, the alarm and curiosity he had excited. The men of keenest insight and best judgment feared his unmasked efforts less than they feared Wilkinson's dark and tortuous treachery.[1] As he drifted down the Mississippi with his little flotilla, he was over-taken by Jefferson's proclamation, which was sent from one to another of the small Federal garrisons. Near Natchez, in January, 1807, he surrendered his flotilla, without resistance, to the Acting-Governor of Mississippi Territory. He himself escaped into the land of the Choctaws and Creeks, disguised as a Mississippi boatman; but a month later he was arrested near the Spanish border, and sent back to Washington.

Thus ended ingloriously the wildest, most spec-tacular, and least dangerous, of all the intrigues for Western disunion. It never contained within itself the least hope of success. It was never a serious

---

[1] E. G. Cowles Meade; see Gayarré, IV., 169.

menace to the National government. It was not by any means even a good example of Western particularistic feeling. It was simply a sporadic illustration of the looseness of national sentiment, here and there, throughout the country ; but of no great significance, because it was in no sense a popular movement, and had its origin in the fantastic imagination of a single man.

It left scarcely a ripple in the West. When the danger was over Wilkinson appeared in New **After-** Orleans, where he strutted to the front for **Effects in** a little while, playing the part of a fussy **the West.** dictator and arresting, among others, Adair of Kentucky. As the panic subsided, they were released. No Louisianian suffered in person or property from any retaliatory action of the Government ; but lasting good was done by the abject failure of the plot and by the exhibition of unused strength by the American people. The Creoles ceased to mutter discontent, and all thought of sedition died away in the province.

The chief sufferers, aside from Blennerhassett, were Sebastian and Innes, of Kentucky. The former re- **Sufferers** signed from the bench, and the latter lost **from the** a prestige he never regained. A few of **Conspiracy.** their intimate friends also suffered. But their opponents did not fare much better. Daveiss and Marshall were the only men in the West whose action toward Burr had been thoroughly creditable, showing alike vigor, intelligence, and loyalty. To both of them the country was under an obligation. Jefferson showed his sense of this obligation in a not uncharacteristic way by removing Daveiss from office; Marshall was already in private life, and all that could be done was to neglect him.

As for Burr, he was put on trial for high treason, with Wilkinson as state's evidence.   Jefferson made himself the especial champion of Wilkin- **The Trial** son ; nevertheless the General cut a con- **of Burr.** temptible figure at the trial, for no explanation could make his course square with honorable dealing.   Burr was acquitted on a technicality.   Wilkinson, the double traitor, the bribe-taker, the corrupt servant of a foreign government, remained at the head of the American Army.

CHAPTER VII.

THE EXPLORERS OF THE FAR WEST, 1804–1807.

THE Far West, the West beyond the Mississippi, had been thrust on Jefferson, and given to the nation, The Far by the rapid growth of the Old West, the West. West that lay between the Alleghanies and the Mississippi. The actual title to the new territory had been acquired by the United States Government, acting for the whole nation. It remained to explore the territory thus newly added to the national domain. The Government did not yet know exactly what it had acquired, for the land was not only unmapped but unexplored. Nobody could tell what were the boundary lines which divided it from British America on the north and Mexico on the south, for nobody knew much of the country through which these lines ran; of most of it, indeed, nobody knew anything. On the new maps the country now showed as part of the United States; but the Indians who alone inhabited it were as little affected by the transfer as was the game they hunted.

Even the Northwestern portion of the land definitely ceded to the United States by Great Britain Need for in Jay's treaty was still left in actual posits Ex- session of the Indian tribes, while the few ploration. whites who lived among them were traders owing allegiance to the British Government. The head-waters of the Mississippi and the beautiful country lying round them were known only in a vague way; and it was necessary to explore and formally take possession of this land of lakes, glades, and forests.

Beyond the Mississippi all that was really well known was the territory in the immediate neighborhood of the little French villages near the mouth of the Missouri. The creole traders of these villages, and an occasional venturous American, had gone up the Mississippi to the country of the Sioux and the Mandans, where they had trapped and hunted and traded for furs with the Indians. At the northernmost points that they reached they occasionally encountered traders who had travelled south or southwesterly from the wintry regions where the British fur companies reigned supreme. The head-waters of the Missouri were absolutely unknown; nobody had penetrated the great plains, the vast seas of grass through which the Platte, the Little Missouri, and the Yellowstone ran. What lay beyond them, and between them and the Pacific, was not even guessed at. The Rocky Mountains were not known to exist, so far as the territory newly acquired by the United States was concerned, although under the name of "Stonies" their northern extensions in British America were already down on some maps.

The West had passed beyond its first stage of uncontrolled individualism. Neither exploring nor fighting was thenceforth to be the work only of the individual settlers. The National Government was making its weight felt more and more in the West, because the West was itself becoming more and more an important integral portion of the Union. The work of exploring these new lands fell, not to the wild hunters and trappers, such as those who had first explored Kentucky and Tennessee, but to officers of the United States army, leading parties of United States soldiers, in pursuance of the command of the Government or of its representatives. The earliest and most important expeditions of Americans into the unknown country which the nation had just purchased were led by young officers of the regular army.

The National Government Undertakes the Work.

The first of these expeditions was planned by Jefferson himself and authorized by Congress. Nominally its purpose was in part to find out the most advantageous places for the establishment of trading stations with the Indian tribes over which our government had acquired the titular suzerainty ; but in reality it was purely a voyage of exploration, planned with intent to ascend the Missouri to its head, and thence to cross the continent to the Pacific. The explorers were carefully instructed to report upon the geography, physical characteristics, and zoology of the region traversed, as well as upon its wild human denizens. Jefferson was fond of science, and in appreciation of the desirability of non-remunerative scientific observation and and investigation he stood honorably distinguished among the public men of the day. To him justly belongs the credit of originating this first exploring

Jefferson Entitled to the Credit.

expedition ever undertaken by the United States Government.

The two officers chosen to carry through the work belonged to families already honorably distinguished for service on the Western border. One was Captain Meriwether Lewis, representatives of whose family had served so prominently in Dunmore's war; the other was Lieutenant (by courtesy Captain) William Clark, a younger brother of George Rogers Clark.[1] Clark had served with credit through Wayne's campaigns, and had taken part in the victory of the Fallen Timbers.[2] Lewis had seen his first service when he enlisted as a private in the forces which were marshalled to put down the whisky insurrection. Later he served under Clark in Wayne's army. He had also been President Jefferson's private secretary.

The young officers started on their trip accompanied by twenty-seven men who intended to make the whole journey. Of this number one, the interpreter and incidentally the best hunter of the party, was a half-breed; two were French voyageurs; one was a negro servant of Clark; nine were volunteers from Kentucky; and fourteen were regular soldiers. All, however, except the black slave, were enlisted in the army before starting, so that they might be kept under regular discipline. In addition to these twenty-seven men there were seven soldiers and nine voyageurs who started only

[1] He had already served as captain in the army; see Coues' edition of the "History of the Expedition," lxxi.

[2] See his letters, quoted in Chap. II. There is a good deal of hitherto unused material about him in the Draper MSS.

to go to the Mandan villages on the Missouri, where the party intended to spend the first winter. They embarked in three large boats, abundantly supplied with arms, powder, and lead, clothing, gifts for the Indians, and provisions.

The starting point was St. Louis, which had only just been surrendered to the United States Government by the Spaniards, without any French intermediaries. The explorers pushed off in May, 1804, and soon began stemming the strong current of the muddy Missouri, to whose unknown sources they in-intended to ascend. For two or three weeks they occasionally passed farms and hamlets. The most important of the little towns was St. Charles, where the people were all Creoles; the explorers in their journal commented upon the good temper and vivacity of these *habitants*, but dwelt on the shiftlessness they displayed and their readiness to sink back towards savagery, although they were brave and hardy enough. The next most considerable town was peopled mainly by Americans, who had already begun to make numerous settlements in the new land. The last squalid little village they passed claimed as one of its occasional residents old Daniel Boone himself.

After leaving the final straggling log cabins of the settled country, the explorers, with sails and paddles, made their way through what is now the State of Missouri. They lived well, for their hunters killed many deer and wild turkey and some black bear and beaver, and there was an abundance of breeding water fowl. Here and there were Indian encampments, but not many, for the tribes had gone westward to the great plains of what is now Kansas to hunt the buffalo. Already buffalo and elk were scarce in Missouri, and the party did not begin to find them in any numbers until they reached the neighborhood of what is now southern Nebraska.

From there onwards the game was found in vast herds and the party began to come upon those characteristic animals of the Great Plains which were as yet unknown to white men of our race. The buffalo and the elk had once ranged eastward to the Alleghanies and were familiar to early wanderers through the wooded wilderness; but in no part of the east had their numbers ever remotely approached the astounding multitudes in which they were found on the Great Plains. The curious prong-buck or prong-horned antelope was unknown east of the Great Plains. So was the blacktail, or mule deer, which our adventurers began to find here and there as they gradually worked their way northwestward. So were the coyotes, whose uncanny wailing after nightfall varied the sinister baying of the gray wolves; so were many of the smaller animals, notably the prairie dogs, whose populous villages awakened the lively curiosity of Lewis and Clark.

In their note-books the two captains faithfully discribed all these new animals and all the strange sights they saw. They were men with no pretensions to scientific learning, but they were singularly close and accurate observers and truthful narrators. Very rarely have any similar explorers described so faithfully not only the physical features but the animals and plants of a newly discovered land. Their narrative was not published until some years later, and then it was badly edited, notable the purely scientific portion; yet it remains the best example of what such a narrative should be. Few explorers who did and saw so much that was absolutely new have written of their deeds with such quiet absence of boastfulness, and have drawn their descriptions with such complete freedom from exaggeration.

Moreover, what was of even greater importance, the two young captains possessed in perfection the qualities necessary to pilot such an expedition through unknown lands and among savage tribes. They kept good discipline among the men; they never hesitated to punish severely any wrong-doer; but they were never over-severe; and as they did their full part of the work, and ran all the risks and suffered all the hardship exactly like the other members of the expedition, they were regarded by their followers with devoted affection, and were served with loyalty and cheerfulness. In dealing Their Deal- with the Indians they showed good humor ings with and common-sense mingled with ceaseless the Indians. vigilance and unbending resolution. Only men who possessed their tact and daring could have piloted the party safely among the warlike tribes they encountered. Any act of weakness or timidity on the one hand, or of harshness or cruelty on the other, would have been fatal to the expedition; but they were careful to treat the tribes well and to try to secure their good-will, while at the same time put-

ting an immediate stop to any insolence or outrage.
Several times they were in much jeopardy when they
reached the land of the Dakotas and passed among
the various ferocious tribes whom they knew, and
whom we yet know, as the Sioux. The French
traders frequently came up river to the country of
the Sioux, who often maltreated and robbed them.
In consequence Lewis and Clark found that the
Sioux were inclined to regard the whites as people
whom they could safely oppress. The resolute
bearing of the new-comers soon taught them that
they were in error, and after a little hesitation the
various tribes in each case became friendly.

With all the Indian tribes the two explorers
held councils, and distributed presents, especially
medals, among the head chiefs and warriors, informing them of the transfer of
the territory from Spain to the United
States and warning them that henceforth they
must look to the President as their protector, and
not to the King, whether of England or of Spain.
The Indians all professed much satisfaction at the
change, which of course they did not in the least
understand, and for which they cared nothing.
This easy acquiescence gave much groundless satisfaction to Lewis and Clark, who further, in a spirit
of philanthropy, strove to make each tribe swear
peace with its neighbors. After some hesitation
the tribe usually consented to this also, and the
explorers, greatly gratified, passed on. It is needless to say that as soon as they had disappeared the
tribes promptly went to war again ; and that in

*Councils
with the
Indians.*

reality the Indians had only the vaguest idea as to what was meant by the ceremonies, and the hoisting of the American Flag. The wonder is that Clark, who had already had some experience with Indians, should have supposed that the councils, advice, and proclamations would have any effect of the kind hoped for upon these wild savages. However, together with the love of natural science inculcated by the fashionable philosophy of the day, they also possessed the much less admirable, though entirely amiable, theory of universal and unintelligent philanthropy which was embodied in this philosophy. A very curious feature of our dealings with the Indians, not only in the days of Lewis and Clark, but since, has been the combination of extreme and indeed foolish benevolence of purpose on the part of the Government, with, on the part of the settlers, a brutality of action which this benevolent purpose could in no wise check or restrain.

As the fall weather grew cold the party reached the Mandan village, where they halted and went **They Winter at the Mandan Villages.** into camp for the winter, building huts and a stout stockade, which they christened Fort Mandan. Traders from St. Louis and also British traders from the North reached these villages, and the inhabitants were accustomed to dealing with the whites. Throughout the winter the party was well treated by the Indians, and kept in good health and spirits; the journals frequently mention the fondness the men showed for dancing, although without partners of the opposite sex. Yet they suffered much from the extreme cold, and at times from hunger, for it was hard to hunt in the winter weather, and the game was thin and poor. Generally game could be killed in a day's hunt from the fort; but occasionally small parties of hunters went off for a trip of several days, and returned laden with meat; in one case they killed thirty-two deer, eleven elk, and a buffalo; in another forty deer, sixteen elk, and three buffalo; thirty-six deer and fourteen elk, etc., etc. The buffalo remaining in the neighborhood during the winter were mostly old bulls, too lean to eat; and as the snows came on most of the antelope left for the rugged country farther west, swimming the Missouri in great bands. Before the bitter weather began the explorers were much interested by the methods of the Indians in hunting, especially when they surrounded and slaughtered bands of buffalo on horseback; and by the curious pens, with huge V-shaped wings, into which they drove antelope.

In the spring of 1805, Lewis and Clark again started westward, first sending down-stream ten of their companions, to carry home the notes *They Start* of their trip so far, and a few valuable *Westward* specimens. The party that started west- *in the Spring.* ward numbered thirty-two adults, all told; for one sergeant had died, and two or three persons had volunteered at the Mandan villages, including a rather worthless French "squaw-man," with an intelligent Indian wife, whose baby was but a few weeks old.

From this point onwards, when they began to travel west instead of north, the explorers were in a country where no white man had ever trod. It was not the first time the continent had been crossed. The Spaniards had crossed and recrossed it, for two centuries, farther south. In British America Mackenzie had already penetrated to the Pacific, while Hearne had made a far more noteworthy and difficult trip than Mackenzie, when he wandered over the terrible desolation of the Barren Grounds, which lie under the Artic circle. But no man had ever crossed or explored that part of the continent which the United States had just acquired; a part far better fitted to be the home of our stock than the regions to the north or south. It was the explorations of Lewis and Clark, and not those of Mackenzie on the north or of the Spaniards in the south, which were to bear fruit, because they pointed the way to the tens of thousands of settlers who were to come after them, and who were to build thriving commonwealths in the lonely wilderness which they had traversed.

From the Little Missouri on to the head of the Missouri proper the explorers passed through a region where they saw few traces of Indians. It literally swarmed with game, for it was one of the finest hunting grounds in all the world.[1] There were great numbers of sage fowl, sharp-tailed prairie fowl, and ducks of all

Wonderful Hunting Grounds.

---

[1] It so continued for three quarters of a century. Until after 1880 the region around the Little Missouri was essentially unchanged from what it was in the days of Lewis and Clark; game swarmed, and the few white hunters and trappers who followed the buffalo, the elk, and the beaver, were still at times in conflict with hunting parties from various Indian tribes. While ranching in this region I myself killed every kind of game encountered by Lewis and Clark.

kinds; and swans, and tall white cranes; and geese, which nested in the tops of the cottonwood trees. But the hunters paid no heed to birds, when surrounded by such teeming myriads of big game. Buffalo, elk, and antelope, whitetail and blacktail deer, and bighorn sheep swarmed in extraordinary abundance throughout the lands watered by the upper Missouri and the Yellowstone; in their journals the explorers dwell continually on the innumerable herds they encountered while on these plains, both when travelling up-stream and again the following year when they were returning. The antelopes were sometimes quite shy; so were the bighorn; though on occasions both kinds seemed to lose their wariness, and in one instance the journal specifies the fact that, at the mouth of the Yellowstone, the deer were somewhat shy, while the antelope, like the elk and buffalo, paid no heed to the men whatever. Ordinarily all the kinds of game were very tame. Sometimes one of the many herds of elk that lay boldly, even at midday, on the sandbars, or on the brush-covered points, would wait until the explorers were within twenty yards of them before starting. The buffalo would scarcely move out of the path at all, and the bulls sometimes, even when unmolested, threatened to assail the hunters. Once, on the return voyage, when Clark was descending the Yellowstone River, a vast herd of buffalo, swimming and wading, plowed its way across the stream where it was a mile broad, in a column so thick that the explorers had to draw up on shore and wait for an hour until it passed by, before continuing their journey. Two or three times the expedition was thus brought to a halt; and as the buffalo were so plentiful, and so easy to kill, and as their flesh was very good, they were the mainstay for the explorers' table. Both going and returning this wonderful hunting country was a place of plenty. The party of course lived almost exclusively on meat, and they needed much; for, when they could get it, they consumed either a buffalo, or an elk and a deer, or four deer, every day.

There was one kind of game which they at times found altogether too familiar. This was the grizzly bear, which they were the first white men to discover. They called it indifferently the grizzly, gray, brown, and even white bear, to distinguish it from its smaller, glossy, black-coated brother with which they were familiar in the Eastern woods. They found that the Indians greatly feared these bears, and after their first encounters they themselves treated them with much respect. The grizzly was then the burly lord of the Western prairie, dreaded by all other game, and usually shunned even by the Indians. In consequence it was very bold and savage. Again and again these huge bears attacked the explorers of their own accord, when neither molested nor threatened. They galloped after the hunters when they met them on horseback even in the open; and they attacked them just as freely when they found them on foot. To go through the brush was dangerous; again and again one or another of the party was charged and forced to take to a tree, at the foot of which the bear sometimes

First Encounters with the Grizzly Bear.

mounted guard for hours before going off. When wounded the beasts fought with desperate courage, and showed astonishing tenacity of life, charging any number of assailants, and succumbing but slowly even to mortal wounds. In one case a bear that was on shore actually plunged into the water and swam out to attack one of the canoes as it passed. However, by this time all of the party had become good hunters, expert in the use of their rifles, and they killed great numbers of their ursine foes.

Nor were the bears their only brute enemies. The rattlesnakes were often troublesome. Unlike the bears, the wolves were generally timid, and preyed only on the swarming game; but one night a wolf crept into camp and seized a sleeper by the hand; when driven **Other Brute Enemies.** off he jumped upon another man, and was shot by a third. A less intentional assault was committed by a buffalo bull which one night blundered past the fires, narrowly escaped trampling on the sleepers, and had the whole camp in an uproar before it rushed off into the darkness. When hunted the buffalo occasionally charged; but there was not much danger in their chase.

All these larger foes paled into insignificance compared with the mosquitos. There are very few places on earth where these pests are so formidable as in the bottom lands of the **The Scourge of Mosquitos.** Missouri, and for weeks and even months they made the lives of our explorers a torture. No other danger, whether from hunger or cold, Indians or wild beasts, was so dreaded by the explorers as these tiny scourges.

In the Plains country the life of the explorers was
very pleasant save only for the mosquitos and the

Pleasant Life in the Plains Country. incessant clouds of driving sand along the
river bottoms. On their journey west
through these true happy hunting grounds
they did not meet with any Indians, and
their encounters with the bears were only just sufficiently dangerous to add excitement to their life.
Once or twice they were in peril from cloud bursts,
and they were lamed by the cactus spines on the
prairie, and by the stones and sand of the river
bed while dragging the boats against the current;
but all these trials, labors, and risks were only
enough to give zest to their exploration of the unknown land. At the Great Falls of the Missouri
they halted, and were enraptured with their beauty
and majesty; and here, as everywhere, they found
the game so abundant that they lived in plenty.
As they journeyed up-stream through the bright
summer weather, though they worked hard, it was
work of a kind which was but a long holiday. At
nightfall they camped by the boats on the river
bank. Each day some of the party spent in hunting, either along the river bottoms through the
groves of cottonwoods with shimmering, rustling
leaves, or away from the river where the sunny
prairies stretched into seas of brown grass, or
where groups of rugged hills stood, fantastic in
color and outline, and with stunted pines growing
on the sides of their steep ravines. The only real
suffering was that which occasionally befell someone
who got lost, and was out for days at a time, until

he exhausted all his powder and lead before finding the party.

Fall had nearly come when they reached the head-waters of the Missouri. The end of the holiday-time was at hand, for they had before Crossing the Mountains. them the labor of crossing the great mountains so as to strike the head-waters of the Columbia. Their success at this point depended somewhat upon the Indian wife of the Frenchman who had joined them at Mandan. She had been captured from one of the Rocky Mountains tribes and they relied on her as interpreter. Partly through her aid, and partly by their own exertions, they were able to find, and make friends with, a band of wandering Shoshones, from whom they got horses. Having cached their boats and most of their goods they started westward through the forest-clad passes of the Rockies; before this they had wandered and explored in several directions through the mountains and the foot-hills. The open country had been left behind, and with it the time of plenty. In the mountain forests the game was far less abundant than on the plains and far harder to kill; though on the tops of the high peaks there was one new game animal, the white antelope-goat, which they did not see, though the Indians brought them hides. The work was hard, and the party suffered much from toil and hunger, living largely on their horses, before they struck one of the tributaries of the Snake sufficiently low down to enable them once more to go by boat.

They now met many Indians of various tribes, all

of them very different from the Indians of the
The   Western Plains. At this time the Indi-
Indians   ans, both east and west of the Rockies,
they Met.   already owned numbers of horses. Although they had a few guns, they relied mainly on
the spears and tomahawks, and bows and arrows
with which they had warred and hunted from time
immemorial; for only the tribes on the outer edges
had come in contact with the whites, whether with
occasional French and English traders who brought
them goods, or with the mixed bloods of the northern Spanish settlements, upon which they raided.
Around the mouth of the Columbia, however, the
Indians knew a good deal about the whites; the
river had been discovered by Captain Gray of
Boston thirteen years before, and ships came there
continually, while some of the Indian tribes were
occasionally visited by traders from the British fur
companies.

With one or two of these tribes the explorers had
some difficulty, and owed their safety to their unceasing vigilance, and to the prompt decision with
which they gave the Indians to understand that they
would tolorate no bad treatment; while yet themselves refraining carefully from committing any
wrong. By most of the tribes they were well received, and obtained from them not only information
of the route, but also a welcome supply of food.
At first they rather shrank from eating the dogs
which formed the favorite dish of the Indians; but
after a while they grew quite reconciled to dog's
flesh; and in their journals noted that they preferred

it to lean elk and deer meat, and were much more healthy while eating it.

They reached the rain-shrouded forests of the coast before cold weather set in, and there they passed the winter; suffering somewhat Lewis and from the weather, and now and then from Clark hunger, though the hunters generally killed reach the plenty of elk, and deer of a new kind, the coast. blacktail of the Columbia.

In March, 1806, they started eastward to retrace their steps. At first they did not live well, for it was before the time when the salmon came They Start up-stream, and game was not common. Eastward When they reached the snow-covered Again. mountains[1] there came another period of toil and starvation, and they were glad indeed when they emerged once more on the happy hunting-grounds of the Great Plains. They found their caches undisturbed. Early in July they separated for a time, Clark descending the Yellowstone and Lewis the Missouri, until they met at the junction of the two rivers. The party which went down the Yellowstone at one time split into two, Clark taking command of one division, and a sergeant of the other; they built their own canoes, some of them made out of hollowed trees, while the others were bull boats, made of buffalo hides stretched on a frame. As before they revelled in the abundance of the game. They marvelled at the incredible numbers

[1] The Bitter Root range, which they had originally crossed. For the bibliography, etc., of this expedition see Coues' book. The MS. diary of one of the soldiers, Gass, has since been discovered in the Draper collection.

of the buffalo whose incessant bellowing at this season filled the air with one continuous roar, which terrified their horses; they were astonished at the abundance and tameness of the elk; they fought their old enemies the grizzly bears; and they saw and noted many strange and wonderful beasts and birds.

To Lewis there befell other adventures. Once, while he was out with three men, a party of eight Blackfoot warriors joined them and suddenly made a treacherous attack upon them and strove to carry off their guns and horses. But the wilderness veterans sprang to arms with a readiness that had become second nature. One of them killed an Indian with a knife thrust; Lewis himself shot another Indian, and the remaining six fled, carrying with them one of Lewis' horses, but losing four of their own, which the whites captured. This was the begining of the long series of bloody skirmishes between the Blackfeet and the Rocky Mountain explorers and trappers. Clark, at about the same time, suffered at the hands of the Crows, who stole a number of his horses.

The Adventure of Lewis and the Indians.

None of the party were hurt by the Indians, but some time after the skirmish with the Blackfeet Lewis was accidentally shot by one of the Frenchmen of the party and suffered much from the wound. Near the mouth of the Yellowstone Clark joined him, and the reunited company floated down the Missouri. Before they reached the Mandan villages they encountered two white men, the first strangers of their own color the party had seen for a year and a half. These

He is Shot by one of his Own Party.

were two American hunters named Dickson and Hancock, who were going up to trap the head-waters of the Missiouri on their own account. They had come from the Illinois country a year before, to hunt and trap; they had been plundered, and one of them wounded, in an encounter with the fierce Sioux, but were undauntedly pushing forwards into the unknown wilderness towards the mountains.

These two hardy and daring adventurers formed the little vanguard of the bands of hunters and trappers, the famous Rocky Mountain men, *They Meet* who were to roam hither and hither across *Two Hunt-* the great West in lawless freedom for the *ers.* next three quarters of a century. They accompanied the party back to the Mandan village; there one of the soldiers joined them, a man name Colter, so fascinated by the life of the wilderness that he was not willing to leave it, even for a moment's glimpse of the civilization, from which he had been so long exiled.[1] The three turned their canoe up-stream, while Lewis and Clark and the rest of the party drifted down past the Sioux.

The further voyage of the explorers was uneventful. They had difficulties with the Sioux of course, but they held them at bay. They killed *They* game in abundance, and went down-stream *Return to* as fast as sails, oars, and current could carry *St. Louis.* them. In September they reached St. Louis and forwarded to Jefferson an account of what they had done.

---

[1] For Colter, and the first explorers of this region, see " The Yellowstone National Park," by Captain H. M. Chittenden.

They had done a great deed, for they had opened the door into the heart of the far West.   Close on their tracks followed the hunters, trappers, and fur traders who themselves made ready the way for the settlers whose descendants were to possess the land.   As for the two leaders of the explorers, Lewis was made Governor of Louisiana Territory, and a couple of years afterwards died, as was supposed, by his own hand, in a squalid log cabin on the Chickasaw trace—though it was never certain that he had not been murdered. Clark was afterwards Governor of the territory, when its name had been changed to Missouri, and he also served honorably as Indian agent.   But neither of them did anything further of note; nor indeed was it necessary, for they had performed a feat which will always give them a place on the honor roll of American worthies.

After-Careers of Lewis and Clark.

While Lewis and Clark were descending the Columbia and recrossing the continent from the Pacific coast, another army officer was conducting explorations which were only less important than theirs.   This was Lieut. Zebulon Montgomery Pike.   He was not by birth a Westerner, being from New Jersey, the son of an officer of the Revolutionary army; but his name will always be indelibly associated with the West.   His two voyages of exploration, one to the head-waters of the Mississippi, the other to the springs of the Arkansas and the Rio Grande, were ordered by Wilkinson, without authority from Congress.   When Wilkinson's name was smirched by Burr's conspiracy

Pike and his Explorations.

the Lieutenant likewise fell under suspicion, for it was believed that his south-western trip was undertaken in pursuance of some of Wilkinson's schemes. Unquestionably this trip was intended by Pike to throw light on the exact nature of the Spanish boundary claims. In all probability he also intended to try to find out all he could of the military and civil situation in the northern provinces of Mexico. Such information could be gathered but for one purpose; and it seems probable that Wilkinson had hinted to him that part of his plan which included an assault of some kind or other on Spanish rule in Mexico; but Pike was an ardent patriot, and there is not the slightest ground for any belief that Wilkinson dared to hint to him his own disloyalty to the Union.

In August, 1805, Pike turned his face towards the head-waters of the Mississippi, his purpose being both to explore the sources of that river, He Ascends and to show to the Indians, and to the the Missis- British fur traders among them, that the sippi. United States was sovereign over the country in fact as well as in theory. He started in a large keel boat, with twenty soldiers of the regular army. The voyage up-stream was uneventful. The party lived largely on game they shot, Pike himself doing rather more hunting than anyone else and evidently taking much pride in his exploits; though in his journal he modestly disclaimed any pretensions to special skill. Unlike the later explorers, but like Lewis and Clark, Pike could not avail himself of the services of hunters having knowledge of the country.

He and his regulars were forced to be their own pioneers and to do their own hunting, until, by dint of hard knocks and hard work, they grew experts, both as riflemen and as woodsmen.

The expedition occasionally encountered parties of Indians. The savages were nominally at peace Encounters with the whites, and although even at this with time they occasionally murdered some soli-Indians. tary trapper or trader, they did not dare meddle with Pike's well armed and well prepared soldiers, confining themselves to provocation that just fell short of causing conflict. Pike handled them well, and speedily brought those with whom he came into contact to a proper frame of mind, showing good temper and at the same time prompt vigor in putting down any attempt at bullying. On the journey up stream only one misadventure befell the party. A couple of the men got lost while hunting and did not find the boat for six days, by which time they were nearly starved, having used up all their ammunition, so that they could not shoot game.

The winter was spent in what is now Minnesota. Pike made a permanent camp where he kept most of his men, while he himself travelled hither Winters on and thither, using dog sleds after the snow the Head-waters of fell. They lived almost purely on game, the Missis- and Pike, after the first enthusiasm of the sippi. sport had palled a little, commented on the hard slavery of a hunter's life and its vicissitudes; for on one day he might kill enough meat to last the whole party a week and when that was exhausted they might go three or four days without anything at all.[1]   Deer and bear were the common game, though they saw both buffalo and elk, and killed several of the latter.   Pike found his small-bore rifle too light for the chase of the buffalo.

At the beautiful falls of St. Anthony, Pike held a council with the Sioux, and got them to make a grant of about a hundred thousand acres in the neighborhood of the falls; and he tried vainly to make peace between the Sioux and the Chippewas.   In his search for the source of the Mississippi he penetrated deep into the lovely lake-dotted region of forests and prairies which surrounds the head-waters of the river.   He did not reach Lake Itasca; but he did explore the Leech Lake drainage system, which he mistook for the true source.

Council with the Sioux.

At the British trading-posts, strong log structures fitted to repel Indian attacks, Pike was well received. Where he found the British flag flying he had it hauled down and the American flag hoisted in its place, making both the Indians and the traders understand that the authority of the United States was supreme in the land.   In the spring he floated down stream and reached St. Louis on the last day of April, 1806.

Hoists the American Flag.

In July he was again sent out, this time on a far more dangerous and important trip.   He was to march west to the Rocky Mountains, and explore the country towards the head of the Rio Grande, where the boundary line between Mexico and Louisiana was very

Returns to St. Louis and Starts Westward.

[1] Pike's Journal, entry of November 16, 1805.

vaguely determined. His party numbered twenty-three all told, including Lieutenant J. B. Wilkinson, a son of the general, and a Dr. J. H. Robinson, whose special business it was to find out everything possible about the Spanish provinces, or, in plain English, to act as a spy. The party was also accompanied by fifty Osage Indians, chiefly women and children who had been captured by the Potowatomies, and whose release and return to their homes had been brought about by the efforts of the United States Government. The presence of these redeemed captives of course kept the Osages in good humor with Pike's party.

The party started in boats, and ascended the Osage River as far as it was navigable. They then pro-

Pike Journeys to the Osage and Pawnee Villages. cured horses and travelled to the great Pawnee village known as the Pawnee Republic, which gave its name to the Republican River. Before reaching the Pawnee village they found that a Spanish military expedition, several hundred strong, under an able commander named Malgares, had anticipated them, by travelling through the debatable land, and seeking to impress upon the Indians that the power of the Spanish nation was still supreme. Malgares had travelled from New Mexico across the Arkansas into the Pawnee country; during much of his subsequent route Pike followed the Spaniard's trail. The Pawnees had received from Malgares Spanish flags, as tokens of Spanish sovereignty. Doubtless the ceremony meant little or nothing to them; and Pike had small difficulty in getting the chiefs and warriors of

the village to hoist the American flag instead.   But
they showed a very decided disinclination to let him
continue his journey westward.   However, he would
not be denied.   Though with perfect good temper,
he gave them to understand that he would use force
if they ventured to bar his passage; and they finally
let him go by.   Later he had a somewhat similar
experience with a large Pawnee war party.

The explorers had now left behind them the fertile, tree-clad country, and had entered on the great
plains, across which they journeyed to the   The
Arkansas, and then up that river.   Like   Swarms of
Lewis and Clark, Pike found the country   Game.
literally swarming with game; for all the great
plains region, from the Saskatchawan to the Rio
Grande, formed at this time one of the finest hunting grounds to be found in the whole world.   At
one place just on the border of the plains Pike mentions that he saw from a hill buffalo, elk, antelope,
deer, and panther, all in sight at the same moment.
When he reached the plains proper the three characteristic animals were the elk, antelope, and, above all,
the buffalo.

The myriads of huge shaggy-maned bison formed
the chief feature in this desolate land ; no other wild
animal of the same size, in any part of the
world, then existed in such incredible   The Bison.
numbers.   All the early travellers seem to have
been almost equally impressed by the interminable
seas of grass, the strange, shifting, treacherous plains
rivers, and the swarming multitudes of this great
wild ox of the West.   Under the blue sky the yellow

prairie spread out in endless expanse; across it the horseman might steer for days and weeks through a landscape almost as unbroken as the ocean. It was a region of light rainfall; the rivers ran in great curves through beds of quicksand, which usually contained only trickling pools of water, but in times of freshet would in a moment fill from bank to bank with boiling muddy torrents. Hither and thither across these plains led the deep buffalo-trails, worn by the hoofs of the herds that had passed and re-passed through countless ages. For hundreds of miles a traveller might never be out of sight of buffalo. At noon they lay about in little groups all over the prairie, the yellow calves clumsily frisking beside their mothers, while on the slight mounds the great bulls moaned and muttered and pawed the dust. Towards nightfall the herds filed down in endless lines to drink at the river, walking at a quick, shuffling pace, with heads held low and beards almost sweeping the ground. When Pike reached the country the herds were going south from the Platte towards their wintering grounds below the Arkansas. At first he passed through nothing but droves of bulls. It was not until he was well towards the mountains that he came upon great herds of cows.

The prairie was dotted over with innumerable antelope. These have always been beasts of the **Other Game.** open country; but the elk, once so plentiful in the great eastern forests, and even now plentiful in parts of the Rockies, then also abounded on the plains, where there was not a tree of any kind, save the few twisted and wind-beaten cotton woods that here and there, in sheltered places fringed the banks of the rivers.

Lewis and Clark had seen the Mandan horsemen surround the buffalo herds and kill the great clumsy beasts with their arrows. Pike records with the utmost interest how he saw a band of Pawnees in similar fashion slaughter a great gang of elk, and he dwells with admiration on the Indians training of the horses, the wonderful horse- Hunting. manship of the naked warriors, and their skill in the use of bow and spear. It was a wild hunting scene, such as belonged properly to times primeval. But indeed the whole life of these wild red nomads, the plumed and painted horse-Indians of the great plains, belonged to time primeval. It was at once terrible and picturesque, and yet mean in its squalor and laziness. From the Blackfeet in the north to the Comanches in the south they were all alike; grim lords of war and the chase; warriors, hunters, gamblers, idlers; fearless, ferocious, treacherous, inconceivably cruel; revengeful and fickle; foul and unclean in life and thought; disdaining work, but capable at times of undergoing unheard-of toil and hardship, and of braving every danger; doomed to live with ever before their eyes death in the form of famine or frost, battle or torture, and schooled to meet it, in whatever shape it came, with fierce and mutterless fortitude.[1]

When the party reached the Arkansas late in

[1] Fortunately these horse-Indians, and the game they chiefly hunted, have found a fit historian. In his books, especially upon the Pawnees and Blackfeet, Mr. George Bird Grinnell has portrayed them with a master hand; it is hard to see how his work can be bettered.

October Wilkinson and three or four men journied
Wilkinson down it and returned to the settled
Descends country. Wilkinson left on record his
the delight when he at last escaped from the
Arkansas. bleak windswept plains and again reached
the land where deer supplanted the buffalo and antelope and where the cottonwood was no longer the
only tree.

The others struck westward into the mountains,
and late in November reached the neighborhood
Pike of the bold peak which was later named
Reaches after Pike himself. Winter set in with
Pike's severity soon after they penetrated the
Peak. mountains. They were poorly clad to resist the bitter weather, and they endured frightful
hardships while endeavoring to thread the tangle of
high cliffs and sheer canyons. Moreover, as winter
set in, the blacktail deer, upon which the party had
begun to rely for meat, migrated to the wintering
grounds, and the explorers suffered even more from
hunger than from cold. They had nothing to eat
but the game, not even salt.

The travelling through the deep snow, whether
exploring or hunting, was heart-breaking work. The
Sufferings horses suffered most; the extreme toil, and
from Cold scant pasturage weakened them so that
and some died from exhaustion ; others fell over
Hunger. precipices; and the magpies proved evil
foes, picking the sore backs of the wincing, saddle-
galled beasts. In striving to find some pass for the
horses the whole party was more than once strung
out in detachments miles apart, through the moun-

tains. Early in January, near the site of the present
Canyon City, Pike found a valley where deer were
plentiful. Here he built a fort of logs, and left the
saddle-band and pack-animals in charge of two of
the members of the expedition; intending to send
back for them when he had discovered some practicable route.

He himself, with a dozen of the hardiest soldiers,
struck through the mountains towards the Rio
Grande. Their sufferings were terrible. **He Strikes**
They were almost starved, and so cold was **Across the**
the weather that at one time no less than **Mountains**
nine of the men froze their feet. Pike and **on Foot.**
Robinson proved on the whole the hardiest, being
kept up by their indomitable will, though Pike
mentions with gratification that but once, in all
their trials, did a single member of the party so
much as grumble.

Pike and Robinson were also the best hunters;
and it was their skill and stout-heartedness, shown
in the time of direst need, that saved **The Party**
the whole party from death. In the Wet **almost**
Mountain valley, which they reached in **Perishes**
mid-January, 1807, at the time that nine of **Starvation.**
the men froze their feet, starvation stared them in
the face. There had been a heavy snowstorm; no
game was to be seen; and they had been two days
without food. The men with frozen feet, exhausted
by hunger, could no longer travel. Two of the
soldiers went out to hunt, but got nothing. At the
same time, Pike and Robinson started, determined
not to return at all unless they could bring back

meat. Pike wrote that they had resolved to stay out and die by themselves, rather than to go back to camp " and behold the misery of our poor lads." All day they tramped wearily through the heavy snow. Towards evening they came on a buffalo, and wounded it; but faint and weak from hunger, they shot badly, and the buffalo escaped; a disappointment literally as bitter as death. That night they sat up among some rocks, all night long, unable to sleep because of the intense cold, shivering in their thin rags; they had not eaten for three days. But they were men of indomitable spirit, and next day trudging painfully on, they at last succeeded, after another heart-breaking failure, in killing a buffalo. At midnight they staggered into camp with the meat, and all the party broke their four days' fast. Two men lost their feet through frost-bite, and had to be left in this camp, with all the food. Only the fact that a small band of buffalo was wintering in the valley had saved the whole expedition from death by starvation.

After leaving this valley Pike and the remaining men of the expedition finally reached the Rio **Pike** Grande, where the weather was milder and **Reaches** deer abounded. Here they built a little **the Rio** fort over which they flew the United **Grande.** States flag, though Pike well knew that he was in Spanish territory. When the Spanish commander at Santa Fé learned of their presence he promptly sent out a detachment of troops to bring them in, though showing great courtesy, and elaborately pretending to believe that Pike had merely lost his way.

From Santa Fé Pike was sent home by a roundabout route through Chihuahua, and through Texas, where he noted the vast droves of wild horses, and the herds of peccaries. He was much impressed by the strange mixture of new world savagery and old world feudalism in the provinces through which he passed. A nobility and a priesthood which survived unchanged from the middle ages held sway over serfs and made war upon savages. The Apache and Comanche raided on the outlying settlements; the mixed bloods, and the "tame" Indians on the great ranches and in the hamlets were in a state of peonage; in the little walled towns, the Spanish commanders lived in half civilized, half barbaric luxury, and shared with the priests absolute rule over the people roundabout. The American lieutenant, used to the simplicity of his own service, was struck by the extravagance and luxury of the Spanish officers, who always travelled with sumpter mules laden with delicacies; and he was no less struck with the laxity of discipline in all ranks. The Spanish cavalry were armed with lances and shields; the militia carried not only old fashioned carbines but lassos and bows and arrows. There was small wonder that the Spanish authorities, civil, military, and ecclesiastical alike, should wish to keep intruders out of the land, and should jealously guard the secret of their own weakness.

Pike is Sent Home by the Spaniards.

When Pike reached home he found himself in disfavor, as was everyone who was suspected of having any intimate relations with Wilkinson. However, he soon cleared himself, and continued to serve in the army. He rose

His Subsequent Career.

to be a brigadier-general and died gloriously in the hour of triumph, when in command of the American force which defeated the British and captured York.

Lewis, Clark, and Pike had been the pioneers in the exploration of the far West. The wandering trappers and traders were quick to follow in their tracks, and to roam hither and thither exploring on their own accord. In 1807 one of these restless adventurers reached Yellowstone Lake, and another Lake Itasca; and their little trading stations were built far up the Missouri and the Platte.

While these first rough explorations of the far West were taking place, the old West was steadily filling with population and becoming more and more a coherent portion of the Union. In the treaties made from time to time with the Northwestern Indians, they ceded so much land that at last the entire northern bank of the Ohio was in the hands of the settlers. But the Indians still held Northwestern Ohio and the northern portions of what are now Indiana and Illinois, so that the settlement at Detroit was quite isolated; as were the few little stockades, or groups of fur-traders' huts, in what are now northern Illinois and Wisconsin. The Southern Indians also surrendered much territory, in various treaties. Georgia got control of much of the Indian land within her State limits. All the country between Knoxville and Nashville became part of Tennessee, so that the eastern and middle portions of the State were no longer sundered by a jutting fragment of wilderness, in-

fested by Indian war parties whenever there were
hostilities with the savages.   The only Indian lands
in Tennessee or Kentucky were those held by the
Chickasaws, between the Tennessee and the Mississippi; and the Chickasaws were friendly to the
Americans.

Year by year the West grew better able to defend itself if attacked, and more formidable in the
event of its being necessary to undertake   Power of
offensive warfare.   Kentucky and Ten-   the West.
nessee had become populous States, no longer fearing Indian inroads; but able on the contrary to
equip powerful armies for the aid of the settlers in
the more scantily peopled regions north and south of
them.   Ohio was also growing steadily; and in the
territory of Indiana, including what is now Illinois,
and the territory of Mississippi, including what is
now northern Alabama, there were already many
settlers.

Nevertheless the shadow of desperate war hung
over the West.   Neither the northern nor the southern Indians were yet subdued; sullen and   Dangers
angry they watched the growth of the   Threaten-
whites, alert to seize a favorable moment   ing the
to make one last appeal to arms before   West.
surrendering their hunting grounds.   Moreover in
New Orleans and Detroit the Westerners possessed
two outposts which it would be difficult to retain in
the event of war with England, the only European
nation that had power seriously to injure them.
These two outposts were sundered from the rest
of the settled Western territory by vast regions ten-

anted only by warlike Indian tribes. Detroit was most in danger from the Indians, the British being powerless against it unless in alliance with the formidable tribes that had so long battled against American supremacy. Their superb navy gave the British the power to attack New Orleans at will. The Westerners could rally to the aid of New Orleans much more easily than to the aid of Detroit; for the Mississippi offered a sure channel of communication, and New Orleans, unlike Detroit, possessed some capacity for self-defence; whereas the difficulties of transit through the Indian-haunted wilderness south of the Great Lakes were certain to cause endless dangers and delays if it became necessary for the Westerners either to reinforce or to recapture the little city which commanded the straits between Huron and Erie.

During the dozen years which opened with Wayne's campaigns, saw the treaties of Jay and Pinckney, and closed with the explorations of Lewis, Clarke, and Pike, the West had grown with the growth of a giant, and for the first time had achieved peace; but it was not yet safe from danger of outside attack. The territories which had been won by war from the Indians and by treaty from Spain, France, and England, and which had been partially explored, were not yet entirely our own. Much had been accomplished by the deeds of the Indian-fighters, treaty-makers, and wilderness-wanderers; far more had been accomplished by the steady push of the settler folk themselves, as they thrust ever westward, and carved states out of the forest and the prairie ; but much yet remained to be done before the West would reach its natural limits, would free itself forever from the pressure of outside foes, and would fill from frontier to frontier with populous commonwealths of its own citizens.

THE END OF VOL. IV.

APPENDIX.

APPENDIX.

It is a pleasure to be able to say that the valuable Robertson manuscripts are now in course of publication, under the
direction of a most competent editor in the person of Mr. W.
R. Garrett, Ph.D. They are appearing in the *American Historical Magazine*, at Nashville, Tennessee ; the first instal-
ment appeared in January, and the second in April, 1896.
The *Magazine* is doing excellent work, exactly where this
work is needed ; and it could not render a better service to
the study of American history than by printing these Robertson papers.

After the present volume was in press Mr. Oswald Garrison
Villard, of Harvard, most kindly called my attention to the
Knox Papers, in the archives of the New England Historical
and Genealogical Society, of Boston. These papers are of
great interest. They are preserved in a number of big
volumes. I was able to make only a most cursory examination of them ; but Mr. Villard with great kindness went carefully through them, and sent me copies of those which I
deemed important. There are a number of papers referring
to matters connected with the campaigns against the western
Indians. The most interesting and valuable is a long letter
from Col. Darke giving a very vivid picture of St. Clair's
defeat, and of the rout which followed. While it can hardly
be said to cast any new light on the defeat, it describes it in
a very striking manner, and brings out well the gallantry of
the officers and the inferior quality of the rank and file ; and
it gives a very unpleasant picture of St. Clair and Hamtranck.

Besides the Darke letter there are several other manuscripts
containing information of value. In Volume XXIII., page
169, there is a letter from Knox to General Harmar, dated

New York, September 3, 1790. After much preliminary apology, Knox states that it "has been reported, and under circumstances which appear to have gained pretty extensive credit on the frontiers, that you are too apt to indulge yourself to excess in a convivial glass"; and he then points out the inevitable ruin that such indulgence will bring to the General.

A letter from St. Clair to Knox, dated Lexington, September 4, 1791, runs in part: "Desertion and sickness have thinned our ranks. Still, if I can only get them into action before the time of the levies expires, I think my force sufficient, though that opinion is founded on the calculation of the probable number that is opposed to us, having no manner of information as to the force collected to oppose us." On the 15th he writes from Ft. Washington about the coming expiration of enlistments and says: "I am very sensible how hazardous it is to approach, under such circumstances, and my only expectation is that the men will find themselves so far engaged that it will be obviously better to go forward than to return, at the same time it precludes the establishment of another post of communication however necessary, but that indeed is precluded also from our decreasing numbers, and the very little dependence that is to be placed upon the militia."

Col. Winthrop Sargent writes to General Knox from Ft. Washington, on January 2, 1792. He states that there were fourteen hundred Indians opposed to St. Clair in the battle, and repeats a rumor that six hundred Indians from the Lakes quarrelled with the Miamis over the plunder, and went home without sharing any part, warning their allies that thereafter they should fight their battles alone. Sargent dwells upon the need of spies, and the service these spies would have rendered St. Clair. A few days afterwards he writes in reference to a rumor that his own office is to be dispensed with, protesting that this would be an outrage, and that he has always discharged his duties well, having entered the service simply from a desire to be of use to his country. He explains that the money he receives would hardly do more than equip him, and that he only went into the army because he valued reputation and honor more than fortune.

The letters of the early part of 1792 show that the survivors of St. Clair's army were torn by jealousy, and that during the winter following his defeat there was much bitter wrangling among the various officers. Wilkinson frequently wrote to Knox giving his estimate of the various officers, and evidently Knox thought very well of him. Wilkinson spoke well of Sargent; but most of the other officers, whom he mentions at all, he mentions with some disfavor, and he tells at great length of the squabbles among them, his narrative being diversified at times by an account of some other incident such as " a most lawless outrage " by " a party of the soldiery on the person of a civil magistrate in the village of Cincinnati." Knox gives his views as to promotions in a letter to Washington, which shows that he evidently felt a good deal of difficulty in getting men whom he deemed fit for high command, or even for the command of a regiment.

One of the worst quarrels was that of the Quartermaster, Hodgdon, first with Major Zeigler and then with Captain Ford. The Major resigned, and the captain publicly insulted the Quartermaster and threated to horsewhip him.

In one letter Caleb Swan, on March 11, 1792, advises Wilkinson that he had been to Kentucky and had paid off the Kentucky militia who had served under St. Clair. Wilkinson in a letter of March 13th, expresses the utmost anxiety for the retention of St. Clair in command. Among the numerous men whom Wilkinson had complained of was Harmar, who, he said, was not only addicted to drink, but was also a bad disciplinarian. He condemned the quartermaster also, although less severely than most of the other officers.

Darke's letter is worth quoting in full. Its spelling and punctuation are extraordinary ; and some of the words can not be deciphered.

Letter from Col. Darke to George Washington, president of the U. S., dated at Fort Washington, Nineth of Novr. 1791,

(Knox Papers, Vol. xxx., p. 12.)

I take the liberty to Communicate to your Excellency the disagreeable News of our defeat.

We left fort Washington the Begining of Septr a Jornel of our march to the place of action and the whole proseeding on our march I hoped to have had the honour to inclose to you but that and all other papers cloathing & &c., was Taken by the Indians. this Jornel I know would have gave you pain but thought it not amis to Give you a State of facts and Give you every Information in my power and had it Ready to Send to you the Very Morning we were actacked.

We advanced 24 miles from fort Washington and bult a Small fort which we I thought were long about from thence we advanced along the banks of the Meamme River where the fort was arected 44½ Miles on a Streight Line by the Compass west ¼ north though farther the way the Road went and bult another fort. which we Left on the 23 October and from that time to the 3d Novr Got 31 Miles where we incamped in two Lines about 60 yards apart the Right whing in frunt Commanded by General Butler, the Left in the Rear which I commanded, our piccquets Decovered Some Sculking Indians about Camp in the Night and fired on them. Those we expected were horsstealers as they had Taken Many of our horses near fort Washington, and on the way and killed a few of our Men.

As Soon as it was Light in the Morning of the 4th Novr the advanced Guards of the Meletia fired the Meletia Being incamped a Small distance in frunt a Scattering fire Soon Commenced The Troops were instandly formed to Reserve them and the pannack Struck Meletia Soon broke in to the Center of our incampment in a few Munites our Guards were drove in and our whole Camp Surrounded by Savages advencing up nere to our Lines and Made from behind trees Logs &c., Grate Havoke with our Men I for Some time having no orders [indevanced ?] to pervent the Soldiers from braking and Stil finding the enemy Growing More bold and Coming to the very Mouths of our Cannon and all the brave artilery officers Killed I ordered the Left whing to Charge which with the assistance of the Gallent officers that were then Left I with deficuaty prevailed on them to do, the Second U S Regt was then the Least disabled the Charge begat with them on the Left of the Left whing I placed a Small Company of Rifelmen on that flank on the Bank of a Small Crick and persued the enemy about four hundred yards who Ran off in all directions but this time the Left flank of the Right whing Gave way and Number of the Indians Got into our Camp and Got possession of the Artilery and Scalped I Sopose a hundred men or more I turned back and beat them quite off the Ground and Got posesion of the Cannon and had it been possible to Get the troops to form and push them we Should then have Soon beat them of the Ground but those that Came from the Lelf whing Run in a huddle with those of the Right the enemys fire being allmost over for Many Munites and all exertions Made by many of the brave officer to Get them in Some order to persue Victory was all in Vain. they would not form in any order in this Confution they Remained until the enemy finding they were not pushed and I dare say Active officers with them and I beleive Several of them white they Came on again, and the whole Army Ran toGether Like a Mob at a fair and had it not been for the Gratest Exertions of the officers would have stood there til all killed the Genl then Sent to me if possible to Get them off that Spot by Making a Charge I found my Endevours fruitless for Some time but at Length Got Several Soldiers together that I had observed behaving brave and Incoraged them to lead off which they did with charged bayonetts Success the whole followed with Grate Rapidity I then endevoured to halt the frunt to Get them in Some order to turn and fire a few Shots but the horse I Rode being Good for little and I wounded in the thigh Early in the Action and having fatigued my Self much was So Stif I could make a poor hand of Running. the Confution in the Retreat is beyound description the Men throughing away their arms not withstanding all the indevour of the few Remaining Brave officers I think we must have Lost 1000 Stand of arms Meletia included. It is impossible to Give any Good account of the Loss of men at this time but from the Loss of officers you may Give Some Gess a list of their Names you have In Closed the Brave and Much to be Lemented G. B. at their Head I have Likewise in Closed you a Small Rough Scetch of the feald of battle. I at this time am Scarcely able to write being worn out with fatigue Not having Slept 6 hours Since the defeat This fatigue has bean occationed by the Cowardly behaviour of Major John F. Hamtramck, and I am Sorry to say Not the Same exertions of the Govenor that I expected. Hamtramck was about Twenty four Miles in our Rear with the first U S Regiment Consisting of upwards of 300 effective men and on hearing of our defeat insted of Coming on as his orders was I believe to follow us Retreated back 7 miles to fort Jefferson we knowing of his being on his march after us and was in hopes of Grate Releif from him in Covering the Retreat of perhaps upwards of 200 or 300 wounded men Many of whom might easily bean Saved with that fresh Regiment with whom I should not have bean atraid to have passed the whole Indian army if they had persued as the would have bean worn down with the Chace and in Grate Disorder when we Got to the fort 31 miles in about 9 hours no one having eat any from the day before the action. we found the Garison without more than than one days bred and no meat having bean on half alowence two days there was a Council Called to which I aftar I beleive they had agreed what was to be done was called it was Concluded to march of & Recommence the Retreat at 10 oclock which was begun I think an hour before that time more than 300 wounded and Tired in our Rear the Govenor assured me that he expected provition on every hour I at first Concluded to stay with my Son who was very dangerously and I expected Mortaly wounded but after Geting Several officers dressed and as well provided for as possible and Seing the Influance Hamtramck had with the Genl about twelve oclock I got a horse and followed the army as I thought from apearences that Major Hamtramck had Influance anough to pervent the Garison from being Supplied with the provition Coming on by Keeping the first Regt as a guard for himself I Rode alone about ten Miles from twelve oclock at night until I overtook the Regiment and the Genl I still kept on until I met the pack horses about daylight Much alarmed at having heard Something of the defeat, the Horse master Could Not prevail on the drivers to Go on with him until I assured then I would Go back with them Lame as I was I ordered the horses to be loaded immediately and I Returned as fast as I could to hault the first Regiment as a guard, and when I met them told them to halt and make fires to Cook immediately as I made Sure they would be sent back with the provitions, but when I met the Govenor and Major Hamtramck I pervailed with Genl St. Clair to order 60 men back only which was all I could possibly get and had the bulock drivers known that was all the guard they were to have they would not have gone on nuther would the horse drivers I believe in Sted of the 120 hors loads Got on all the Rest went back with the army and though the Men had bean So Long Sterving and we then 47 miles from the place of action I could not pervail on them the Genl and his fammily or [advisers ?] to halt for the sterved worn down Soldiers to Cook, nor did they I believe even Kill a bullock for their Releaf I went back to fort Jefferson that Night with the flour beaves &c. where they was No kind of provision but a Miserable Poor old horse and many Valuable officers wound there and perhaps 200 soldiers it was Night when I Got back I Slept not one moment that Night my son and other officers being in Such Distress. the next day I was busy all day— Getting—   made to Carry of the wounded officers there being no Medison there Nor any Nurishment not even a quart of Salt but they were not able to bare the Motion of the horses.   That Night I Set off for this place and Rode til about 12 oclock by which time my thigh was amassingly Sweld Near as large as my body and So hot that I could feel the warmth with my hand 2 foot off of it I could Sleep none and have Slept very Little Since the wounds begin to Separate and are much esier I am aprehensive that fort Jeferson is now beseiged by the indians as Certain Information has bean Received that a large body were on Sunday night within fifteen miles of it Coming on the Road we Marched out and I am Sorey to Se no exertions to Releive it I Cannot tel whether they have the Cannon they took from us or Not if they have not, they Cannot take it Nor I don't think they Can with for want of Ball which they have No Grate Number of. They took from us eight pieces of ordenence 130 bullocks, about 300 horses upwards of 200 Tents and a Considerable quantity of flour amunition and all the officers and Soldiers Cloathing and bagage except what they had on I believe they gave quarters to none as most of the Women were Killed before we left the Ground I think the Slaughter far Grater than Bradocks there being 33 brave officers Killd Dead on the Ground 27 wounded that we know of and Some Mising exclusive of the Meletia and I know their Cole. and two Captains were Killed I do not think our Loss so Grate as to Strike the Surviving officers with Ideas of despair as it Seems to. the Chief of the Men Killd are of the Levies and indeed many of them are as well out of the world as in it as for the Gallent officers they are much to be Lamented as the behaviour of allmost all of them would have done honour to the first Veterans in the world. the few that escaped without wounds it was Chiefly axedent that Saved them as it is impossible to Say more in their praise than they deserve.

In the few horse officers though they had no horses Good for anything Capt. Truman Lieut. Sedam Debuts Boins and Gleer behaved Like Soldiers. Capt. Snowder is I think Not Calculated for the army and Suliven Quartermaster and Commt is as Grate a poltoon as I ever saw in the world.[1] Ensign Shambury of the first United States Regiment is as brave Good and determined a Hero as any in the work Lieutenent James Stephenson from Berkeley of the Levies aded to one of the most unspoted and Respectable Carectors in the world in private Life as Good an officer as ever drew breth, his Gallent behavior in Action drew the attention of every officer that was Near him more than any other, There is one Bisel perhaps a volenteer in the Second U S Regiment who Richly deserved preferment for his bravery through the whole action he made the freeest use of the Baonet of any Man I noticed in the Carcases of the Savages. John Hamelton I cant say too much in praise of who was along with the army a packhorse master he picked up the dead mens guns and used them freely when he found them Loaded and when the Indians entered the Camp he took up an ax and at them with it. I am Intirely at a loss to Give you any idea what

[1] Written and lined as above.

General St. Clair intends to do. I well know what I would do if I was in his place and would venture to forfet my Life if the Indians have not moved the Cannon farther than the Meamme Towns if I did not Retake them by Going there in three days insted of two months I well know the have Lost many of their braves & wariors and I make no doubt the have Near 100 wounded Their killed I cannot think Bare any perpotion to ours as they Lay so Concealed but many I know were killd and those the most dareing fellows which has weakened them Grately and I know we were able to beat them and that a violent push with one hundred brave men when the Left whing Returned from persuing them would have turned the Scale in our favor indeed I think fifty would in the Scatered State they were in and five or Six hundred Mounted Riflemen from Conetuck aded to the force we have would Be as Sure of Suchsess as they went many have offer to Go with me a number of officers ofer to Go as privates and I never was Treated with So much Respect in any part of the world as I have bean this day in this wilderness in the time I am offered My Choice of any horse belonging to the town as I Lost all my own horses I shall Se the General in the morning and perhaps be no more Satisfied than I am now. Though I have Spoke of all the officers with that Respect they Richly deserve I Cannot in Justice to Capt. Hannah help mentioning him as when all his men were killed wounded and Scatered except four Got a (?) that belonged to Capt. Darkes Company when the Cannon was Retaken the Artilery men being all killed and Lying in heaps about the Peases who he Draged away and Stood to the Cannon himSelf til the Retreat and then within a few yards of the enemy Spiked the Gun with his Baonet Capt. Brack (?) and all the Captains of the Maryland Line I cannot Say too much in their praise. I have taken the Liberty of Writing So perticculer to you as I think no one Can Give a better account nor do I think you will Get an account from any that Saw So much of the action Genl. St. Clair not Being able to Run about as I was if his inclination had been as Grate I hope in the Course of the winter to have the pleasure of Seeing you when I may have it in my power to answer any questions you are pleased to ask Concerning the unfortunate Campain.   I

> Have the Honour to be
> your Excellencys most obt.
> and most humble servent
>
> WM. DARKE

10 Novr. I have prevailed on the Good Genl. to send a Strong party To Carry Supplies to fort Jeferson which I hope will be able to Releve it and as I have polticed wound and the Swelling much Asswaged if I find myself able to Set on hors back will Go with the party as I Can be very warm by Laping myself with blankets

> WM. DARKE

His Excellency
The President of the United States.

INDEX.

All Four Volumes Available in Bison Book Editions

THE WINNING OF THE WEST.

By THEODORE ROOSEVELT.